DRAWING TOWARD HOME

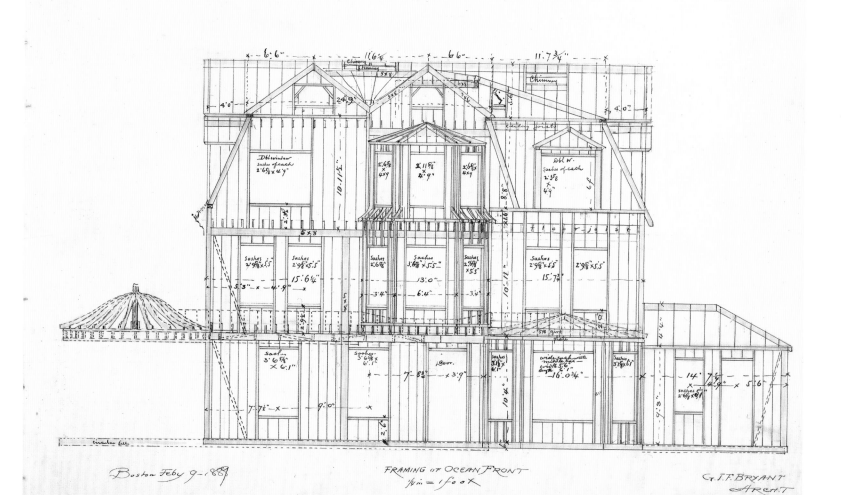

Boston Feby 9 – 1889

FRAMING of OCEAN FRONT
¼ in = 1 foot

G.J.F. BRYANT
Arch't

DRAWING TOWARD HOME

DESIGNS FOR DOMESTIC ARCHITECTURE FROM HISTORIC NEW ENGLAND

JAMES F. O'GORMAN, *Editor*

With LORNA CONDON, CHRISTOPHER MONKHOUSE,
ROGER G. REED, *and* EARLE G. SHETTLEWORTH, JR.

HISTORIC NEW ENGLAND

Boston 2010

FRONT COVER: Edward Shaw (1784–1859), William Wilkins Warren House, Arlington, Massachusetts, 1840. Gift of Earle G. Shettleworth, Jr., 1995.

BACK COVER: Henry B. Hoover (1903–1989), Terrace for the Edgar Moor House, Tabor Knoll, Lincoln, Massachusetts, 1964. Gift of the Family of Henry B. Hoover: Henry B. Hoover, Jr., Lucretia Hoover Giese, and Elizabeth Hoover Norman, 2009.

FRONT FLAP: Little and Browne (1890–c. 1939), Forecourt Fence and Gates for the Henry Clay Frick Estate, Eagle Rock, Prides Crossing, Beverly, Massachusetts, 1902–05 (detail). Gift of Herbert W. C. Browne, 1939.

BACK FLAP AND FRONTISPIECE: Gridley J. F. Bryant (1816–1899), Elevation of "FRAMING OF OCEAN FRONT" for the Thomas Wigglesworth House, Manchester, Massachusetts. Signed: "G. J. F. BRYANT ARCHT." Dated: "Boston Feby 9, 1889." Black ink, watercolor, and graphite on starch-coated fabric; 13¼ × 20¼". Gift of Rebecca Gardner Campbell, 1996.

PAGE 6: A. H. Davenport and Company (active 1880–1908 and beyond), Model of an Unidentified Interior (shown flat), early twentieth century. Library and Archives purchase, 1994.

Exhibition Itinerary

Boston University Art Gallery at the Stone Gallery
Boston, Massachusetts
November 18, 2009 – January 17, 2010

The National Building Museum
Washington, D. C.
February 13 – August 15, 2010

Published by Historic New England
141 Cambridge Street
Boston, Massachusetts 02114
www.HistoricNewEngland.org

Distributed by Tilbury House, Publishers
103 Brunswick Avenue
Gardiner, Maine 04345
www.tilburyhouse.com
800-582-1899

First Edition 2010

Library of Congress Cataloging-in-Publication Data
Drawing toward home : designs for domestic architecture from Historic New England / James F. O'Gorman, editor ; with Lorna Condon . . . [et al.]. – 1st ed.
    p. cm.
  Includes bibliographical references and index.
  ISBN 978-0-88448-328-1
1. Architectural drawing—New England—19th century. 2. Architectural drawing—New England—20th century. 3. Architecture, Domestic—New England—Designs and plans. 4. Architecture—New England—History—19th century. 5. Architecture—New England—History—20th century. I. O'Gorman, James F. II. Condon, Lorna. III. Title: Designs for domestic architecture from Historic New England.
  NA2706.U6D69 2010
  728'.022274—dc22
                    2009051591

Book and cover design by Julia Sedykh Design
Printed by Capital Offset Company, Concord, New Hampshire
Bound by Acme Bookbinding, Charlestown, Massachusetts

Contents

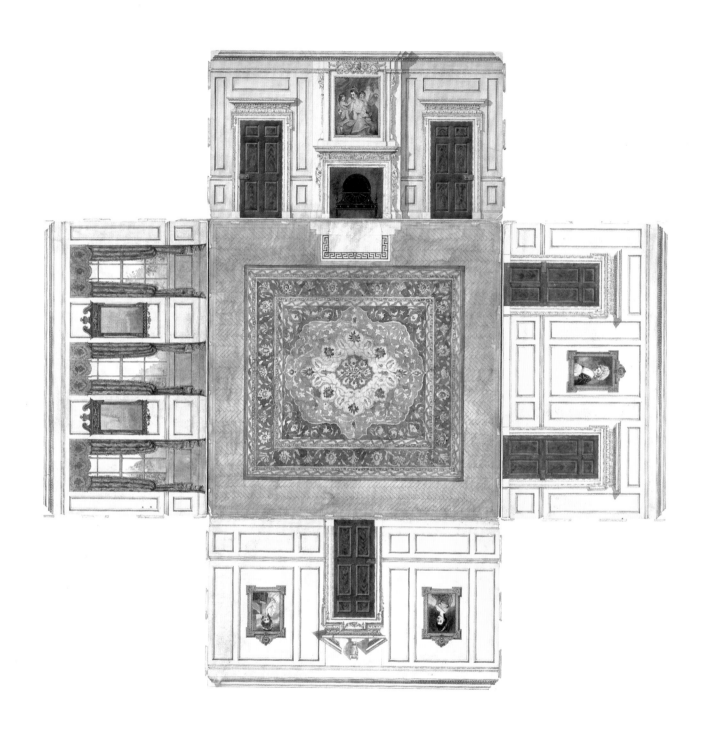

Contributors

Grace Slack McNeil Professor Emeritus of the History of American Art, Wellesley College — James F. O'Gorman

Curator of Library and Archives, Historic New England — Lorna Condon

Eloise W. Martin Chair of European Decorative Arts, The Art Institute of Chicago — Christopher Monkhouse

Historian, National Register of Historic Places — Roger G. Reed

Director of the Maine Historic Preservation Commission and Maine State Historian — Earle G. Shettleworth, Jr.

Independent Researcher — Donald C. Carleton, Jr.

Charles F. Montgomery Professor Emeritus of American Decorative Arts, Yale University, and former Executive Director of Historic New England — Abbott Lowell Cummings

Landscape Historian — Elizabeth Hope Cushing

Director of Preservation Studies and Associate Professor of American and New England Studies, Boston University — Claire W. Dempsey

Independent Researcher — Stuart A. Drake

State Architectural Historian, New Hampshire Division of Historical Resources — James L. Garvin

Team Leader, Visitor Experience, Historic New England — Peter Gittleman

Carolyn and Peter Lynch Curator of American Decorative Art, Peabody Essex Museum — Dean T. Lahikainen

Architectural Historian — Maureen Meister

Architectural Historian — Pauline C. Metcalf

Professor of Art History and Director of Architectural Studies, Boston University — Keith N. Morgan

Curator Emeritus, Historic New England — Richard C. Nylander

Architectural Historian — Timothy Orwig

Architectural Historian — Annie Robinson

Executive Director, Cambridge Historical Commission — Charles M. Sullivan

Gary Wolf Architects, Boston — Gary Wolf

Preservation Specialist, Historic New England — Sally Zimmerman

Supporters

Historic New England is grateful to the following organizations and persons for supporting Drawing Toward Home:

Anonymous

The Henry Luce Foundation

The Felicia Fund

<table>
<tr><td>HOST COMMITTEE</td><td>HONORARY COMMITTEE</td><td>LEADERSHIP COMMITTEE</td></tr>
</table>

HOST COMMITTEE	HONORARY COMMITTEE	LEADERSHIP COMMITTEE
Ann M. Beha, FAIA	Abbott Lowell Cummings	*Partner*
Richard Cheek	Christopher Monkhouse	F. H. Perry Builder
Peter Madsen, FAIA	Keith N. Morgan	Stephen Harby
James McNeely, AIA	James F. O'Gorman	Caren & Randy Parker
Henry Moss, AIA, LEED	Roger G. Reed	
Elizabeth S. Padjen, FAIA	Chase W. Rynd	*Drafter*
Colin L. M. Smith, FAIA	Earle G. Shettleworth, Jr.	James G. Alexander, FAIA, LEED
Frederick A. Stahl, FAIA		Leland Cott, FAIA
Charles M. Sullivan		S. Fiske Crowell, Jr.
William Veillette		Pamela W. Fox
		David M. Hart, AIA
		Jim Righter
		Steve Rosenthal
		Sea-Dar Construction
		A. Anthony Tappé, FAIA
		Donor
		Jonathan Levi Architects, Inc.
		OMR Architects
		Peter Vanderwarker

Seventeenth-century immigrants to New England occupied their first hours on these shores with the tasks of obtaining food and building shelter, initially following the example of Native American structures. The need for shelter remains a priority for us all in the twenty-first century. So it is that throughout four hundred years of history, New Englanders have designed and built homes using a vast array of materials, construction techniques, and styles. The architectural profession has long been trained in this region's universities and experimented in its widely varied climate and terrain. The domestic buildings created here provided models for much of the nation for style, for use of technology, and in defining the social uses of domestic spaces.

From its founding by William Sumner Appleton in 1910 as the Society for the Preservation of New England Antiquities, Historic New England has focused on preserving the history of New England homes. We collect landscapes and buildings, photographic images, drawings, archival records, architectural fragments, and domestic artifacts. Prompted by Appleton's encouraging the first members to send in postcards, photographs, and drawings of threatened buildings, to continuing efforts today to preserve representative examples of the work of New England architects, the collection of architectural drawings has grown to 30,000 items. Never before has this collection been systematically assessed by scholars and used as the basis for an exhibition and publication.

Drawing Toward Home: Designs for Domestic Architecture from Historic New England is the immediate result of years of effort on the part of Curator of the Library and Archives Lorna Condon and our contributors, but it would not have been possible without the collecting foresight of our founder and our predecessor staff throughout our first one hundred years. As Historic New England begins its second century, our commitment to studying, understanding, and interpreting domestic architecture is stronger than ever. The need to continue to build the collections is evidenced by what survives to form this exhibition and also by what has been lost. Architectural drawings are often considered to be ephemeral and expendable, too often allowed to deteriorate when a project is finished, and too large, fragile, and expensive to preserve for comprehensive collecting. The treasures shown here, complemented by historic photographs and insightful commentary, give us a glimpse of what knowledge and pleasure can be had in exploring the collection from a variety of perspectives. These drawings inform our understanding of the past and enrich our appreciation for what New Englanders contributed to the American built environment.

The stewardship of historic sites and collections is a costly business, made possible at Historic New England by the generosity of donors and members who share our commitment to preserving and presenting New England heritage. We are grateful to all who have contributed to the collections through the years, including some recent gifts made to round out this view of domestic architecture. Our trustees recognize the value of building and sustaining diverse collections, whether or not the designs depicted are currently popular. Our members and donors steadily support our work, often translating personal appreciation of their own historic homes—whether seventeenth century or late twentieth century—into support for our region-wide and era-spanning preservation efforts.

To those who have led this project we give special thanks. Lorna Condon and her colleague lead authors James F. O'Gorman, Christopher Monkhouse, Roger G. Reed, and Earle G. Shettleworth, Jr., have all worked with the collection for many years. They bring a depth of knowledge that comes only from hours spent looking, analyzing, and comparing. We are also grateful to Julia Sedykh, whose handsome design reveals both images and scholarship to best advantage.

We are all enriched by having access to these collections. I find them to be fascinating, beautiful, and fun. I hope the same will be true for you.

CARL R. NOLD
President and CEO, *Historic New England*
Boston, Massachusetts
January 2010

Edward Pearce Casey (on left) at work in his office with
an unidentified assistant. Casey's design for his aunt
and uncle's country house is discussed and illustrated
on pages 158–60.

A major component of the American pursuit of happiness has long been a home of one's own. (The automobile is a distant second; the one a castle, the other a chariot.) Early on it might have been a four-square, neoclassical box or cozy Gothic cottage. Of late, for the middle class, it has taken the form of a detached, single-family dwelling set on a weed-free lawn in suburbia, preferably with a two- or three-car garage, although townhouses, apartments, condos, and seaside or country trophy houses may also qualify. It might be a ranch house, a "Cape," a "Colonial," or a "McMansion." It might have been designed by a "name" architect or a faceless drafter working for a developer. In any case, the center of the nuclear family looms large in the American psyche. "American Dream Homes"; "American Dream Realty"; "American Dream Builders"; "American Dream Mortgages": the Internet abounds with commercial enterprises seeking to help us—at a profit to themselves—achieve the perfect framework for our birthright domestic bliss. (The origins of the current societal gloom may be sought in the failure to properly finance The Dream.)

"A man's home is his castle"; "Be it ever so humble, there's no place like home"; "East and west, home is best": books of familiar quotations ring with poetic endorsements of this focal architectural feature of the pursuit of happiness in the United States. As Robert A. M. Stern, Dean of the School of Architecture at Yale University and designer of many upscale residential projects, once noted, it is possible in this country, as it is not in Europe, for an architect to have a complete and often distinguished career designing almost nothing but single-family homes: think of Frank Lloyd Wright or, in New England, Royal Barry Wills.[1]

The literature on American residential architecture is vast. Its history parallels the range of drawings included in this catalogue, from the *Rural Residences* of Alexander Jackson Davis (1837), Orson Squire Fowler's *Home for All; or, The Gravel Wall and Octagon Mode of Building* (1848), and Gervase Wheeler's *Homes for the People* (1855) to Tracy Kidder's best-selling *House* (1985), Daniel McGinn's recently released *House Lust,* and the currently popular *Dwell* magazine. People are endlessly curious about other people's homes. There are guided tours sponsored by civic organizations, historic house museums, the long-lasting "This Old House" on PBS, the weekly Home section of the *New York Times*. Recent historians have tracked the development of domestic accommodations in New England from Abbott Lowell Cummings's *The Framed Houses of Massachusetts Bay, 1625–1725* (1979) and Bainbridge Bunting's *Houses of Boston's Back Bay* (1967) to Christopher Glass's *At Home in Maine* (2004), and, on the national level, in works like David Handlin's *The American Home: Architecture and Society, 1815–1915* (1979) or Alan Gowans's *The Comfortable House* (1986).

The meaning of the American home ranges from refuge to showplace. Frank Lloyd Wright designed hearth-centered houses with sheltering roofs and inconspicuous entryways, following the age-old symbols of familial focus, domestic comfort, and security. His 1950s Zimmerman House in Manchester, New Hampshire, is a canonical example. Silas Lapham, in William Dean Howells's eponymous novel of 1885, saw the dream house rising for his family's use in Boston's fashionable Back Bay district as proof of his upward mobility. As the center of self expression, the home is perhaps the most characteristic building type in a capitalistic democratic society. Its central position in American life makes it an architectural design problem worthy of attention. The drawings selected for this catalogue and for the exhibition of the same name from Historic New England's Library and Archives reflect that fact. They are all for domestic architecture in New England in the late eighteenth, nineteenth, and twentieth centuries. Although specific to life in the Northeast, they parallel the history of architecture, and hence architectural graphics, at the national level.[2]

A house, like any building, is the result of a two-stage process: conception and execution. The design drawing is "the mediator between the mind of the architect and the material forms of the building."[3] It makes graphically manifest the translation of the clients' wishes, expressed as the building program, into their physical embodiment. Before a new house is a home, it is commonly a desire, a dream, an air castle that may be made concrete by the repetitive product of a speculative developer, or by a custom home designed by a registered architect. The developer's clients take more or less what is offered; an architect trades on personalized work. The commission comes from people who describe what they want in the house, where it will be located, the size of the family as well as the budget, the number of pets, and other matters affecting the product, including the personalities of the owners and the image they want to project to the world. The designer translates this verbal information into preliminary drawings that he or she hopes will satisfy the clients' needs and wants, and eventually produces the working or contract drawings that will, with a set of written specifications, form a legal contract and direct the builder in the construction of the house.[4]

This now-common graphic process is of relatively recent origin. The history of architectural drawing begins in earnest with the artist-architects of the Renaissance in Italy. Raphael described the basic types—the orthographic or flat plan, the elevation, and the section—that he said were the province of the architect; he reserved for the artist the perspective view of a building that anticipates its realization in three dimensions. In the period before 1800, and even for decades afterward, on the eastern seaboard of North America, settled mainly by the British, there was little need for more than basic, flat, geometrical diagrams that could be prepared by the client himself, or a gentleman amateur, or a builder, because that was an era of traditional technology and commonly understood classical design principles. The drawings by Salem's Samuel McIntire shown in this catalogue are characteristic of the type, and, as late as 1851, the architect Samuel Sloan could still write that for "the most simple houses two [drawings] are sufficient, a Ground Plan and Elevation."[5] Time-sanctioned load-bearing wood and masonry technology produced structures that were ordered according to the forms of classical antiquity as codified in publications by Italian authorities such as Andrea Palladio or Jacopo Barozzi da Vignola, or eighteenth-century English architects such as William Chambers or Robert Adam.

All that changed with the dawn of the modern world. Architectural design became much more complex. The Industrial Revolution of the late eighteenth and early nineteenth centuries made available new building materials, such as cast iron, wrought iron, and plate glass, and new techniques for using them. It brought the musings of the philosophers about the esthetics of the Beautiful, the Sublime, and the Picturesque, which further expanded the range of approved taste. It saw the rise in the western world of pluralistic, middle-class, democratic, consumer-oriented societies that required new building types like public libraries, department stores, and railroad stations as well as demotic domestic retreats. It saw the broadening historical study of architectural styles beyond that of ancient Rome, which had dominated western architecture since the Renaissance, studies made possible by the increased availability of books that rolled off the new, steam-driven, high-speed printing presses. It also introduced the concept of a usable past, of the association of certain older styles with certain new types of buildings (Gothic for a church, for example), and of the eventual mingling of those styles in creatively eclectic compositions. The study of architectural history became a necessary part of the architect's training and of his practice. In domestic design, the four-square Federal box gradually gave way to the picturesque villa or cottage; builders' guides by Asher Benjamin explaining the classical orders were replaced by house pattern books by Andrew Jackson Downing or Gervase Wheeler, prescribing homes in Gothic, Italianate, castellated, and other exotic styles. The end of the nineteenth century brought the Queen Anne, Shingle, and English Colonial Revival modes to domestic architecture.

The twentieth century introduced reinforced concrete, steel, and the industrialization of the building trades; mechanized heating, ventilating, and air-conditioning (HVAC); the automobile; the airplane; suburban sprawl; and Modernism. The historical styles gradually gave way in the schools—if not always on the ground—to International Style architecture championed by immigrants from Europe, such as Walter Gropius (who settled near Boston and taught at Harvard) and Ludwig Mies van der Rohe (who established his practice in Chicago). Period houses, especially those designed to express the American nostalgia for revival styles, be they English, Dutch, or Spanish Colonial, continued to outnumber Modern flat-roofed boxes deep into the century in the work of some architects and many builders. A house pattern book entitled *Colonial Architecture for Those About to Build* could coexist with the catalogue of an exhibition on the International Style published by The Museum of Modern Art. Historians of the architecture of mid-twentieth-century America continue to ignore these traditional manifestations, but as the drawings in this catalogue demonstrate, they were there. As late as 1935, Arland Dirlam designed his own English Colonial Revival house, drawings for which are included here.

In the wake of these and other developments, more and more design drawings were needed to explain unfamiliar concepts, sources, systems, styles, and procedures. Thus the professional architect began to appear in this country in the early nineteenth century. This person, familiar with the history of styles and new technologies, was neither the client nor the builder but a third party who prescribed building operations through drawings. During the course of the century, what had been a "person" evolved into a partnership, firm, or corporation. These changes were accompanied by changes on the drafting boards. New machine-made papers, improved drawing tools like the T square and the ruling pen, new inks and watercolors, and new methods of copying and distributing drawings, all were introduced over the course of time.[6] At first, the drafter gained expertise by early apprenticeship in the building trades, from the proliferation of architectural books and periodicals, from travel both domestic and foreign made easier by the railroad, steamboat, and eventually the ocean liner and the jet plane. New England architects, such as Robert Swain Peabody (*Note Book Sketches,* 1873) and Julius A. Schweinfurth (*Sketches Abroad,* 1888), published drawings of older and recent buildings made during foreign travel. These cemented their studies, educated their hand, recalled sites that had caught their interest, instructed others not fortunate enough to travel abroad themselves, and—not the least—established their reputations as well-traveled professionals. Architectural information was disseminated by both drawings and reference books.[7] With the introduction of the handheld Brownie camera in 1900, photographs largely replaced travel sketching. In the twentieth century, the 35mm slide-producing camera held sway.

In the first half of the nineteenth century, a prominently displayed architectural library and a set of drawing instruments were the badges of the rising professional, like the sign in the form of a tooth for a dentist or a pair of eyeglasses for an oculist.[8] Before the Civil War, architects were trained as apprentices in the offices of older men. This catalogue contains a drawing executed as late as 1860 by Henry M. Francis, when he was a student in the Boston office of Alexander R. Esty. After the war, with the appearance of schools of architecture, the first of which opened

TOP LEFT: Advertisement for Henry Austin, showing his remodeling of Ithiel Town's New Haven house for Joseph E. Sheffield, 1860. RIGHT: Advertisement for L. [uther] Briggs & Co., Boston, 1871–73. Joy's Building was the location of many architectural offices in the mid-nineteenth century. BOTTOM LEFT: Daguerreotype of carpenter-turned-architect Aaron Morse (1806–49), with drafting instruments and open book signifying his new profession, 1840s.

at the Massachusetts Institute of Technology in 1868, university courses in history and design more and more became a standard part of the architect's training, as did European travel, and an impressive Latin-language diploma from one of those schools hanging on his (or, increasingly, by the end of the century, her[9]) office wall now became proof of professionalism. Over the course of the century, the worker who once shaped buildings at the construction site gradually became the recipient of explicit graphic design directions created by an artist-architect in a drafting room probably located far from that site.[10] In general, the process of producing those graphics remained largely unchanged from the nineteenth century until the late twentieth, when computer-aided design programs (or CAD) created a revolution in office practice—and the design of buildings—greater even than what had occurred in the early nineteenth century.

Architectural drawings intended to explain a proposed building to a client or builder, whether handcrafted or computer generated, are of various kinds.[11] These include Raphael's fundamental *plans,* or horizontal slices through a proposed dwelling, that are the diagrams of the clients' intended pattern of living. Plans show the shapes of and relationships among the rooms. Several examples occur here in the projects of Luther Briggs, Jr. A plot or block plan locates the house on its site, as does J. G. Hales's for the James A. Rundlet house. A later variation of this is Edwin Goodell's use of a diagram showing the orientation of the proposed Dabney house in Westport, Massachusetts, in relation to summer and winter sunshine. *Sections,* or vertical slices through the house, illustrate the relationship of superimposed spaces, the structure, and the interior elevations of rooms. Ogden Codman, Jr.'s, for Martha Codman reveal a spectacular domed stair hall. A. H. Davenport and Company created a variation of this type by showing the elevations of the walls enclosing a square room, so that all four can be simultaneously seen in relation to the plan they surround.

Exterior *elevations* reflect the expression of those interior arrangements on the outside of the home through the placement and shape of windows, doors, wings, roofs, porches, and so on. In this catalogue, they range from the simple balanced façades of houses in the English Colonial Revival style by A. W. Longfellow or Arland Dirlam to the irregular, picturesque exterior of Peabody and Stearns's Appleton house. There are also *details,* drawings at a larger (sometimes full) scale that explain typical or important aspects of joinery, construction, or design. These can be framing diagrams, such as Gridley Bryant's for the Wigglesworth house, or details of window frames, like those Luther Briggs, Jr., drew for the Bigelow house, or interior finishes like the ones Frank Chouteau Brown produced for the Tyler house.

There are other types of architectural graphics as well. In rough *preliminary sketches,* the architect probes the clients' program for a suitable arrangement and expression. Frank Chouteau Brown's studies for "A House on the Connecticut" are a case in point; so is John Calvin Stevens's scratchy proposal for a small, Shingle Style summer cottage on Great Diamond Island off the coast of Maine. Architects also prepare drawings for ancillary elements of a complex, such as landscaping, outbuildings, and gateways to estates. Henry Hoover laid out a terrace for the Edgar Moor house. The Little and Browne office produced a handsome fence and gateway for the Frick estate. This catalogue even includes the elevation of a two-story martin house complete with cupola, designed by Luther Briggs, Jr., to provide upscale nesting quarters for the clients' avian neighbors.

With the exception of the sketches, the graphic types just mentioned are included in Raphael's list of diagrams typically drawn by architects. These are flat graphics that are not intended to suggest the three-dimensional reality of the finished design, but are, like those of Samuel McIntire, mere diagrams that show undistorted, measurable relationships between the parts of a house. They are useful for instructing the builder, or, like the colored elevation by Alexander Esty, for impressing the client. In either case, they are two dimensional. Not until well into the nineteenth century did American architects, especially in New England, frequently begin to intrude upon the domain of the artist to project three-dimensional views, or anticipatory presentation *perspectives,* that became a standard part of their graphic repertory.[12] In his book of the 1830s, *Civil Architecture,* Bostonian Edward Shaw repeated Raphael's trio of planar drawings but added that, since it is difficult to judge the appearance of a building from orthographs, "it is most satisfactory and indeed, but just to the proprietor, to furnish him with views of the intended structure from different points of sight, accompanied by . . . outbuildings, shrubbery, &c., such as they may be expected to be when brought to perfection." After the Civil War, as a function of architects' new stature as artists removed from the building site, perspective views served primarily as visual aids to their sales pitch. As Benjamin Linfoot put it in 1884, the "architect . . . must keep his client's enthusiasm alive and active by sending or submitting bright, jaunty little perspectives of his contemplated work."[13]

Some architects were gifted enough to do their own perspectives, which were of course useless as instructions to the builder but useful to persuade the client to build, or—published in the new professional journals—to show off their skills to their peers. Soon there appeared men called "perspectivists," "renderers," or "delineators," who specialized in such eye-catching drawings. These artists existed either in-house, on the staff of an architect, or were itinerant, traveling from office to office, even city to city, to rent their pencils, pens, or brushes to any who wanted them. Many perspectives appear in this catalogue. The colorful bird's-eye view of the Cochrane garden by Arthur Shurcliff, signed on the reverse by a commercial artist named P. O. Palmstrom, Otto Eggers's perspective of Parker Hooper's Charlton house, the ink line perspective of William F. Goodwin's Paine house, initialed "R N W," or John C. Clapp, Jr.'s, drawing of Fox and Gale's Stone house well exemplify the type. A renderer who styled himself merely "Full" signed the soft pencil sketch of the house intended for Northeast Harbor, Maine, from the office of Bigelow, Wadsworth, Hubbard and Smith.

By late in the nineteenth century, such views of intended buildings came to exist independent of the construction process. This gave priority to their artistic rather than their utilitarian value. They were exhibited at galleries, museums, and clubs, and published in journals and books, with the drafter's intention of reaching beyond a specific client to a wider audience. Bigelow, Wadsworth, Hubbard and Smith, for example, showed the sketch of the house at Northeast Harbor at an annual exhibition of the Architectural League of New York, as had Parker Hooper his Charlton house depicted by Otto Eggers. Maine's prolific John Calvin Stevens exhibited his own sketches as far afield as Boston, New York, and Philadelphia. They were then published in catalogues or yearbooks, and in Stevens's promotional *Examples of American Domestic Architecture* (with text by Albert Winslow Cobb, 1889).

The first formal exhibition of drawings by the Boston Society of Architects took place at the Boston Art Club in February 1886. The show included more than two hundred works, some sent over by English architects, in pen, pencil, and watercolor. A residential design by John Calvin Stevens drew particular attention.[14] Another early show of architectural drawings opened in October 1890 at Boston's fashionable St. Botolph Club, a select social gathering founded in 1880 by a group of men including painters, sculptors, architects, and amateurs interested in the arts. The exhibition numbered eighty works. Because the club hoped to reach an audience beyond the drafting room or conference table, the exhibition committee said it wanted to have "largely perspectives, and, in general, such drawings as would interest not only the profession, but the outside public generally." The printed catalogue lists works from local offices, including those of Little and Browne and John Hubbard Sturgis, examples of whose drawings are included here.[15] More than twenty-five of the entries represented domestic projects. Periodically in the following years, St. Botolph found space for exhibitions of individual architects as well as of the Boston Architectural Club. Some architects had by then literally joined the ranks of the artists; indeed, E. C. Cabot had one foot firmly planted in each field.

The presence of such presentation drawings in this catalogue gives a somewhat skewed idea of the production of architectural offices. Many are beautiful objects in their own right, suitable to hang on living room walls, and they can often be found in dealers' shops and in museum or gallery exhibitions. Their attractiveness helps to preserve them. But the basic plans, sections, and details—the essential working drawings that take up the bulk of the architect's office time—often lack sufficient eye appeal for the general public, and as such, often do not survive. Unlike the preparatory sketches of artists, which are recognized as collectible works of art, architectural drawings created as means to an end are not always valued for themselves, especially if the architect is not famous. They get manhandled or are discarded altogether; they are not considered precious objects. Architects retain them only as they find them useful in the production of the finished product. At the terminus of the construction cycle, or the demise of the architect, they become obsolete; their sheer volume overwhelms, and people lose interest in them. Architectural archives are necessarily selective, necessarily unbalanced in favor of attractive rendered perspectives. Historic New England is fortunate in having a wide variety of graphic types, for they are all essential tools in explaining our cultural heritage. The preservation of these documents—however selective—ensures that the history of domestic design in the Northeast will be recorded as fully as possible, not only by what got built and still stands but also by what was contemplated, whether built or not.

This catalogue, as is the exhibition, is organized chronologically. The earliest works, from around 1800 onward, reflect the emergence of an architectural profession in this country, with drawings ranging from the linear diagrams of Samuel McIntire and Asher Benjamin to the colorful elevations of Luther Briggs, Jr., and Alexander Esty. The second half of the century saw the consolidation of the profession and the founding of architectural schools in which drafters became artists, adding attractive perspectives to the standard graphic repertory. Drawings by Henry Francis and John M. Allen represent this type. Early twentieth-century architects continued this trend as they turned out period houses in which past styles were given fresh development. Perspective views from the offices of Coolidge and Carlson, and Bigelow, Wadsworth, Hubbard and Smith, as well as from the hand of Halfdan Hanson, represent the most sought-after design graphics from this period. They exemplify what historian David Gebhard meant when he wrote that "presentation drawings for this architecture . . . were loose and free, suggesting the architect's quick, sensitive, and therefore romantic effort to symbolize a nonurban world."[16] Finally, the mid-twentieth century introduced Modernism, with houses presented in the crisp linear graphics of the era, such as those of Remmert Huygens. The catalogue closes there because the introduction of the computer in the 1980s effectively ended the history of handcrafted architectural graphics.

As a whole, the drawings in this catalogue trace projects in the evolving history of styles in New England domestic architecture of the last two centuries.[17] There are designs for the spectrum of classical and picturesque homes. In the nineteenth century, some architects turned their attention to earlier New England buildings in the classical style as sources of inspiration or for reasons of preservation, or both. Men like John Hubbard Sturgis recorded in measured drawings the forms and details of outstanding relics of the region's colonial heyday. With the publication of books on exotic styles and architects' travels to Europe and beyond to discover wider varieties of expression, the homogeneity of Roman classicism as the accepted standard of excellence since the Renaissance began to give way to a pluralism that included Greek forms, then the Gothic, Byzantine, and Romanesque. Following Napoleon's venture up the Nile in the early years of the nineteenth century, Neo-Egyptian buildings began to appear. Soon styles even more exotic to Western eyes—Chinese, Indian, Moorish, and so forth—became available. Although not all modes seemed suitable for domestic work, this catalogue demonstrates many of them. Samuel McIntire and Asher Benjamin drafted Roman-based Federal houses; Joseph Howard and Edward Shaw designed Grecian

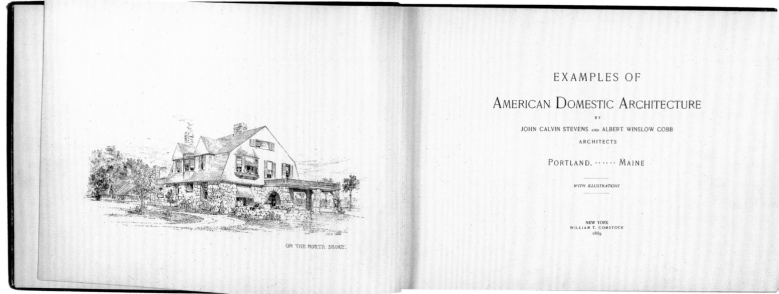

TOP LEFT: Royal Barry Wills (1895–1962) in front of his own house in
Winchester, Massachusetts. TOP RIGHT: Frontispiece and title page
from Royal Barry Wills's *Better Houses for Budgeteers*, 1946 (first edition,
1941), one of the many publications in which New England's favorite
Colonial Revival architect promoted his services. BOTTOM: Frontispiece
and title page from *Examples of American Domestic Architecture*, by
Albert Winslow Cobb, with illustrations by John Calvin Stevens, 1889.
This is another example of an architect's promotional literature.

temple-form dwellings, and Shaw also produced Gothic Revival cottages. At mid-century, Gervase Wheeler, Luther Briggs, Jr., Alexander Esty, and Edward Dow created Italianate villas, and Joseph Hayward designed a castellated mansion. Briggs drafted a rare design for a "Cottage Villa in the Rhenish Picturesque Style," while other architects, Gridley Bryant, for example—or his clients, like the Beebes and Brewers—chose the more elegant and more fashionable French Mansard.

The Queen Anne and Stick Styles emerged. New England summer architecture became synonymous with the Shingle Style after 1880; Maine's John Calvin Stevens was the master of the mode. Toward the end of the century, a learned classicism returned in the work of Ogden Codman, Jr., and A. H. Davenport and Company. Other styles proliferated too: the English Colonial Revival in the hands of A. W. Longfellow; the French Norman and American bungalow in the drawings of Frank Chouteau Brown. Boston's Arthur Little became famous for his revival of the Bulfinchian or Federal mode. Historical styles lingered well into the twentieth century, as in the Davis house by Coolidge and Carlson, but Modernism appeared early in the work of David Abrahams and Henry Hoover and later in that of Edwin Goodell, Huygens and Tappé, and others. The drawings in this catalogue, with a few additions, could illustrate a work on the stylistic evolution of New England domestic architecture of the nineteenth and twentieth centuries.

Architectural drawing runs parallel to building history. Choices of techniques made by architects at their drafting boards were closely connected to the development of the architectural profession. Unfamiliar technology, evolving society, and the influential styles in the early nineteenth century called for more complex graphics and a new visual clarity in drawing, and that required new drafting tools, materials, and techniques.[18] The catalogue shows important aspects of the evolution of graphic types during the years covered, from the introduction and development of materials and methods that transformed the black-ink diagrams made by McIntire or Benjamin at the beginning, to the colorful renderings of the firm of Fox and Gale in the middle, and the fresh perspectives of Remmert Huygens toward its end. Shades and shadows, tints and washes were gradually added to enliven and encode the linear diagrams of the eighteenth and early nineteenth centuries.

Until the nineteenth century, the basic architectural drawings were largely black on white; they were drawn in pencil on writing stock or heavy paper, then inked using a drafting or ruling pen. They contained few notes or dimensions, since that information was usually conveyed verbally or in a few jotted instructions. During that century, with the increasing separation of designer from building site, the introduction of formally written specifications, and, especially, more informative drawings using not only dimensions and notations but watercolor washes that brought a visual language to represent building materials, architectural graphics became complex and standardized. A color code described various materials: red or pink meant brickwork; yellow, woodwork; gray, stonework; and so on. Luther Briggs, Jr.'s, window details are typical, so too are Frank Chouteau

Brown's sheet of profiles and joinery for the Tyler house. Early on, the copying of drawings had to be done, according to a Boston architect of the period, by the laborious process of "laying a sheet of detail paper under the drawing and pricking through all the lines, then the original was taken up and the pin points traced in pencil and connected."[19] By the 1880s, with the appearance of larger, more detailed drawings for larger, more complex buildings—drawings intended for a growing number of specialized building trades—mechanical methods of copying were introduced to produce the ubiquitous blueprint, at first using natural light and then electric. The new process required that the ground upon which a drawing was made be translucent, so tracing paper and tracing cloth, or linen, became common. The drawings for the Appleton house were produced by the office of Peabody and Stearns using ink and watercolor on linen.

With the development of classes on life drawing and watercolor painting in the university schools of architecture after the Civil War, drafting became freer, with architects picking up soft lead pencils, colored pencils, charcoal sticks, crow quill pens, pastel crayons, watercolor brushes, and other artists' tools to create design drawings. At the same time, the emergence of professional "perspectivists"—Raphael's artists—resulted in elaborate, eye-popping views of proposed work. At times, the new materials appear alone; at others, combined into mixed media presentations. Parallel developments in the history of art, such as Impressionism in painting, also had an impact on drafting room practices. The graphic freedom with which Halfdan Hanson presented the Drake house makes it seem a distant—and belated—cousin to that flickering landscape mode. Such drawings were produced beyond the middle of the twentieth century, but much of this handcraft disappeared, of course, with the introduction of the computer.

The drawings included here are purposively not restricted to those of celebrity architects. The designs of the "starchitects" appear, of course, of men whose names grace any history of American architecture: Samuel McIntire, Asher Benjamin, Gervase Wheeler, Edward Shaw, Gridley J. F. Bryant, A. W. Longfellow, Peabody and Stearns, McKim, Mead and White, Ogden Codman, Jr., Frank Chouteau Brown, Arthur Shurcliff, and John Calvin Stevens. There are others by architects well remembered in New England if not in the rest of the country, men such as Luther Briggs, Jr., Coolidge and Carlson, Nathaniel Bradlee, Alexander Esty, Arthur Little, John Hubbard Sturgis, and Walter Bogner. More representative of the architectural profession as a whole, however, of the solid majority of domestic designers in the years covered by the catalogue, are the even lesser known or unknown men, some of whom are included for drawings that carry a particular interest of their own: Joseph Hayward, John M. Allen, Joseph Howard, Charles Roath, and Jacob Luippold. These hierarchical differences show up in the drawings themselves, in the gulf in skill displayed between, say, Halfdan Hanson's accomplished perspective of the Drake residence compared to Joseph Hayward's awkward elevations for the Oakes Ames castle. The domestic landscape of New England, however, resulted from the labors of the entire spectrum of designers.

To the extent that the collections in Historic New England's Library and Archives permit, this catalogue and the exhibition cover the sweep of domestic building types, of society in general, from cottage to castle. There are designs by Samuel Rantin and Son and by Jacob Luippold for the region's ubiquitous urban, middle-class, three-decker housing units. There are townhouses, both middle class, by Luther Briggs, Jr., and Charles Roath, and upper class, by Gridley Bryant. Apartments are represented, both urban, by Fox and Gale, and suburban, by Walter Crabtree. Cottages by John M. Allen and John Calvin Stevens, a bungalow by Frank Chouteau Brown, villas by Gervase Wheeler and Edward Dow, mansions by Edward Casey, Ogden Codman, Jr., and Little and Browne, all appear here, as do houses for the suburbs by David Abrahams, Henry Hoover, and Peabody and Stearns, and the seashore by Bigelow, Wadsworth, Hubbard and Smith.

Finally, there are projects for additions and alterations, additions to existing houses by Frank Chouteau Brown and Little and Browne and the Emmerton house by Arthur Little, and alterations to the Emerson house by Luther Briggs, Jr. Not all alterations or additions are the work of the initial architects. Over time, houses get changed, and some of those changes bury the original concept of the designer and client. Drawings preserve the process.

The clients for many of these domestic establishments naturally came from the affluent segment of New England society, those with the means to commission designs for high-rent areas of the landscape. On the list appear the industrialist and financier Henry Clay Frick of Pittsburgh and New York, the wealthy Boston merchant Thomas Wigglesworth, and William Sumner Appleton, Sr., father of the founder of the Society for the Preservation of New England Antiquities (now Historic New Eng-

land). Here are residential designs for Bigelows, Bloodgoods, Charltons, Cochranes, Codmans, Stones, Paines, Drakes, Ameses, Spauldings, Noyeses, Shermans, and Coolidges intended for or erected at Northeast Harbor, Maine; Newport, Rhode Island; Dublin, New Hampshire; and Plymouth, Brookline, Beverly, and Wellesley, Massachusetts; and other choice locations. But, as we have seen, there are designs here for the working and middle classes as well, ranging from generic rental properties such as three-deckers or apartment houses and living quarters above shops to the detached, single-family houses of suburbia. As a whole, the catalogue represents a large segment of the entire spectrum of New England domestic architecture.

Historic New England now holds more than 30,000 architectural drawings in its Library and Archives. It collects them as part of its mission to preserve the material and cultural history of the region. The many house museums administered by Historic New England are not the only portals to the past that help it fulfill that aim. The full story of architecture and society in the Northeast cannot be told from surviving buildings alone. The historian needs both buildings and drawings. As architect Robert A. M. Stern wrote, "we hope our buildings will be better than our drawings . . . but . . . the drawings provide a record of our intentions, a standard for measure."[20] The growing collection of architectural graphics owned by Historic New England represents a major resource for the study of northeastern architecture and adds a significant dimension to our understanding of the evolution of the domestic environment of the Northeast, and, by extension, of the entire United States. What is shown in this catalogue is the mere tip of the iceberg, a small sampling of an extraordinarily rich and indispensable resource for the fulfillment of Historic New England's mission.

Suitable for Framing:
Architectural Drawings as Works of Art

CHRISTOPHER MONKHOUSE

Over the last twenty-five years, the quest for appropriate period frames for oil paintings has become something of an obsession for connoisseurs, judging from the proliferation of specialist dealers, frame makers, and even curators engaged in this activity. The literature on historic frames has expanded exponentially, as have exhibitions specifically devoted to the subject. However, in one of the most insightful and comprehensive surveys to emerge thus far, simply titled *The Art of the Picture Frame*, at the National Portrait Gallery in London in 1997, its curator Jacob Simon noted in his introduction to the accompanying catalogue: "There is also a demand for an exhibition on the framing of prints, drawings, and photographs as I found out in the course of my research."[1] In other words, the study of period frames for works of art on paper has continued to be neglected, if not ignored altogether. In the following essay, this sad state of affairs pertaining to the framing of architectural drawings will be addressed by considering some surviving evidence.

Historic New England, since its founding in 1910 as the Society for the Preservation of New England Antiquities, has played a leadership role in the region, if not the nation, in the care and conservation of historic properties. Despite its goal of telling the entire story of a property's history through the accretions of generations on site, the associated architectural drawings and records that came with many of the properties have been transferred to its Boston headquarters. There they can be better cared for and studied with the aid of flat files, compact shelving, and a reference library close at hand. A notable exception is the framed perspective watercolor of Roseland Cottage, the Gothic Revival summer residence designed by Joseph C. Wells for New Yorkers Henry and Lucy Bowen in Woodstock, Connecticut, in 1846 (see pages 64–65).[2]

The framed watercolor is remarkable not only because of the highly decorative composition frame with multiple cusped arches, but also because the view was rendered in perspective at a time when such a treatment for architectural drawings was still uncommon in America.[3] In fact, it is the earliest example of an architectural perspective in Historic New England's extensive collection, irrespective of building type. More in keeping with architectural practice at that time would have been for the architect to provide only a set of floor plans and front and side elevations for his clients and their builders, as Wells also did for Roseland Cottage. Shortly before designing Roseland Cottage, Wells had produced a similar set of Gothic Revival designs for another New York client, Jonathan Sturgis, who wished to build a summer residence in Fairfield, Connecticut.

Like Roseland Cottage, the Sturgis house, along with a set of architectural drawings, still remains intact.[4] Based on the surviving graphic evidence for at least the Bowen commission, Wells was capable of providing clients, as part of his design package, with a perspective portrait of their home suitable for framing.[5]

Related objects have a habit of finding one another. Historic New England has recently had the good fortune to acquire an even earlier example of a presentation architectural elevation still housed in its original frame and glass (see page 20). Probably dating from the late 1810s or early 1820s, the drawing depicts a substantial three-storied brick Federal-style residence set off by a *verre églomisé* black and gold mat within a gilt wooden frame incorporating an internal spiral-twisted molding. The label for the frame's maker, John Doggett, is still affixed to the back. As the leading picture framer in Federal and Greek Revival Boston, Doggett frequently provided similar frames with *verre églomisé* black and gold mats for schoolgirl embroidery executed by the daughters of Boston's first families, as well as more substantial neoclassical gilt frames for portraits painted by Gilbert Stuart.[6] But as this drawing comes with no other history, the circumstances surrounding its commission and framing must remain for the present a matter for conjecture. It seems plausible, however, to imagine that the domestic character of the frame and mat made it appropriate for hanging in the building depicted, perhaps even as a gift from a grateful architect or builder to his satisfied patron, as appears to have been the case with the Roseland Cottage perspective drawing for Mr. and Mrs. Bowen.

A century later, the architects' practice of presenting clients with portraits of their homes still seems to be in evidence with the framed presentation pencil and gouache perspective by Otto Eggers of Parker Morse Hooper's Pond Meadow in Westport Point, Massachusetts, for the Edward Perry Charlton family (see pages 180–81). Another example is the nearly contemporaneous perspective by "J.E.C." (probably John E. Carlson) from the office of Coolidge and Carlson for Mrs. Minerva Davis's gambrel-roofed residence in Agawam, Massachusetts (see pages 188–90). The latter's mount, outlined in pencil and wash, suggests the drawing was intended for framing, and given its modest size, perfectly suited for hanging in the diminutive dwelling it depicts.

Midway in time between the images of Roseland Cottage, dating from 1846, and Pond Meadow, dating from 1915, another perspective of a summer cottage might fall into the category of an architect's token

TOP: Front elevation of an unidentified residence in original gilt frame with a *verre églomisé* border. The unsigned drawing is done in ink and wash on paper. The frame was made by John Doggett of Boston, c. 1820. BOTTOM: Detail of John Doggett's paper label, which is attached to the back of the frame shown above.

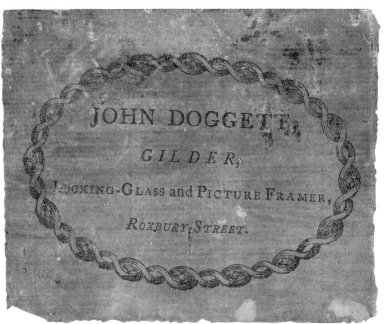

of appreciation for a client's commission—a modest Stick Style cottage in Marion, Massachusetts, for the Reverend John Cotton Brooks (see pages 116–17). While this drawing no longer retains its original frame, the house has been made memorable because the architect, John M. Allen, or his draftsman, has placed it within a format reminiscent of a fan. The image is dated 1882, at the height of the rage for all things Japanese (think Gilbert and Sullivan's *Mikado*). Maybe Allen thought of the drawing more as a decorative element to be attached directly to the wall sans frame and hence better able to blend in with real fans, parasols, and fishnets that likely adorned the interior. If the work was meant to be framed and glazed, however, the frame might have been ebonized with incised gold lines in keeping with the taste of the Aesthetic Movement, not unlike the one used by architect Charles Kimball in 1877 for the perspective delineated by W. H. Field of the Stick Style summer cottage for Dr. J. Heald in Lovell, Maine (now in the collection of the Maine Historic Preservation Commission).[7]

As will be shown, there is further evidence that architects provided presentation drawings as personal gifts for their valued clients, especially if the architect was an accomplished artist in his own right, whether in watercolor, pastel, ink, or even pencil. Such skills were often picked up or further developed while on sketching holidays at home or abroad, and often in the company of other artists, both professional and amateur. One such group, known as The Brushins, provided camaraderie and constructive criticism for Portland, Maine, architect John Calvin Stevens. He is included in this catalogue with a sketch from 1888 for a Shingle Style cottage on Great Diamond Island in Casco Bay (see pages 118-21).

Cass Gilbert is an example of an artist/architect who excelled in the mediums of both pastel and watercolor. In 1892, for one of his most loyal patrons, the lawyer William Lightner of St. Paul, Minnesota, he provided a pastel perspective in an Eastlake gilt oak frame of a Richardsonian Romanesque residence just on the verge of succumbing to the Classical Revival.[8] His painterly use of reddish brown sandstone for string courses and entry arch voussoirs set off by walls of rough-faced gray quartzite, in light of the picturesque play of contrasting stone, made the house an ideal subject. The drawing hung in the entrance hall, just like the watercolor perspective of Roseland Cottage. While presentation drawings tended to pass from one homeowner to the next, the Cass Gilbert pastel has recently come to be appreciated as a valuable work of art—rather than as a mere document—and hence did not get left behind by a recent owner, despite having remained in situ for one hundred years.[9] Better, of course, than being consigned to the rubbish bin, but such drawings are most meaningful when they are allowed to remain where the architect envisioned them hanging for the duration of the building's existence.[10]

As Gilbert's pastel has recently been reframed and re-matted, the author must rely on his memory of what the original Eastlake gilt frame looked like when he first saw it a dozen years ago in its then unaltered state. The gilding on the original oak frame was laid directly on the wood rather than on gesso as recommended by the English tastemaker and author, Charles Eastlake: "The effects of oak-grain seen through leaf-gold

is exceedingly good, and the appearance of *texture* is infinitely more interesting than the smooth monotony of gilt 'compo.'"[11] Such gilded surroundings proved felicitous for the pastel perspective, as they were compatible with the warm earth tones used to depict the house, while the oak grain showing through the gilding provided a variegated surface in keeping with the chalky texture of the pastel.

Another artist/architect in the same vein as Cass Gilbert is William Ralph Emerson of Boston. Best known for the seminal role he played in introducing the Shingle Style to the New England coast, Emerson also excelled as a watercolorist and pastelist, as acknowledged by his contemporaries.[12] In an exhibition highly unusual for its time (or any time for that matter), the Salmagundi Club and the American Black-and-White Society, representing professional artists and illustrators, respectively, joined forces with the Architectural League of New York, representing professional architects, to present a joint exhibition in the winter of 1886 at the American Art Association in New York City. Emerson was singled out for special praise. Perhaps because he knew he was going to be shown in the company of professional landscape painters, he decided to introduce color into his architectural perspectives, and with stunning results according to the reviewer for *The American Architect and Building News*:

> . . . No. 226 by Mr. W R Emerson of Boston [is] a study of a rambling red house, almost buried in summer foliage, which to our mind is, without exception, the most beautiful piece of work in the whole collection. Every architect knows Mr. Emerson's pencil sketches, and remembers the picturesqueness with which he manages to fill those unapproachable compositions; but a colored drawing bearing his name is a novelty. We cannot say certainly whether the rendering is wholly from his hand or not [it would have been!] but whoever did it has known not only how to retain all the picturesqueness of a thoroughly characteristic design, but to intensify it, at the same time that he clothed it with the tenderness and feeling that only color laid by a master hand can give. Anything more full of artistic sentiment it would be hard to conceive, and we may all be proud that such a charming work should close the American portion of the collection hung on the walls of the gallery.[13]

Much encouraged by such reviews, Emerson continued to explore and exploit color when rendering architecture on paper, whether in watercolor or pastel. In 1897, while designing a Shingle Style cottage for the landscape architect, Joseph H. Curtis, on a site overlooking the entrance to Northeast Harbor on Mount Desert Island in Maine, Emerson used the opportunity to produce a house portrait in highly saturated pastels (see page 22). He further enriched the composition by selecting a wide gold mat set within a narrow black frame incorporating a gold liner.[14] In keeping with the tradition of an architect giving a portrait of the house he has just designed to his client, Emerson's pastel perspective may have hung briefly in Joseph Curtis's Shingle Style cottage, and perhaps in the front hall, as in the case of Gilbert's pastel for William Lightner in St. Paul, Minnesota, and Wells's watercolor of Roseland Cottage in Woodstock,

TOP: Perspective of a cottage for Joseph H. Curtis in Northeast Harbor, Maine, signed by the architect and delineator William Ralph Emerson, 1897. Pastel. BOTTOM: Perspective of the Islesboro Hotel (Inn) in Islesboro, Maine, designed by Wheelwright and Haven and delineated by Robert Closson Spencer, Jr., 1888–89. Ink and watercolor on heavy paper.

Perspective of the Samoset Hotel, Rockland, Maine,
signed by the architect and delineator Harry C. Wilkinson,
dated 1903, in original oak frame. Pencil on tracing paper.

Connecticut.[15] While the Emerson pastel no longer hangs there, it has happily not strayed far. It presently can be found on view just up the hill in Thuya Lodge, a botanical library designed and built by Joseph Curtis in 1912, and since 1933 open to the public.[16] The library is now owned and maintained by the Mount Desert Land and Garden Preserve along with its adjacent garden, designed by Charles Savage in 1958.

Perspective portraits of hotels, unlike those for houses, were hung in front lobbies for reasons of profit. Whether provided by the architect or an independent architectural delineator, such views were used initially to attract investors. They could then be adapted for advertising purposes, as illustrations in brochures sent to potential guests in advance of the opening. In the course of time, alterations and enlargements would be acknowledged and celebrated through additional framed perspectives recording these changes as a way of signaling progress and success. One hotel that went out of its way to fill its lobby and corridors with such views (with photographs in time supplanting the drawings) was the Poland Spring House in Poland, Maine, the legendary flagship resort for a chain of hotels managed by the Hiram Ricker family, including the Mt. Kineo on Moosehead Lake and the Samoset in Rockland, both also in Maine.[17]

Hotels could reach a broader audience when their architectural perspectives were shown in exhibitions of architectural drawings, which started to proliferate in America in the 1880s, following a highly visible display by both American and foreign architects at the Centennial Exposition in Philadelphia in 1876. One hotel that gained valuable exposure through such venues was the Islesboro Inn (see page 22), a hostelry located on an island of the same name in the middle of Penobscot Bay in Maine.[18]

Designed in the late 1880s by the Boston architectural firm of Wheelwright and Haven, the presentation perspective for the Islesboro Inn (initially called Hotel) made its debut in 1890 in an exhibition of architectural drawings at the exclusive St. Botolph Club, Boston's leading social club for people involved in the arts. Since the club's founding in 1880, architecture has played a visible role there, in terms of both its membership and its programs. Organizing a loan exhibition of architectural drawings was in keeping with its mission and reflective of a burgeoning interest in the genre. The Islesboro Inn is listed as #9 in the accompanying catalogue, out of a total of eighty drawings on view.[19]

When the history of architectural drawing exhibitions is finally written, the St. Botolph Club exhibition of 1890 might well be singled out for the effort it made to give credit not only to the architects but also to the delineators. At a time when delineators frequently went unacknowledged, the St. Botolph Club went out of its way to list his or her name (there is one woman delineator mentioned here—"Miss S. S. Howe"). As the Islesboro Inn drawing is signed only with the delineator's initials "RCS" in the lower left corner, they might have been thought to stand for the well-known Boston architect R. Clipston Sturgis. But thanks to the catalogue entry, the drawing's delineator is recorded as "R. C. Spencer Jr." His name appears frequently as a delineator for drawings in the exhibition,

and not only in the service of Wheelwright and Haven, but also of Shepley, Rutan and Coolidge.[20] And Spencer was in very good company, including such talented delineators as E. Eldon Deane, George P. Fernald, David A. Gregg, Theodore O. Langerfeldt, and W. W. Bosworth.

The second time the Islesboro Inn presentation perspective was included in an exhibition in Boston occurred exactly a year later in the fall of 1891. The show was organized jointly by the Boston Society of Architects and the Boston Architectural Club and staged in a highly visible venue—McKim, Mead and White's newly opened Boston Public Library—during the annual convention of the American Institute of Architects. All 453 exhibits had the benefit of review by the leaders of the architectural profession, including #422, listed in the accompanying catalogue as simply "Islesboro Inn. Wheelwright and Haven Architects." A visitor would look in vain to discover the name of the delineator whose initials appeared on the drawing.[21]

After the Boston Public Library exhibition, the Islesboro Inn presentation perspective finally got to hang in the lobby of the building it depicted. There the drawing presumably remained until the inn finally closed its doors in 1951, followed by demolition in 1955. In the course of the first half of the twentieth century, it would have witnessed a fire in 1915, and a rebuilding from designs by a Philadelphia architect in 1917.[22] The drawing avoided a long trip west to Chicago in the spring of 1893, because in the architecture section of the fine arts display at the World's Columbian Exposition, the Boston architect Edmund Wheelwright (who also served as a juror for the architecture entries) submitted a photograph instead of the drawing for his Islesboro Inn.[23]

By the time the presentation perspective finally reached Historic New England just over a century since its execution, its original frame—as is so often the case—had disappeared, along with its exhibition history, which might well have been recorded by labels attached to the back. In all likelihood, the original frame was made of quarter-sawn oak, with the proportions dictated by the size of the drawing. In an era when many resort hotel lobbies were furnished with Mission Style oak furniture, such a frame would have been very much in keeping with its surroundings. Similar frames have survived on closely related drawings, like the one illustrated on page 23 by architect and delineator Harry C. Wilkinson for the Samoset Hotel in Rockland in 1903, just down the bay from the Islesboro Inn.[24]

To end where this essay began, it is the author's hope that in the future the importance of keeping architectural drawings in their original frames will be more deeply appreciated. Although removing drawings from their frames has, ironically, often been undertaken in the name of preservation and due to limited storage space, frames also have significant stories to tell about the use of architectural drawings as works of art intended for public display. In other words, a presentation architectural drawing without its original frame becomes a mere historical document, providing little opportunity for the viewer to imagine the more public role originally envisioned for it by both its architect and its delineator.

The Development of the Architectural Profession in New England: An Overview

ROGER G. REED and EARLE G. SHETTLEWORTH, JR.

istoric New England's wide-ranging collection of drawings and documents allows scholars to trace the evolution of the architectural profession in New England. The earliest drawings are rudimentary outlines for functional buildings constructed in a traditional manner. Much was left to the skills of carpenters and joiners who fabricated architectural elements by hand. These men knew their trades, and they worked with knowledge of historical styles and building traditions imported from Great Britain. Prior to the nineteenth century, knowledge not gained through apprenticeship was derived from builders' guides or style books published in England, such as William Pain's *The Practical Builder* (first edition, 1774). In rare instances, English architects relocated here and brought their expertise. Peter Harrison, who lived in Newport, Rhode Island, and designed several important Boston buildings, is an example.[1] Benjamin Henry Latrobe, in Washington, D. C., was perhaps the most famous among the first generation of professional architects. Less well known were people like English-born Peter Banner, who came to New England via New York.[2] Few visited Europe to learn about architecture; Charles Bulfinch was a rare exception among early native-born architects because he traveled abroad.[3]

In the eighteenth century, most buildings were designed on paper with crudely measured floor plans or framing plans, supplemented by a sketch of the front elevation. Finish work—what we would refer to as ornamentation—was added later for those clients who could afford hand-carved details. Because it was expensive, carved decoration was mostly limited to the interior, where it would be out of the weather. The drawings of Samuel McIntire of Salem provide a good illustration.[4] Trained by his father as a housewright, McIntire worked as a wood-carver and furniture maker. He provided minimal floor plans and elevations that gave masons, carpenters, and joiners the basic dimensions, but reserved the finish work for his own skilled hands.

The traditional method of acquiring knowledge of building began with apprenticeship to someone in the trades. If a young carpenter wished to improve his station by offering architectural services, his options were to train himself using various builders' guides or find an established architect in whose office he could work.[5] Until practicing architects became more common in the early 1800s, studying and copying from books provided the best means of developing drawing skills. In 1809, a group of architects and skilled craftsmen, recognizing the importance of books, established the Architectural Library of Boston, a collection intended for members of the building trades.[6] The five men who founded it were: Ithiel Town, an engineer and architect; Solomon Willard, a sculptor, stonemason, and architect; Samuel Waldron and Nathaniel Critchet, housewrights; and John Gill, a stucco worker.

The nature of early architectural drawings is represented in this catalogue by some of the finest architects first produced in New England: Asher Benjamin, Samuel McIntire, and the unknown designer for the James A. Rundlet house. Benjamin, along with Charles Bulfinch, was one of the earliest to call himself an architect—that is, someone who would plan and design an entire house for a client. He and Bulfinch also represent two important aspects of the architectural profession in its infancy in America.

Asher Benjamin came from modest origins. Born in Greenfield in western Massachusetts, he designed important houses in the Connecticut River valley before relocating to Boston. His abilities as a designer were not especially sophisticated, but he understood the principles of design. In one sense, he surpassed his more cultivated contemporary, Bulfinch, by publishing several builders' guides, which contributed significantly to the development of the profession. Having begun as a carpenter, Benjamin understood the need for such guides to provide supplemental direction for carpenters, joiners, and aspiring architects. His *Country Builder's Assistant* (1797) was the first carpenter's book by an American published in America.[7] Benjamin also offered a drawing school in Boston, although little is known about it. In these early years, formal architectural training probably did not extend much beyond taking lessons in the various skills otherwise learned on the job. The value of working for an established architect provided such an advantage that, in the early nineteenth century, young students would be willing to pay to work at menial tasks in the office. If you were fortunate, as in the case of Alexander Parris, your architect owned an extensive library of architectural books to be studied in your spare time.[8] The tradition of having a well-stocked architectural library available in an architect's office remains common today.

Charles Bulfinch was a gentleman architect from the upper class, who had other sources of income, such as real estate speculation, and served for many years on the Boston Board of Selectmen. His name could not be found in the Boston city directories as offering design services. When his business ventures failed, he became more dependent upon his design skills and devoted more time to architecture, moving to Washington, D. C., to continue the work on the nation's capitol.

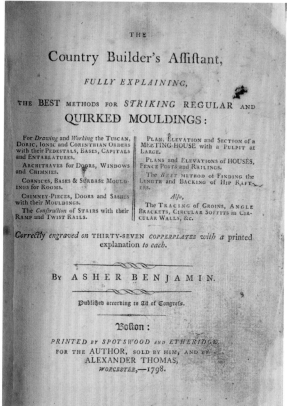

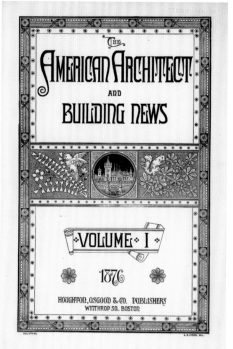

LEFT: Title pages of *The Rules of Work of the Carpenters in the Town of Boston* (1800) and *The Constitution of the Proprietors of the Architectural Library of Boston* (1809). TOP RIGHT: Title page of Asher Benjamin's *Country Builder's Assistant* (1798). BOTTOM RIGHT: Title page of *The American Architect and Building News* (1876).

In Boston, the first man to identify himself in the local directory as an architect was Peter Banner, in 1805. By 1840, this number had grown to a dozen.[9] The style of the early drawings, which was often spare in detail, began by the 1830s to give way to more professionally polished designs. The blossoming of the architectural profession is represented in this catalogue in drawings by Edward Shaw, Charles Roath, and Joseph Howard in Boston, and by William F. Pratt in Northampton, Massachusetts. These men all originated in the working class. Shaw and Pratt both trained as carpenters (Pratt worked for his father).[10] The drawings in this catalogue from this group exhibit characteristics we would find more recognizable today, the principal difference being the absence of the number of detail drawings we now expect. This was partly a function of the earlier buildings' lack of complexity, and partly due to the fact that craftsmen in the building trades accepted certain "rules of work," outlining performance and pay.[11] It was also true that the written specifications could be lengthy documents providing detailed instructions not shown on the drawings.[12]

The growing number of architects in Boston illustrates the rise of a profession then achieving recognition by a public that, since the founding of the colonies, had traditionally deferred to local carpenters or housewrights. The major change involved convincing clients of the need to pay architects to supervise construction and, indeed, to respect the architects' right of ownership of the drawings. Until architectural supervision became more accepted, no architect could be assured that his designs would be carried out as he intended.

The next major change came after the Civil War. Many of the new generation of architects traveled to Europe, even obtaining architectural education in the Ecole des Beaux-Arts in Paris. William G. Preston was the first Bostonian to train there, although he was preceded by the New York transplant H. H. Richardson.[13] It became increasingly common toward the end of the nineteenth century, as schools began to offer courses in design, to obtain a formal education in architecture. The first institution to establish a school of architecture in this country was the Massachusetts Institute of Technology in 1868. Led by William Robert Ware, this school trained a great many New England architects. The number who studied there is particularly significant if we include those who attended courses but did not obtain a degree, for example, Louis H. Sullivan. Harvard and Yale followed with their own professional degrees. In 1867, the Boston Society of Architects was established as the first local chapter of the national American Institute of Architects.[14] Led by Edward Clarke Cabot, the BSA was not intended to be an elitist organization, as every architect in the city received an invitation to attend.[15]

The post-Civil War period also saw an increase in partnerships, and the larger office staffs needed to support them. Peabody and Stearns is an example of a large firm with a national practice.[16] This trend reflected both the increased competition for large-scale projects in the late nineteenth century and the greater complexity of buildings to be designed. Professional organizations, such as the Boston Society of Architects and the Boston Architectural Club, started in 1889, provided a forum for the discussion of ideas and the advancement of professional standards in what could still be a ruthlessly competitive profession. The Boston Architectural Club evolved into the Boston Architectural College, which has become one of the nation's major independent architectural schools.

While avenues for formal academic training became increasingly available, there remained the parallel track for carpenters to establish themselves as architects. Early in the nineteenth century, Charitable Mechanic Associations in Massachusetts, Maine, Rhode Island, and Connecticut offered drawing classes, but these organizations were expensive to join. It became easier for carpenters and builders to develop architectural skills by the 1870s, when there was an extraordinary increase in architectural publications. Architectural journals, such as *The American Architect and Building News* of Boston, which began publication in 1876, were edited for architects. Other journals, such as *Carpentry and Building* of New York, which first appeared in 1879, were directed at contractors.[17] Trade journals supplemented these, as, of course, did pattern books, from which a contractor without professional training could purchase plans for houses and compete with architects. The cases of Irish immigrant Samuel Rantin and German immigrant Jacob Luippold in the late nineteenth century, and Norwegian immigrant Halfdan Hanson in the early twentieth century, whose drawings appear in this catalogue, are excellent examples of men who followed this track. In the case of Joseph Hayward of Brockton, Massachusetts, however, we have one example of a carpenter who did not make the transition.

By the end of the nineteenth century, the profession of architecture had been established much as we know it today. The training available to students, both formal and informal, continued into the twentieth century. The arrival of the dynamic Parisian professor Désiré Despradelle introduced the French system of architectural education to Boston in 1893. Recruited by the Boston architect Francis Ward Chandler, who headed the MIT program, Despradelle brought to his classroom both the teaching methods and the elaborate classical style that characterized the Ecole des Beaux-Arts. Until his death in 1912, Despradelle influenced a generation of aspiring architects such as Guy Lowell, designer of the Museum of Fine Arts on Huntington Avenue in Boston, one of New England's most visible statements of neoclassical design.

A major change came in the mid-twentieth century, when American architecture again followed the lead of Europe, although now by rejecting historical styles. Harvard University's program in architecture set the trend in New England, and nationally. Established in 1893 under the direction of architect H. Langford Warren, the program initially trained students to design in the historical styles. The great building campaign at Harvard in the years between the wars had affirmed American interpretation of Georgian Colonial architecture as the dominant style. In 1936, Harvard hired the German architect, Walter Gropius, to run what was then called the Graduate School of Design, and this resulted in a decline in emphasis on traditional styles in favor of what soon came to be called the

International Style. The Gropius-designed graduate school dormitories, the Harkness Commons (1949–50), represent this break with the past.

Boston architect James Lawrence, who attended the program at MIT under the influence of modern Scandinavian design, provided a somewhat jaded account in 1989 of the Gropius-led changes underway in the 1930s: "The air was heavy, and a cleansing was needed, but when it came in the form of the International Style, stripping away what was false and irrelevant, it also limited too severely the role of the imagination in design, resulting in an impoverishment of our architecture—from which we are still reacting today, not always successfully."[18] Apart from stylistic change, Gropius also redirected the teaching of architecture. Under his leadership, the GSD combined the departments of architecture, landscape architecture, and city planning. This holistic approach profoundly altered the perspective of the students, who were encouraged to collaborate with each other at the GSD and with different departments within Harvard.[19] Notwithstanding these changes in architectural education, the continued popularity of traditional styles for the homeowner is reflected in some of the postwar drawings featured in this catalogue.

With the Great Depression and World War II behind it, the profession in New England benefited from a building boom, especially as a result of cities seeking to reinvent themselves in the face of aggressive competition from the fast-growing suburbs. Two collections recently acquired by Historic New England reflect this trend. The first—sketches and drawings by Gerhard Kallmann and Michael McKinnell dating from the early 1960s—documents the design phases of Boston's new City Hall, a dramatic concrete structure commanding an open plaza in the heart of the city which replaced the Scollay Square neighborhood.[20] In contrast to these records, the second collection consists of extensive files tracing the partnership that architect Frederick A. Stahl and developer Roger Webb formed with the Society for the Preservation of New England Antiquities (now Historic New England) to preserve and revitalize Boston's Faneuil Hall market, itself an ambitious project to renew the waterfront in the 1820s. The groundbreaking 1968 study produced by Stahl, Webb, and the Society established the feasibility for historic rehabilitation and recommended the plan, which was achieved through the urban renewal process. Thus, in the 1960s and 1970s the architectural profession began to pursue parallel aims, creating new designs while finding an increasing role for renewing old buildings. In the domestic field, the writings of Vincent Scully and the work of Robert A. M. Stern steered a new generation of architects on a course of postmodernism, which again found place for historical references in design, whether it be the vernacular expression of the neo-Shingle Style or the formal red brick of the neo-Georgian. By 1980, the look of many New England homes had come full circle, returning to the architectural styles of the seventeenth and eighteenth centuries.

TOP LEFT: Stahl Associates' study of Faneuil Hall Marketplace, showing the pair of original, no longer extant Alexander Parris buildings. Rendering by John Hagan, 1968. TOP RIGHT: Walter Gropius in his home in Lincoln, Massachusetts, c. 1965. BOTTOM: Kallmann, McKinnell and Knowles's competition drawing, final stage, for Boston City Hall. Drawing by Michael McKinnell, 1962.

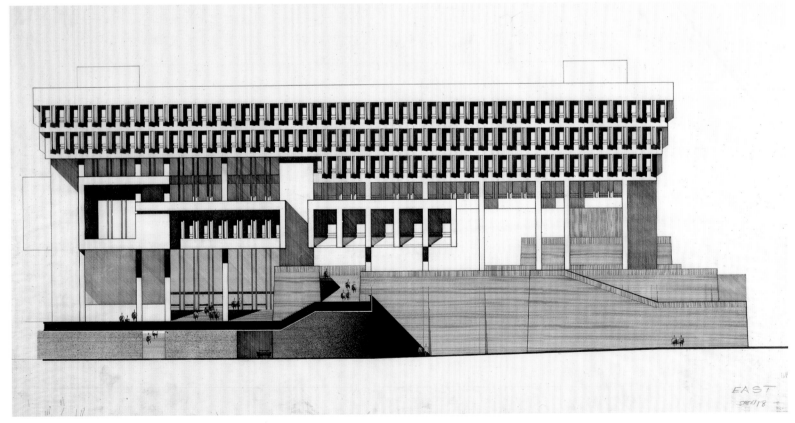

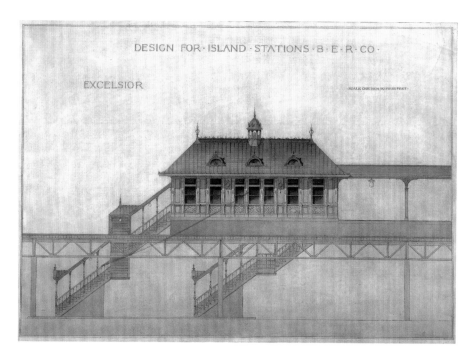

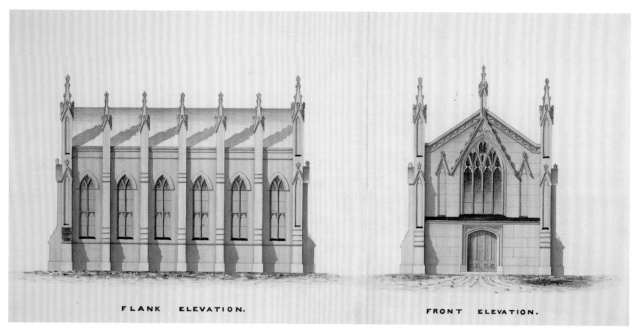

TOP LEFT: Alexander W. Longfellow, Jr.'s, winning entry for the Boston Elevated Railway Company's 1898 competition for a station design.
TOP RIGHT: William Sumner Appleton, founder of the Society for the Preservation of New England Antiquities, now Historic New England, 1929. BOTTOM: Detail of Richard Bond's competition entry for the chapel at Mount Auburn Cemetery, Cambridge, Massachusetts, 1843.

LORNA CONDON

One hundred years have passed since the Society for the Preservation of New England Antiquities, now Historic New England, began to collect records of New England buildings and of the people who created and used them. Today, Historic New England holds one of the country's most important architectural archives, including drawings, photographs, prints, books, artworks, manuscripts, and ephemera. Its collections are a major resource for anyone undertaking research on the region's built environment. That this archives came into being is directly the result of one man's vision.

William Sumner Appleton (1874–1947) was born to a family of wealth and privilege. His grandfather, Nathan Appleton, who had made a fortune in the textile industry, was a member of the Boston Athenaeum and the Massachusetts Historical Society, and his father, William Sumner Appleton, Sr., who had a scholarly interest in genealogy and numismatics, was a founder of the Bostonian Society, the Boston Numismatic Society, and the American Historical Society. Growing up on Boston's Beacon Hill, Sumner, as he was known, moved in a cultivated milieu, surrounded by the work of some of New England's most influential architects. Charles Bulfinch's Massachusetts State House was just blocks away from his own home at 39 Beacon Street, which had been designed for his grandfather by Alexander Parris, architect of the Quincy Market. The young Appleton probably would have known the work of Asher Benjamin at 54 Beacon Street, which had also once belonged to his grandfather. Even away from the city proper, he was exposed to the work of leading architects. His family's Stick Style country house, Holbrook Hall, in Newton, Massachusetts, was designed by Peabody and Stearns. He spent a great deal of time in Manchester, Massachusetts, at the country home of his aunt Harriot Appleton Curtis and her family. Sharksmouth, as it was called, was the work of another Boston firm, Ware and Van Brunt. At Sharksmouth, Appleton would have used the staircase that had been removed from the 1737 Hancock House in Boston at the time of its controversial demolition in 1863 and reinstalled in the Curtis house. No doubt, Appleton's passion for architecture was nurtured by his childhood exposure to these remarkable buildings.

After an extended stay in Europe with his family and attendance at St. Paul's School in Concord, New Hampshire, Appleton entered Harvard in the fall of 1892. His program included courses in history, French, philosophy, and art, among others. Charles Eliot Norton, Harvard's first professor of the history of art, taught him Ancient, Roman, and Medieval art.

Appleton came under the spell of the influential and charismatic Norton and became familiar with the thinking of William Morris and John Ruskin. Upon graduating in 1896, he left for a six-month grand tour of England and the Continent. When he returned, he entered into business as a real estate and investment broker, but after a few years, he suffered a breakdown due, according to him, to severe eye strain, and gave up the business world.

As he recuperated from his breakdown, Appleton began to explore in a serious way the historical and antiquarian activities that had been a tradition in his family. He turned to pursuits more in keeping with his interests and joined several patriotic, historical, and antiquarian organizations, including the Massachusetts Society of the Sons of the Revolution, the Massachusetts Historical Society, the Bostonian Society, the Essex Institute, and the New England Historic and Genealogical Society. Through the Sons of the Revolution, Appleton became active in 1905 in the effort to preserve the Paul Revere House in Boston's North End, one of the oldest surviving houses in the city. Serving as secretary of the Paul Revere Memorial Association, he worked with architect Joseph Everett Chandler and others on the restoration. In 1906, Appleton took the lead in another preservation effort, one intended to thwart the Boston Transit Commission's plan to alter the Old State House. In the face of opposition from a number of groups, the Transit Commission was forced to back down.

Appleton's experiences in the fourteen years following his graduation from Harvard, which included work in real estate, additional academic studies at Harvard, involvement in civic affairs and non-profit organizations, hands-on preservation work, and extensive travel, matured him into a more rounded individual and laid the foundation for his professional career.[1]

In 1909, Appleton learned of plans to significantly alter the Jonathan Harrington house, which overlooks the green in Lexington, Massachusetts, and was the site of a dramatic incident during the confrontation with British troops on 19 April 1775. Outrage at yet another loss to the region's historic fabric had a galvanizing effect on him, and he took the necessary legal steps to establish the Society for the Preservation of New England Antiquities, taking care to ensure that it would enjoy non-profit status. He later commented, "From that minute on my life's work seemed to be cut out for me."[2] As he gathered members for his society, the charm, zeal, diplomacy, and tenacity that characterized his professional work for the rest of his life came into play. He assembled officers and a board of trustees made up of both men and women who could provide financial support and/or prestige; several of them had academic experience or had worked with other historical and patriotic organizations.

Appleton conceived of an energetic and dynamic organization that would be able to move swiftly whenever a historic building was threatened. He described his goals for the Society: "to own for purposes of preservation, appropriate old houses throughout New England, or else to take such steps, by means of advice or financial assistance, as may lead other societies to undertake the work of such ownership and preservation."[3]

As Corresponding Secretary, he communicated to the members through the quarterly *Bulletin*, informing them of current activities, preaching to them about preservation, persuading them to donate objects, and asking for contributions to support special projects. It is through the *Bulletin* that Appleton's vision for preservation on paper was first articulated.

In 1911, in only the fourth issue, Appleton wrote, "The Society wishes to form a complete collection of views and accounts of all the notable old buildings and sites in New England. To accomplish this it must depend largely on gifts of photographs, drawings, engravings, picture postal cards, and books. All persons are urged to present such material to the Society." This call to members was repeated many times in the succeeding issues. Only four years later, the Society's first librarian, Ernest L. Gay, reported that more than 14,500 views had been added to the Library's collection. During this time, the collecting policy had expanded to include contemporary views of New England architecture and daily life: "The idea in view has simply been that what is new to this generation will be old-fashioned to the next and antique to that following." By 1920, Appleton's vision of the role the Society would play in the preservation of a visual record of New England had greatly expanded: "The point cannot be too often reiterated that any and every picture of a New England subject, be it landscape, seascape, old or modern house, ship or what not, is suitable for our collection." It is important to note that Appleton was assisted in his collection building by successive librarians, trustees, officers, and donors; after his death, these same groups, along with his successors, worked to both refine and expand the holdings.[4]

A second collecting priority was noted in 1912, when librarian Gay called for an endowment fund to provide for "photographing and making measured drawings [i.e., drawings to scale] of old houses of merit." For Appleton, the measured drawing was a tool for historic preservation, a way to both save a building on paper and to study it. Long before the Historic American Buildings Survey (HABS), Appleton stressed the importance of a systematic approach to recording buildings through measured drawings and photography. Appleton's goal was to hire a competent draftsman to travel throughout New England documenting "meritorious old work" and to be available, when necessary, to secure information from buildings undergoing demolition or alteration. Appleton did not succeed in his plan for a traveling draftsman, but he was able to inspire a number of members who were architects and others to measure buildings and deposit the drawings in the Society's Library. These individuals included William T.

Aldrich, Frank Chouteau Brown, Herbert W. C. Browne, Ogden Codman, Jr., William Ware Cordingly, Henry Charles Dean, George Francis Dow, Norman Isham, James F. Kelley, Donald Macdonald-Millar, Alfred Shurrocks, and Thomas T. Waterman, among others.[5]

So strong was Appleton's belief in the efficacy of documenting buildings on paper, that in the 1930s, he willingly supported the efforts of the newly formed Historic American Buildings Survey to employ out-of-work architects to record the country's architectural heritage by means of measured drawings, photographs, and written records, despite his general aversion to the involvement of the Federal government in anything. He purchased for the collection hundreds of copies of HABS drawings and photographs of New England buildings. In June 1935, he even hosted an exhibition of drawings and photographs of Massachusetts buildings that had been prepared by HABS under the direction of his friend Frank Chouteau Brown, who at the time was serving as Massachusetts District Officer of the survey. Special invitations were sent to members of the Boston Society of Architects and the Boston Architectural Club. The exhibition proved to be so popular that its closing date was extended, and the drawings and photographs were subsequently sent to the Yale University Gallery of Fine Arts for display.

By the early 1940s, the Library collection included more that 3,000 measured drawings. Later, the number would swell when Frank Chouteau Brown's archive, including a nearly complete set of HABS drawings of New England buildings as well as his field notes, came to the organization after his death.

The discussion of Historic New England's collection of measured drawings would not be complete without noting two sets of drawings described by former director Abbott Lowell Cummings as of "cornerstone significance." In 1863, a battle to prevent the demolition of the Boston home of the patriot John Hancock was waged and lost. Just before the house was torn down, architect John Hubbard Sturgis made a set of measured drawings to record it. These drawings are of major importance because they are considered to be the earliest measured drawings of an American domestic building and because of their significance in the development of the preservation movement in New England. The drawings remained with Sturgis's successors for just over one hundred years, until Abbott Cummings acquired them for the collection in 1965. (That they should have come into the Society's collection is particularly appropriate—Appleton had included a photograph of the Hancock House on the cover of the first *Bulletin*, described the house's fate as "a classic in the annals of vandalism," and used it as a symbol to rally members to his fledgling organization.)

Also of significance is the set of measured drawings documenting Boston's Brattle Square Church, built in 1772 for an illustrious congregation according to designs by Thomas Dawes. According to architectural historian Frederic C. Detwiller, "An early plan gives the pew locations of many of the town's leading citizens and reads like a veritable *Who's Who* in Boston at the time of the Revolution." John Hancock, James Bowdoin, John Adams, Samuel Adams, Harrison Gray Otis, and Theodore Lyman were

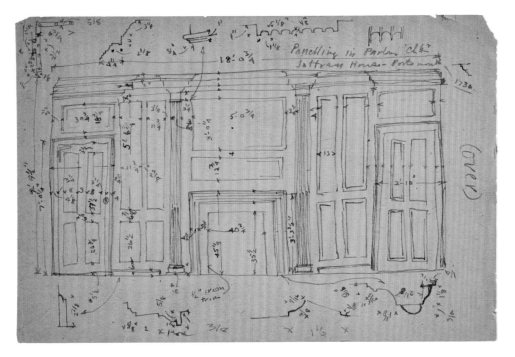

TOP LEFT: A measured drawing of paneling, the Jaffrey house, Portsmouth, New Hampshire, by Donald Macdonald-Millar, early twentieth century. TOP RIGHT: Architect Eleanor Raymond's 1931 house for her sister, Rachel, Belmont, Massachusetts. BOTTOM: View along Hancock Street, Boston, showing Suffolk University's Ridgeway Building with an underground basketball court, designed by the firm of James McNeely. Rendering by Monika Pauli, 1991.

all members. By the early 1870s, the congregation had moved to Boston's Back Bay, and the church was demolished, but not before a set of measured drawings was done, at least in part by architect Gridley J. F. Bryant. The Brattle Square Church drawings were donated anonymously to the Society in 1925.[6]

As is obvious from his eagerness to acquire measured drawings, Appleton encouraged practicing architects, landscape architects, and others to share their expertise and to be members and donors. In the organization's first nine years, at least sixteen of these individuals gave a variety of items to the Library. The list of donors includes William T. Aldrich, Ernest W. Bowditch, Frank Chouteau Brown, Herbert W. C. Browne (who also served as a trustee), Joseph Everett Chandler, John C. Clapp, Jr., Ogden Codman, Jr., Lester Couch, Henry C. Dean, Norman Isham, Alexander Wadsworth Longfellow, Warren H. Manning, Lawrence Park, Henry Davis Sleeper, John Calvin Stevens, and R. Clipston Sturgis. The work of six of these men is represented in this volume.

At least by 1921, Appleton's interest in architectural drawings had expanded to include drawings of actual or proposed commissions by New England architects—the Society's journal, by then renamed *Old-Time New England,* records the gift of "1 set of architectural drawings of the James H. Beal estate, Boston, June 26, 1852," by Gridley J. F. Bryant. The year 1921 also brought a rare opportunity to acquire a collection of designs by Asher Benjamin, comprising "his own drawings . . . for some of the best and earliest of his work as well as a nearly complete set of the plates of the rare 1798 edition of his 'Country Builder's Assistant'." The collection was being offered for sale for $100. Appleton had to abandon his usual policy of acquiring items by gift and develop a creative strategy to purchase it. He asked his Harvard classmate, architect Lawrence Park, to serve as a committee of one and to write to architects throughout the region requesting donations to support the acquisition. At least thirty-one architects received the appeal in late May. The records show that twenty-five sent contributions of between one and ten dollars each. Four of the architects represented in this catalogue responded, three positively—Herbert W. C. Browne, Stanley B. Parker, and John Calvin Stevens—but George Marlowe was, "Just now not in a position to make any contribution." On June 4, Appleton wrote to W. R. Greeley of the firm Kilham and Hopkins, "We have enough raised now to purchase the Asher Benjamin drawings." This fund-raising campaign netted Appleton one of his most significant acquisitions.[7]

Throughout the years, the collection of original architectural drawings has grown by gift and purchase to include thousands of items, representing the work of more than four hundred architects active from the late eighteenth century to the present. Some of the architects are represented by only one or two drawings; others by large collections. In addition to Benjamin and Bryant, the list includes some familiar names and some unfamiliar: Samuel McIntire, Thomas Rundle, Thomas Sumner, Alexander Parris, Richard Upjohn, Luther Briggs, Jr., Richard Bond, Ammi B. Young, Henry Austin, Ware and Van Brunt, Little and Browne, McKim, Mead

and White, George Clough, Henry Francis, John Calvin Stevens, Ogden Codman, Jr., Edward P. Casey, Robert Allen Cook, Alexander Wadsworth Longfellow, Jacob Luippold, Halfdan Hanson, Arthur Shurcliff, Maginnis and Walsh, Hutchins and French, Frank Chouteau Brown, Henry Hoover, Arland Dirlam, Remmert Huygens, James McNeely, Frederick A. (Tad) Stahl, and Kallmann, McKinnell, and Wood, among others. Clearly, there are notable names missing from the list, architects whose work for one reason or another did not make it into the collection. H. H. Richardson is one, while the work of women architects is only marginally represented, but those collections are growing. For example, in 1997, Historic New England acquired Eleanor Raymond's own archive of photographs of her work.[8]

The range and variety of the drawings in the collection are remarkable. From the elegant neoclassical townhouses and country estates of Little and Browne and Ogden Codman, Jr., to Robert Allen Cook's workers' housing for the Draper Company in Hopedale, Massachusetts, and Jacob Luippold's three-deckers and other modest residential and commercial buildings; from the bank buildings of Hutchins and French to the churches and synagogues of Arland A. Dirlam; and from the public buildings of George Clough, including schools and courthouses, to the Modern bank and office buildings of Stahl Associates.

The collection also includes a number of important renderings from architectural competitions, including the one in 1843 for the chapel at Mount Auburn Cemetery in Cambridge, Massachusetts. The competition attracted submissions from Gridley J. F. Bryant, Ammi B. Young, Richard Bond, and, presumably, the winner Dr. Jacob Bigelow. The drawings were a gift to the Society from the estate of Dr. Bigelow's grandson, Dr. William Sturgis Bigelow, a major collector of Japanese art and donor to the Museum of Fine Arts, Boston. Another competition—for the stations of the Boston Elevated Railway in 1897—generated the handsome winning entry, signed "Excelsior," by Alexander Wadsworth Longfellow, Jr. A relatively recent competition, for the design of Boston City Hall in 1961, which attracted 256 entrants, is represented in the collection by the drawings of the winning team, Kallmann, McKinnell, and Knowles.

By focusing on a few of the major acquisitions throughout the decades, the richness and depth of the collection can be better understood. In the late 1930s, Elizabeth A. Huebener donated "a valuable lot of material from the estate of her father, Mr. Edward A. Huebener of Dorchester [Massachusetts], including 131 views, 106 pamphlets, 71 circulars, 243 clippings, scrapbooks and maps; also 187 measured drawings . . ."[9] An antique dealer, appraiser, upholsterer, and avid collector of materials related to Dorchester, Edward Huebener also had been involved with the organization since at least 1915, as a member, generous donor, and chair of the nominating committee. Over the years, he also had conducted business with Sumner Appleton, selling him items for the collection, including period wallpapers for reinstallation in the Society's houses. From the Appleton-Huebener correspondence, one can deduce a cordial and respectful relationship, one that encouraged sharing of information and, from Appleton's point of view, donations. Without question, the "187 measured drawings," are original drawings by Dorchester architect Luther Briggs, Jr., for middle-class residences, business blocks, monuments, and public buildings, dating from the late 1840s to the 1850s. (In the *Bulletin* and *Old-Time New England*, the words "measured drawing" seem to apply equally to describe both scale drawings of historic buildings and new work.) The importance of the Briggs collection was recognized even at the time of its acquisition, and plans were underway to illustrate a selection of the drawings in an article in *Old-Time New England*; however, it would be forty years before Edward F. Zimmer would publish "Luther Briggs and the Picturesque Pattern Books," in the winter-spring 1977 issue of *Old-Time England*.

In 1939, after nearly fifty years in business, architect Herbert W. C. Browne decided to close his firm. His partner Arthur Little had been dead for fourteen years, his chief draftsman, Lester Couch, had just died, and Browne himself was nearly eighty. In the course of the firm's history, the partners had catered to an elite clientele, designing numerous country houses and townhouses for patrons like industrialist Henry Clay Frick, diplomat Larz Anderson and his wife, Isabel, and politician Charles Sprague. Given Browne's lengthy association with the organization, it is no surprise that he offered items in his office to the Society. Sumner Appleton responded in a letter: "We could use practically all grouped or framed photographs and architectural pictures, plans, sketches, elevations, and so forth." In addition, Appleton asked for ". . . The Office safe . . . Typewriter's desk and chair . . . Wastepaper baskets . . . Drafting table . . . Taylor house capital . . . Coat rack . . ."[10] After cataloguing, the Little and Browne collection was found to include drawings for more than forty-five commissions, four extremely detailed account books, listing the names of contractors and subcontractors and associated costs for approximately 298 projects, five albums of professional photographs documenting their work, and an album of furniture designs. Appleton's acquisitiveness resulted in the survival of a major resource for the study of one of Boston's most successful architectural practices.

At the other end of the spectrum are the Jacob Luippold and Robert Allen Cook collections. Jacob Luippold's modest residential and commercial buildings are of particular interest today. As former librarian Ellie Reichlin wrote: "The collection is remarkable in its documentation of a small practice at the turn of the [twentieth] century and gives insights into working- and middle-class building styles during a period when the city was experiencing rapid growth."[11] Milford, Massachusetts, architect Robert Allen Cook left a remarkable record of his prolific practice. A generalist who designed buildings of all types in Milford and the surrounding area, Cook organized and saved his correspondence, contracts, specifications, client lists, account books, project photographs, and drawings. Following his death in 1949, the records were left untouched until the early 1990s, when Historic New England acquired the bulk of the collection. It includes drawings and supporting documentation for hundreds of commissions. Cook's records for his work for the Draper Company in

Hopedale, Massachusetts, provide remarkable information about the development of an early twentieth-century company town. In recent years, Historic New England has become the steward of important twentieth-century collections from Boston architects Remmert Huygens, Gerhard Kallmann and Michael McKinnell, James McNeely, and Frederic A. (Tad) Stahl. The papers of the Architectural Heritage Foundation, founded by Roger Webb, are also part of the holdings of the Library and Archives.

Writing in 1946, Buchanan Charles, who served as the Society's librarian from 1945 to 1960, noted it had ". . . never been the Society's policy to form a large general Library on historical subjects, as this would be expensive to maintain and would be likely to duplicate other historical and genealogical libraries not far away."[12] The Society had, however, acquired either through gift or purchase works on local history, the decorative arts, and, of course, preservation and architecture.

Only a year later, the Society's "gratitude was unbounded," when it received as a bequest the 330-volume library of architect Herbert W. C. Browne. Browne had been a collector since his youth, and his library included examples of important English, American, Italian, and French architectural books from the seventeenth to the late nineteenth century, as well as works on landscape design and decoration. Browne's own catalogue, which accompanied the bequest, provides detailed information about many of these rare volumes and indicates his extensive bibliographic knowledge.

Librarian Charles noted that the books "are all of great value to the Society in showing many of the sources of New England architecture. Five or six of them . . . are of such fame . . . that I shall mention them individually. Charles's list included, among others, Vitruvius's *De Architectura* (Amsterdam, 1649); Palladio's *I quattro libri dell'architettura* (Venice, 1570); Colen Campbell's *Vitruvius Britannicus* (London, 1715–25); *The Designs of Inigo Jones* by William Kent (London, 1727); and Thomas Chippendale's *The Gentleman and Cabinet-Maker's Director* (London, 1754).[13] In addition to the Browne collection, the Library and Archives also holds late eighteenth- and nineteenth-century American builders' guides, house pattern books, decorating manuals, and works on gardens and landscape.

During the intervening years, other architects and scholars either donated or bequeathed their reference libraries to the organization; in some cases, their surviving family members made the gift. Historic New England now holds volumes from the libraries of architects Edward P. Casey, Ambrose Cramer, James E. (Jack) Robinson, III, and George T. Kelly; from curator Rodris Roth; and from architectural historians and professors Abbott Lowell Cummings and Margaret Henderson Floyd. Members of the Perry family donated the library of the Perry Paint Company.

By the mid-1960s, the Library had become more proactive in its collecting. The annual report for 1964–65 lists a number of important acquisitions in addition to the Hancock House drawings described above. One such acquisition was an exceedingly rare pamphlet, *The Constitution of the Proprietors of the Architectural Library of Boston*, which also included a catalogue of its holdings in 1809. According to architectural historian Martha McNamara, it was the "first public library in New England devoted exclusively to architecture and allied arts." At the time, the Society's librarian, Wendell D. Garrett, noted that the fifty-five items listed in the catalogue "give us a perfect indication of the range and variety of these architectural works available to Boston builders at the time." The addition of this small pamphlet inspired a new collecting initiative—to acquire actual volumes that had been in the Library or representative examples. In 1966 came Lionel Charlton's *The History of Whitby and of Whitby Abbey* (York, 1779) with the Library's bookplate; in 1968, Abraham Swan's *A Collection of Designs in Architecture* (London, 1757), and William Pain's *Pain's British Palladio* (London, 1790), both with the Library's stamp.[14]

Over time, the Library and Archives also has acquired numerous volumes bearing the bookplates of New England architects. In 1975, for example, a superb copy of *The Cabinet-Maker and Upholsterer's Guide,* by George Smith (London, 1826), came into the collection. It had belonged to Boston architect Thomas W. Sumner, designer of the East India Marine Hall, in Salem, Massachusetts, among other works. The volume nicely complemented architectural drawings by Sumner already in the collection.[15] Since that time the number of books with known provenance has steadily grown.

The discussion of the Library and Archives' architectural holdings would not be complete without describing some of the collections of architectural photographs. Many of the half million photographic images in the collection today capture New England's built environment; in addition, some were created expressly for the purpose of documenting the region's architecture.

In 1913, librarian Gay appealed to members to contribute funds for the acquisition of a complete set of prints from the Halliday Historic Photograph Company. According to him, the images constitute "one of the best general collections of views of old New England houses and historic sites anywhere in existence. A regrettably large proportion of the houses shown in these photographs has vanished forever, and of many of them the Halliday print is supposed to be the only known representation." By 1916, Appleton could report that "the Society now finds itself in the possession of a set of this unrivaled collection of photographs of old New England houses . . . The acquisition of such a collection is an important step towards the goal the Society should set for itself. It must be our ambition to make of our photograph collection the best source for pictorial information concerning every noteworthy old house in New England."[16] (Later, in 1957, the Halliday collection of glass plate negatives from which the prints were made also became part of the holdings.) Baldwin Coolidge, a Boston photographer known for both his technical skill and his artistry, donated approximately 2,200 negatives in 1918. The Louis A. Woodbury collection of more than eight hundred negatives representing every house in the town of Groveland, Massachusetts, came as a gift from Woodbury's widow in 1921. Prolific author and photographer Mary Harrod Northend's collection of thousands of negatives and prints, which came to the Society in the late 1950s, documents architecture in New Eng-

land of many styles and periods. In the 1950s and 1960s, Abbott Lowell Cummings negotiated the purchase of two remarkable photographic archives. Photographer George Noyes's collection of more than 1,500 negatives of old houses, commercial buildings, streetscapes, and landscapes in the Newburyport, Massachusetts, region was a major acquisition in 1957. A little more than ten years later, the several thousand negatives exposed by Arthur C. Haskell were added to the holdings. Haskell, who had a background in architectural drafting, turned to photography in the 1920s. He became the principal photographer for the *White Pine Monograph Series,* worked for many of Boston's leading architectural firms, including Royal Barry Wills and David J. Abrahams, both of which are represented in this catalogue, and recorded many of the New England buildings for the Historic American Buildings Survey. The Library and Archives holds important collections of the work of many other nineteenth-, twentieth-, and twenty-first century architectural photographers, including David Bohl, William Clark, Richard Cheek, A.W. Folsom, Wilfred French, Steve Rosenthal, the Soule Photographic Art Company, Peter Vanderwarker, and Paul Weber, among others.

It is important to note another category of photographic documentation. In 1919, William Sumner Appleton undertook the restoration of the Abraham Browne house in Watertown, Massachusetts. To record the process, Appleton not only made copious descriptive notes, but also commissioned a full set of professional photographs to record the building before, during, and after the work. The work at the Browne house established a precedent for careful photographic documentation of restoration projects. In 1982, the Library and Archives collection was immeasurably enriched by the gift from photographer Peter Zaharis of hundreds of negatives that had largely been commissioned by Abbott Lowell Cummings during the course of restoration activities at several properties. Through the years Historic New England has continued to emphasize this aspect of photographic recording keeping.

In addition to architectural drawings, books, and photographs, the Library and Archives holds collections of builders' account books; building accounts, bills, receipts, and correspondence; and architectural contracts and specifications. The architectural ephemera, such as illustrated billheads, business cards, and advertisements, and the nineteenth- and twentieth-century catalogues of house plans and of products used in the construction and interior decoration of the home stand as evidence of the material world in which architects practiced their profession.

Writing in 1974, Abbott Lowell Cummings noted: "the student of New England architectural history will find in the Society's Library an almost limitless range of documentary source material, without recourse to which no serious study of the subject can be considered definitive."[17] As Historic New England enters its second century, it is committed to continuing in the tradition of Appleton and his successors by collecting the records created by both women and men that document the ever-changing New England environment. These records, no longer only on paper (or glass or film) but in digital form as well, will be preserved and made accessible to all.

TOP: Palladio's *I Quattro libri dell'architettura* (1570), from the Herbert W. C. Browne rare book collection. BOTTOM LEFT: Architect Thomas W. Sumner's bookplate in the *Cabinet-Maker and Upholsterer's Guide* (1826). BOTTOM RIGHT: Examples of architectural ephemera—correspondence, specifications, and trade and business cards.

Architect Jacob Luippold's house on Mozart Street,
Jamaica Plain, Boston, about 1890. The man on the
porch may be Luippold himself. Luippold's designs are
discussed on pages 130–33.

CATALOGUE ENTRIES

All dimensions are in inches, height by width.

Endnotes and references begin on page 225.

Asher Benjamin (1773–1845)

Frontispiece of an Unidentified House, 1797

Asher Benjamin, builder-architect, raised in Hartland, Connecticut, turned twenty-one in January 1794. He is first found in that year in nearby Suffield, where his earliest documented work brought him into direct contact with two or three of the leading master carpenters in the upper Connecticut River valley.

First and highly important was Thomas Hayden (1745–1817) of Windsor, whose house designed for John Watson at East Windsor Hill, 1788–89, is the earliest surviving neoclassical house of three stories in the valley. Hayden is particularly distinguished for having produced for this house the earliest known architectural working drawings in western New England.

Equally important was the local Suffield builder Joseph Howard (1736-1810), whose account book beginning in 1783 shows that he, too, like Hayden, executed working drawings, for example: "a Draft of a Cornice" (May 1792); "Draft ing a meaten Hous" (March 1794); "a Draft for a bridg" (September 1794).[1]

Benjamin's exposure to these important local figures came about specifically through the single most important building campaign in Suffield during the 1790s, which produced the north wing of the Phelps-Hatheway house. On 15 May 1794, Oliver Phelps contracted with local builder Ashbel King to erect an addition to his imposing house on the main street "agreeable to a Plan thereof now given him . . ."[2] The building accounts reveal that Hayden, King, and Howard were all involved in the project, and Hayden was responsible for the fabrication of neoclassical finish trim within and without the north wing. Though Asher Benjamin was probably a minor player, his earliest documented work here, as shown in the Phelps cash books, extended from 25 October 1794 to 26 February 1795, including the entry on the latter date of eleven dollars "in full pay for two Ionic Capitals," thought to be those of the principal frontispiece of the north wing.

The overall design of the Phelps-Hatheway house frontispiece mirrors that which Hayden had earlier designed for the John Watson house in the late 1780s, including the newly fashionable neoclassical arrangement of a circular-headed fanlight projecting upwards into a broken pediment. The ultimate source of this scheme for the American rural builder would have been designs published by William Pain in both the *Practical Builder* (edition Boston, 1792) and *Practical House Carpenter* (edition Boston, 1796). The client for the "Ionick Front" shown here, signed by Benjamin and dated at Greenfield, Massachusetts, 4 March 1797, may have been either William Coleman or Jonathan Leavitt, for both of whom Benjamin designed houses there that year. The drawing is highly finished, and reveals clearly that the young builder's drafting abilities were fully developed by this time. We can only assume that he received training at the hands of Hayden and Howard. ALC

Phelps-Hatheway house, Suffield, Connecticut, in 1958.

Elevation of an "Ionick Front." Dated and signed:
"Greenfield 4th of March 1797 / A Benjamin." Black
ink and gray wash on laid paper; 9¼ × 6". Library and
Archives purchase, 1921.

Asher Benjamin (1773–1845)

Jonathan Leavitt House,
Main Street, Greenfield, Massachusetts,
(now the Greenfield Public Library), c. 1797

Jonathan Leavitt, son of the Rev. Jonathan Leavitt of Heath, in northwestern Franklin County, Massachusetts, was born there 27 February 1764, and graduated from Yale in 1786. He came to Greenfield to practice law about 1790, and the intention of his marriage to Emelia, daughter of President Ezra Stiles of Yale, was recorded in April 1796. Thus well positioned in life, he acquired an impressive site on Main Street in the center of Greenfield, and on 7 August 1797, in a deed of mortgage for $1,200, which would presumably have financed construction, he described this property as the "Lot on which I now live."[1] A year later, the newly completed house was assessed at the same figure in the federal Direct Tax of that year. Most of the other house values in Greenfield at the time ranged below $500.[2]

In a letter written a few years later on 30 July 1815, Jonathan Leavitt's son, Jonathan III, refers to the property as "Social Villa,"[3] and according to local sources, Jonathan Leavitt, the father, had his law office in the west wing and his dining room in the east wing. It is the distinctive design of these appendages with their hyphens which permits a secure attribution to Asher Benjamin. The drawing shown here, in all major respects the source of the east wing, survived among the drawings that can be identified with the architect's Greenfield period, roughly 1796 to 1800.

The specific form of a house with matching outer dependencies had not appeared in Benjamin's work before this time, although the general concept could not have been unfamiliar to him. In the 1796 Boston edition of William Pain's *Practical House Carpenter*, which Benjamin used extensively in the compilation of his own *Country Builder's Assistant*, published at Greenfield in 1797, the English author had shown in plate 99 a plan and elevation of a central block flanked by matching wings, which may have provided inspiration for a somewhat similar scheme appearing in plates 31 and 32 of the second edition of Benjamin's *Country Builder's Assistant*, published at Boston in 1798.

There is little or no connection, however, between Benjamin's drawing, published in 1798, and the design of the wings of Jonathan Leavitt's house, particularly with respect to the fenestration of the hyphens. Nor is there any direct similarity with the house Samuel McIntire designed for Theodore Lyman in Waltham, Massachusetts, erected following Lyman's acquisition of the site 30 March 1793.[4] The Lyman house represents one of the rare examples of the form in New England for the period just before 1800, and one that Benjamin might have easily seen when he visited Boston in the mid-1790s.

In any event, it is the closely spaced circular-headed windows of the hyphens and the disposition of neoclassical decorative elements in the façades of the wings as designed by Benjamin that are without any known parallels. At present, and unless an unambiguous precedent is found, we can only suggest that this quite individualistic treatment must be credited to Benjamin's creative design talents in the period before he became a full-fledged architect in Boston. ALC

Jonathan Leavitt house about 1907.

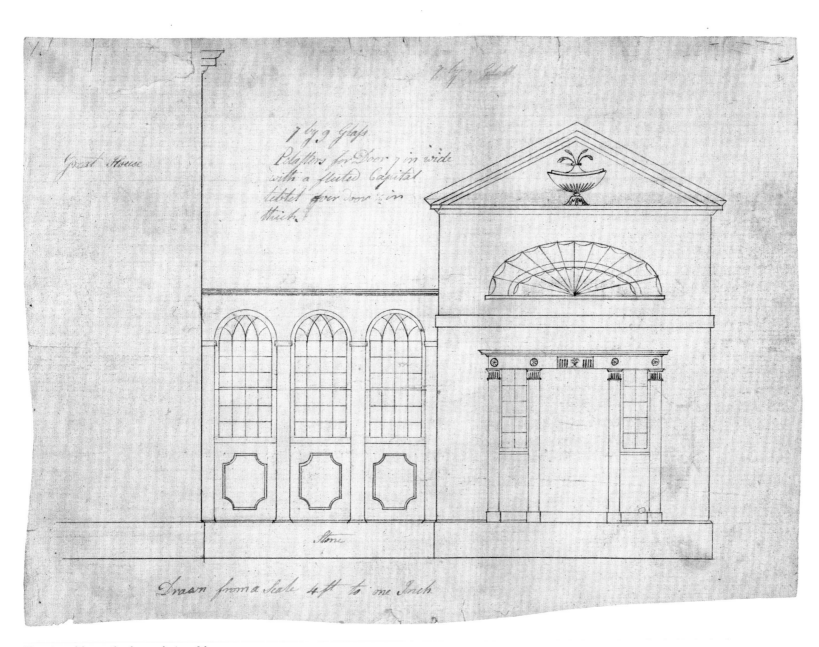

Elevation of the east hyphen and wing of the
Jonathan Leavitt house, undated and unsigned.
Brown and black ink on laid paper; 7⅜ × 10".
Library and Archives purchase, 1921.

Attributed to Asher Benjamin (1773–1845)

Unidentified Building, Early Nineteenth Century

The elevation of an unidentified building shown here is executed in the spare manner of draftsmanship typical of architectural drawings in New England dated just before and after 1800. The component elements of the design would point to Asher Benjamin as the most likely author. Two of his major early influences were Charles Bulfinch and the architectural handbooks of the English author William Pain. We have assumed that Benjamin visited Boston before 1800, and studied certain of Bulfinch's early buildings there at first hand, particularly the Tontine Crescent. He would later write that "The construction of the Franklin Street houses [Tontine Crescent] . . . gave the first impulse to good taste; and architecture, in this part of the country, has advanced with an accelerated progress ever since."[1]

Benjamin was also heavily influenced by two Boston editions in 1792 and 1796 of the works of William Pain, remembered largely for having translated the progressive neoclassical architecture of Robert Adam into a carpenter's vernacular. Benjamin's fascination with Pain's architectural vocabulary begins to take shape in his design for the wings of the Leavitt house in Greenfield, Massachusetts (see pages 42–43), which reveals that he was rapidly developing his own individualistic neoclassical style. This would be most forcefully expressed in the design of three houses, which he claimed at the time to have built in Windsor, Vermont.[2] In style, they represent a high-water mark of neoclassical exuberance in Benjamin's work in the years before 1802, when he moved to Boston to begin life as a city architect.[3]

In any effort to establish a claim for Asher Benjamin as author of the design shown here, one notices at once the general massing of the composition which, in terms of the central attic story, seems to have been inspired by the central block of the Tontine Crescent. Of the individual features, the most distinctive is the frontispiece, with its strong similarity to Benjamin's Hubbard-Fullerton house of about 1801 in Windsor. Also of interest is the fact that the side lights of the frontispiece are identical in pattern to the original side lights of the frontispiece of the Benjamin-designed Coleman-Hollister house in Greenfield. While a number of neoclassical decorative accessories became stock items of manufacture during this period, and while specific design details in architectural handbooks were available to all comers, it seems significant nevertheless that both of these features find their identical counterparts in Asher Benjamin's early work.

It should be noted as well that the tracery of the semicircular fanlight in the pediment of the attic story is identical to an example that appears in plate 16 of Benjamin's *American Builder's Companion*, published at Boston in 1806, and perhaps an adequate reason for dating this unidentified drawing as no earlier. Finally, the inclusion in the upper left-hand corner of the drawing of a profile detail of the building's cornice is executed in precisely the same manner as a set of similar molding profiles included in a drawing signed and dated by Benjamin at Greenfield, 29 January 1797,[4] in which he wields his pen as an engraver's burin to achieve shaded effects. ALC

Hubbard-Fullerton house, Windsor, Vermont, about 1935.

Front elevation and detail of an unidentified building,
undated and unsigned. Ink with ink washes on wove paper;
6⅞ × 5½". Gift of Earle G. Shettleworth, Jr., 1995.

Samuel McIntire (1757–1811)

Unidentified House, c. 1802–05

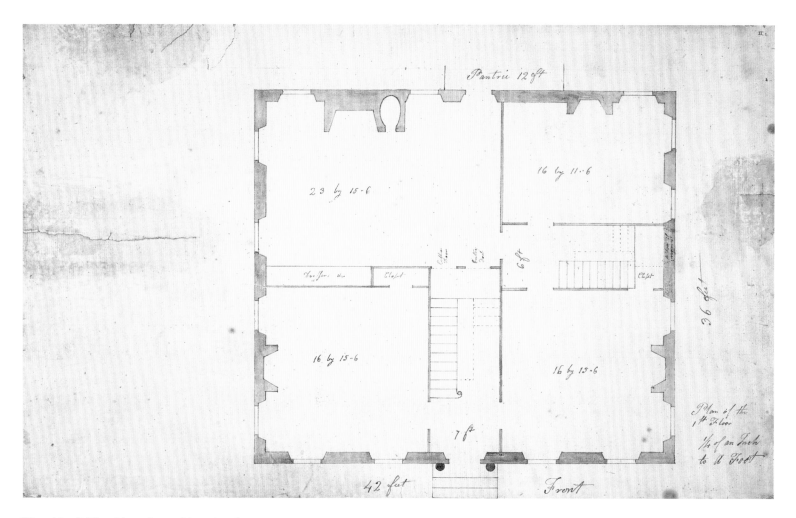

"Plan of the / 1ˢᵗ Floor" (one of a set of three sheets),
undated and unsigned. Ink and gray wash on laid (J. Larking 1802)
paper; 11¾ × 19". Library and Archives purchase, 1935.

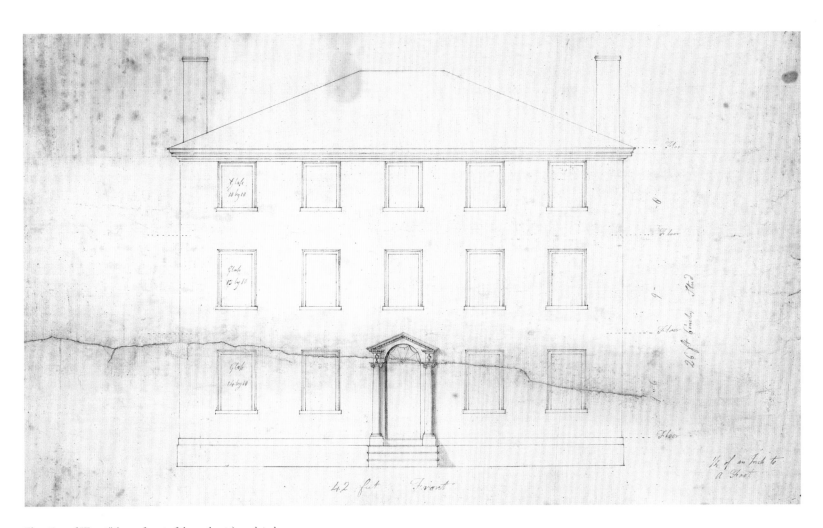

Elevation of "Front" (one of a set of three sheets), undated and unsigned. Ink and gray wash on laid (watermark with a fleur-de-lis above a shield with GR) paper; 11¾ × 19". Library and Archives purchase, 1935.

Samuel McIntire (1757–1811)
Unidentified House, c. 1802–05

These are two of four surviving drawings by the celebrated Salem architect Samuel McIntire that relate to an unidentified house. The 1802 date incorporated into the watermark of the paper used for the first-floor plan marks the earliest possible date of execution. A preliminary drawing for this house, inscribed in McIntire's hand "Sketch of a Brick House planned for Mr," was found in the scrapbook of his drawings given to the Essex Institute in the nineteenth century and is now owned by the Peabody Essex Museum. Three other drawings, including these two and a second-floor plan, came from the Samuel Fowler house in Danversport, Massachusetts. The separation of the sketch is explained by McIntire's practice of executing a preliminary design to show to a client and retaining it to produce a finished set of plans for the actual construction. Finished drawings were generally kept by the client.

The plan gives the dimensions of each room and shows the placement of the fireplaces with the chimneys incorporated into the exterior walls, which allowed McIntire the opportunity to create spacious rooms and one of his most effective patterns of circulation. The plan follows a traditional New England double-pile arrangement, with a central entry hall with straight stairs, a formal parlor to the left, and a "keeping room" or dining room to the right (suggested by the china closet and easy access to the kitchen).

At the back of the house, there is an informal parlor or library next to a side hall with stairs for the servants and extra space for an optional side door. The largest room is the kitchen with built-in "dressers" with shelves and cupboards for storage and a brick baking oven or a tin Rumford roaster incorporated into the fireplace. A separate pantry for additional storage, constructed of wood, is indicated at the rear of the house.

The front elevation shows a well-proportioned three-story townhouse of five bays with a central entry, a building form most often found in urban settings. The inscription on the preliminary design and the thickness of the walls on the floor plans indicate the house was to be constructed of brick, the favored building material in the Salem area after 1800. The simplicity of the façade suggests that the client wanted an economical structure. The drawing bears no indications of window lintels, string courses, decorative cornice, or roof balustrade, extra features often found on McIntire's other surviving neoclassical- or Federal-style houses.

Economy is also suggested by the use of a single door for the main entrance. Most of McIntire's larger townhouses of similar date have entry doors with a fanlight and side lights as well as a protective portico; doors of this design are most often found as secondary entrances. One plausible reason for its use here was the seven-foot width of the interior hall, which may not have been sufficient to accommodate side lights. The frontispiece here, with engaged columns and a semicircular fanlight set into a broken pediment with dentils, is similar to the door in plate 39 in William Pain's *Practical House Carpenter* (edition Boston, 1796) and relieves the spare simplicity of the façade. The Roman Ionic order is embellished with classical urns or vases on the blocks above the capitals, resulting in one of McIntire's most elegant and beautiful designs.

Several historians have wondered if the drawings might relate to the building of the brick Fowler house in 1810, but, in addition to being only two stories, the Danversport house has an entirely different floor plan, and no other details correspond to the drawings. Samuel Page Fowler, the son of the original owner, was a noted antiquarian who amassed a large collection of historical material relating to Danvers and Salem, and he may have acquired the drawings secondhand. DTL

Plot Plan of the James A. Rundlet House,
Middle Street, Portsmouth, New Hampshire, 1812

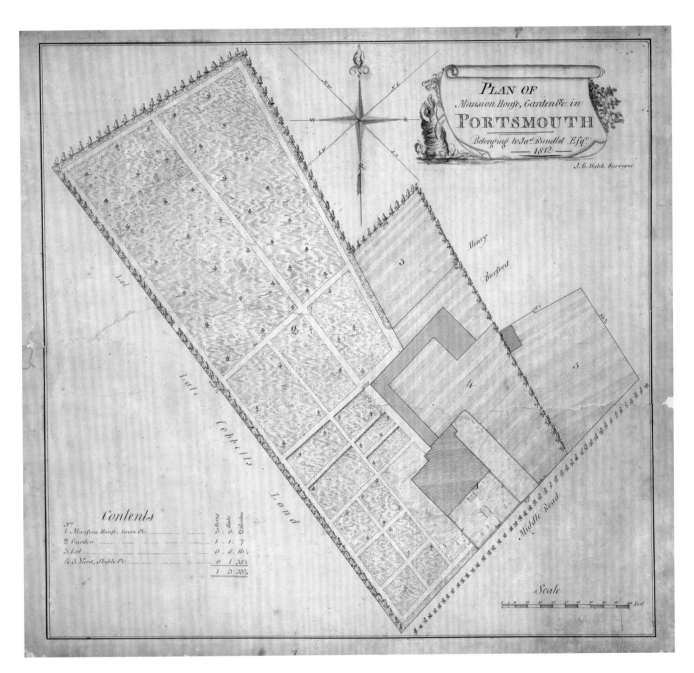

"PLAN OF / Mansion House, Garden&c. in / PORTSMOUTH /
Belonging to Jaˢ Rundlet Esqʳ 1812." Signed: "J. G. Hales Surveyor."
Ink on heavy paper; 17¾ × 18¾". Gift of Ralph May, 1971.

John Grove Hales (1785–1832)
Plot Plan of the James A. Rundlet House

Unattributed
James A. Rundlet House

These drawings of the Rundlet house and grounds are part of a significant collection of family papers that came to Historic New England with the house and land in 1971 as a gift from Ralph May (1882–1975), great-grand-son of the first owner of the house, James Rundlet (1772–1852). The manuscript collection contains many of the records associated with building and furnishing the house in 1806 and 1807, including a labor schedule of craftsmen, bills for their work, and purchases of furniture, wallpaper, and other household items.

James Rundlet was born in Exeter, New Hampshire, and educated at Phillips Academy before relocating to Portsmouth in 1794. He married Elizabeth Hill the next year, and for twelve years the family lived in rented housing. Rundlet began small, as a textile trader and commission merchant, but rose rapidly through the ranks of the merchant community to become one of the city's wealthiest men. After retiring from retail and trade, he invested in real estate, bank stocks, and textile manufacturing in Amesbury, Massachusetts, and Salmon Falls, New Hampshire. In 1804, he built a store in the fashionable brick block of Market Square and later acquired land in the expanding western portion of the town, where the mercantile elite would construct large and fashionable houses on the roads that radiated out from the older core.

The drawing on the opposite page is unsigned, and while Rundlet himself is known to have purchased drawing paper, the author is not certainly known. The work schedule and bills indicate that two of the region's rising builder-architects, Ebenezer Clifford and Jacob Marston, were associated with the construction of the house, either of whom might have prepared this sheet. Indeed, these records provide an important case study of the network of craftsmen who contributed to the planning and execution of large projects like this one. Like other early drawings, this one includes only a first-floor plan and one elevation of its principal façade. The drawing uses wash to enhance its appearance, but the inner spaces are simply delineated with single lines. Door openings that would elucidate circulation and room names that would clarify function are missing. One critical detail was included—an elaborate series of moldings planned for the exterior cornice. A similar design was executed on the cornice, the window caps, and the best parlor's cornice. This Gothic pattern, as well as the apparently unexecuted design for the roof balustrade, would have been familiar to Portsmouth-area craftsmen and their clients from Asher Benjamin's builders' guides, as well as from their use on other town buildings.

The house was to be a large one, as befitted the needs of a prosperous merchant and his family, rising to three stories and employing the signature central passage plan. The rooms are amply sized, and the plan included all the components necessary for genteel living: three public rooms on the main floor, likely used as a best parlor, a family sitting room, and a dining room, with supporting service spaces and circulation paths. Indeed, it is the various and up-to-date provisions for fundamental household functions, including a Rumford roaster and boilers, as well as a separate scullery, that distinguish the plan for the house. Changes made to this design in the course of its construction and in the early years of its use also concentrated on providing improvements to domestic facilities at the rear of the house.

The plot plan of the house lot, by surveyor John Grove Hales, illustrated on the previous page, is another component of the collections associated with the house. Hales prepared this and other estate portraits for Portsmouth-area properties, likely in association with his work on a map of the city in 1812. He is probably best known for the maps he prepared of Boston in 1814 and its environs in 1819, but he also produced many maps of other towns, large and small, during his brief career. As the Hales plot plan records, Rundlet placed his house on a large lot, which provided both a refined setting and functionally segregated spaces. The house was set on a rise with terraces directly in front of the building. The angled range of the wood house and stable created a service yard to the east and rear, off the kitchen and scullery. The gardens, by contrast, were to the west of the house, the out-of-town side, and extended the full depth of the lot. The parcel and its buildings remain intact, an extraordinary survival within Portsmouth's historic landscape. CWD

The Rundlet-May house in 1922.

James A. Rundlet House,
Middle Street, Portsmouth, New Hampshire, 1806

Plan, detail, front elevation, undated and unsigned.
Ink and wash on laid paper; 18⅛ × 25⅞".
Gift of Ralph May, 1971.

Unattributed

Unidentified Doorway, Early Nineteenth Century

American examples of the neoclassical frontispiece encased within a heavily rusticated frame are exceptionally rare, but not unknown. In spring 1789, as the inauguration of the first president of the newly united nation approached, Boston's celebrated gentleman-architect, Charles Bulfinch, journeyed first to Philadelphia and then to New York to attend the event. In Philadelphia, Bulfinch was particularly impressed with the "house of Mr. Bingham, which is in a stile which would be esteemed splendid even in the most luxurious parts of Europe. Elegance of construction; white marble staircase, valuable paintings, the richest furniture and the utmost magnificence of decoration make it a palace, in my opinion too rich for any man in this country."[1]

The William Bingham house in turn was modeled upon Hertford House in London's Manchester Square, where Bingham and his wife had often been entertained by George Montagu, fourth Duke of Manchester. As reported by his biographer, Bingham "sketched a plan of this mansion, enlarging it somewhat, and employed an architect 'to execute it properly.'"[2] So affected was the young Boston architect with this sumptuous display of up-to-date London grandeur that he made a sketch of the façade at the time of his visit. The drawing, preserved among the designs of Bulfinch in the Library of Congress, is now widely recognized as the primary inspiration for the first Harrison Gray Otis house on Cambridge Street in Boston. For his distinguished Boston client, Bulfinch departed from the Bingham house model in only one major respect: by exchanging the heavily rusticated frontispiece of the Philadelphia house for one that follows in form and detail his devotion to the open and delicate treatment of door, fanlight, and side lights, derived from the work of Robert Adam.

The sketch of a frontispiece exhibited here is strikingly close in all details to Bulfinch's rendering of the frontispiece of the Bingham house. The similarity extends as well to the sketch of a fanlight detail in the upper left-hand corner, in which the pattern of the tracery agrees precisely with that shown in the third story of the Bingham house. On the other hand, the draftsmanship of the sketch is not that of the Boston architect. With no further evidence of provenance, we are thus left with the tantalizing question of a relationship that seemingly exists but cannot be documented. If the unknown draftsman had produced his image from direct observation, the sketch would presumably have been executed before 1823. Both Bingham and his wife died at a relatively young age, and their splendid mansion became a hotel in 1806 or 1807. An 1817 aquatint, showing the newly erected Washington Hall, reveals that there had seemingly been little alteration of the original rusticated frontispiece of the adjoining Bingham house. The latter building, however, was badly damaged in a fire of 17 March 1823, which destroyed Washington Hall. Although William Bingham's mansion was repaired and maintained in use as a hotel, there was a second fire in 1847, following which whatever remained of the original structure was razed about 1850.[3] ALC

Elevation by Charles Bulfinch of the William Bingham house, Philadelphia, 1789.

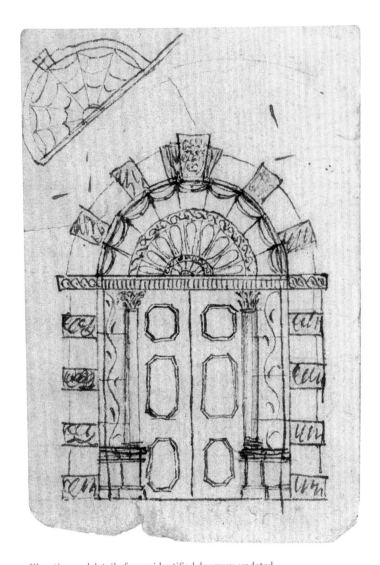

Elevation and detail of an unidentified doorway, undated
and unsigned. Brown ink and graphite on wove paper;
3⅝ × 2½". The drawing was found inside a copy of
William Pain's *The Builder's Companion* (c. 1757–1762)
when Historic New England acquired the book.
Library and Archives purchase, 1972.

Joseph C. Howard (1820–1846)

Unidentified Greek Revival House, c. 1844–45

This pen and ink and watercolor drawing of an unidentified Ionic temple-front house in the Greek Revival style is one of two drawings in Historic New England's Library and Archives that is signed on the reverse in pencil by Joseph C. Howard, whose very brief career in Boston was cut short by his early death in Roxbury, Massachusetts, of consumption on 27 October 1846, at the age of twenty-six. Called "architect" in the death record, he was the son of John and Clarissa H. (Carter) Howard of Roxbury, where he was born on 10 December 1820.[1] Very little is known of his youth and training, but when no more than twenty-four years of age, he formed a partnership with Luther Briggs, Jr., both of whom are listed as "architects, 10 Joy's Building" in the Boston directories for 1844 and 1845.

Luther Briggs, Jr., born at Pembroke, Massachusetts, in 1822, worked in the Boston office of the well-known architect and engineer, Captain Alexander Parris, whose wife was Luther's aunt. Young Briggs left the Parris office about 1842 and went to work as a draftsman for Gridley J. F. Bryant, who would later establish his reputation among Boston's commercial architects. Briggs's biographer, Edward Zimmer, reports that "A high spirited, sophomoric letter he [Howard] sent to Briggs from Nashua, New Hampshire, in April of 1843, while Luther was working for Bryant, indicates that Howard was familiar with Bryant and his office, suggesting that perhaps Howard had been another of Bryant's draftsmen."[2] In any event, the association with Briggs, however long or short, is perhaps the most significant thing that we know about Howard.

Given the very limited working dates of Howard's career, it will be seen at once that the design, with its colonnaded temple-front, is entirely in the Greek Revival mainstream, and the execution of the drawing is highly competent. On the other hand, it is puzzling to find the appendages at the sides somewhat uncharacteristically truncated, and (in the absence of an accompanying plan) we are left in doubt as to the location of the principal entrance. Contemporary pattern books and many examples that have survived at the vernacular level reveal that the building form itself was almost invariably furnished with a front entrance either in the center or to one side of the colonnaded façade. It would be interesting to know what alternate arrangement Howard had proposed. ALC

Elevation of an unidentified Greek Revival house, undated.
Signed on verso in graphite: "J. C. Howard Archt." Ink
and watercolor on wove (J Whatman Turkey Mill) paper;
11⅜ × 10". Gift of Elizabeth Huebener, 1937.

Edward Shaw (1784–1859)

William Wilkins Warren House,
Arlington, Massachusetts, 1840 (destroyed by fire)

During the three decades before the Civil War, the Greek Revival style enjoyed great popularity in New England, and was adapted widely by architects and builders to create many distinctive homes. One of the more novel residential interpretations of the style is to be found in the remarkable set of drawings that the Boston architect Edward Shaw drafted for merchant William Wilkins Warren's 1840 country seat on the western shore of Spy Pond in Arlington. As Warren noted in his 1884 autobiography:

> Soon after our return [from St. Thomas] I purchased from my brother-in-law, William Schouler, a five-acre lot bordering on Spy Pond in West Cambridge [Arlington]. This was laid out on a plan I had drawn while at sea; a Doric villa was erected and hundreds of trees and shrubs set out the same year, the whole being completed so that we were in full enjoyment of it the spring following. The place was much admired, and from its novel construction was called the West India House.

Although William Warren recalled drawing a plan during his voyage from the West Indies to Boston, once returned, he must have passed his initial ideas to Edward Shaw, who translated them into a portfolio which consisted of elevations, floor plans, and landscaping designs, all that was necessary to construct this unusual dwelling and its surrounding grounds. When Warren offered the house for sale in 1846, a real estate advertisement in the *Boston Daily Evening Transcript* described it as follows:

> The house is built in the most thorough manner, with slated roof and cupola, has two wings connected in the rear, and joining the main building, and which has also a spacious piazza on three sides. The basement story contains kitchen, stove, wash rooms, dining-room, bed room and large cellar. The principal story contains 3 parlors, 4 chambers, and large bathing room.

William Warren's West India House changed hands twice in the next quarter century before being acquired in 1871 by Samuel D. Hicks, a Boston coppersmith, who added a mansard roof and made other changes. The house was in use as a genteel boarding establishment in 1934, when it was destroyed by fire. EGSJr

W. W. Warren house about 1910, after alterations.

"FRONT ELEVATION."(first of bound set of six sheets). Signed:
"Edward Shaw, Boston, Architect." Inscription on verso of fifth
sheet reads: "Wm. W. Warren's Plans of / house to be built by /
Adam S. Cottrell as per / contract signed this day / July 30, 1840.
Adam S. Cottrell / Wm. W. Warren." Black ink and watercolor on
wove paper; 12 × 14¾". Gift of Earle G. Shettleworth, Jr., 1995.

Edward Shaw (1784–1859)

Unidentified Gothic Revival House, 1846

Asher Benjamin, Minard Lafever, and Edward Shaw rank as the three major authors of American builders' handbooks used in New England during the second quarter of the nineteenth century. Each man began his career in modest circumstances as a rural carpenter and rose to become a major architect, Lafever practicing in New York, and Benjamin and Shaw in Boston.

Shaw worked as a housewright in Boston from 1822 to 1828, when he started listing himself as an architect, the profession he would pursue until his retirement in 1855. During his Boston years, Edward Shaw designed houses, public buildings, and commercial structures, primarily in the Greek Revival and Gothic Revival styles popular in the 1830s and 1840s. In 1842, Andrew Jackson Downing's *Cottage Residences* helped to promote the American Gothic cottage as the house of choice, and Shaw soon followed with two such designs in his 1843 Boston publication, *Rural Architecture*. Plates 45 and 46, which show the more modest of the two residences, are identified as "a Gothic dwelling," while plates 47 and 48 depict the recently completed Brookline, Massachusetts, country house of David Sears, Boston's wealthiest citizen.

The southeast elevation of an unidentified Gothic cottage shown here is one of ten sheets of elevations, floor plans, framing plans, and details drawn by Edward Shaw on 21 April 1846. The medium is pen and ink with selective watercolor highlighting. While the northeast, or front, elevation displays the traditional symmetry of a New England façade masked in a crenellated central entrance tower and a pair of trimmed gables, the southeast elevation more successfully captures the romantic asymmetrical massing characteristic of medieval revival domestic architecture in general and Shaw's Sears house in particular. The architect's professional presentation of his work is reflected in his characteristic practice of binding his drawings together in a folio. Several such folios of Edward Shaw's drawings survive, some with elaborately lettered title pages identifying and dating the project. All of this reminds us of Shaw's statement at the beginning of *The Modern Architect*, his 1854 revision of *Rural Architecture*:

In answer to many inquiries respecting my practical knowledge as a Carpenter and Joiner, I would say, that I served in that capacity twenty years, - fourteen of which, as a contractor and builder, drawing all of my own plans and designs for private and public dwellings costing from five hundred to forty thousand dollars. Since which time I have spent fifteen years in the theoretical practice and science of Architectural Drawings and Plans, both ancient and modern. EGSJr

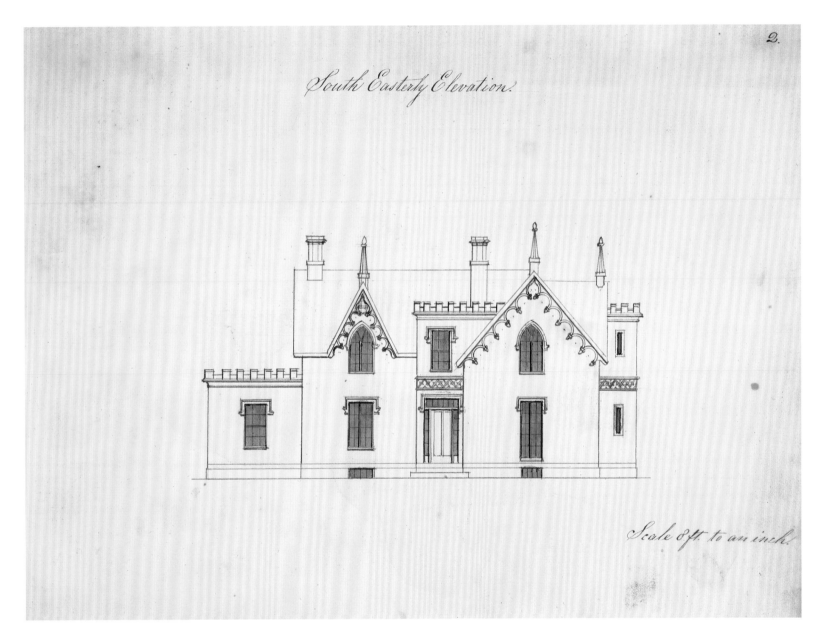

South Easterly Elevation.

Scale 8 ft. to an inch.

"South Easterly Elevation" of an unidentified Gothic Revival
house (second of bound set of ten sheets). Signed and dated
on fourth sheet: "Drawn 8 ft to an inch. / By Edward Shaw
Architect. / Boston Apr. 21 1846." Ink and watercolor on wove
(J Whatman Turkey Mill 1845) paper; 9¾ × 13¾". Library
and Archives purchase, 2006.

William F. Pratt (1814–1900)

Augustus Clarke House,
Hawley Street, Northampton, Massachusetts, 1842

William Pratt learned the building trades from his father, Thomas, a Northampton carpenter, with whom he worked in the 1830s, after he came of age. By 1850, when he designed the Northampton Town Hall, Pratt had established himself as an architect. He provided the Connecticut River valley towns with a full range of architectural designs in the latest styles, and left a collection of drawings, now owned by the Northampton Historical Society.[1] The drawings for the Clarke house, however, document the earliest known project by Pratt.

Pratt spent a year in Jamaica, from 1840 to 1841, working as a builder. The Clarke house must have been designed shortly after his return, and it may reflect some influence of the residential architecture of the West Indies. Although in the Greek Revival style, the second-story veranda and floor-length windows suggest the architecture of a more temperate climate. Augustus Clarke, a local merchant and auctioneer, had this house built about 1842. Notwithstanding its monumental façade, the house was erected on a residential street near the center of Northampton. (It survives, but altered almost beyond recognition.)[2] While we do not know where Pratt received his training, these drawings demonstrate a refined talent in architectural rendering.

What distinguishes this otherwise traditional Greek Revival-style façade is the second-floor balcony, which projects out in the center bay, allowing for a large parlor. The parlor and adjoining dining room in the center of the house form a double room. Paired full-length windows provide natural light at either end of these rooms. RGR

Augustus Clarke house in 2007.

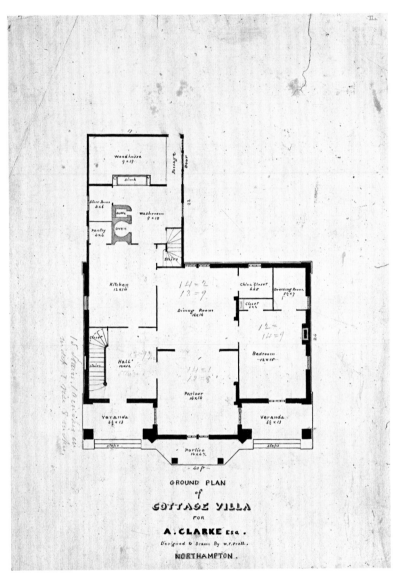

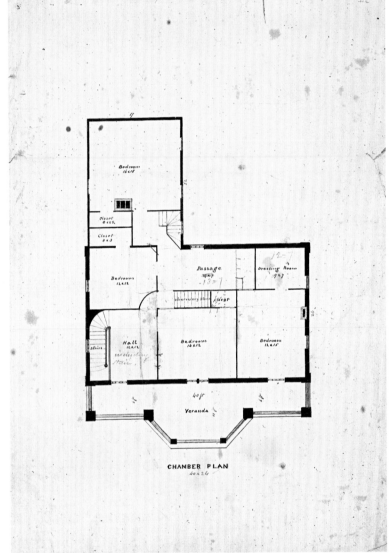

"GROUND PLAN / of / COTTAGE VILLA / FOR / A. CLARKE ESQ."
(number three of a set of four sheets; number inscribed on verso).
Signed: "Designed & Drawn By W. F. Pratt. / NORTHAMPTON."
Dated on verso: February 17, 1842. Ink, watercolor, and graphite
emendations on wove paper; 12⅛ × 8½". Gift of W. B. Clarke, 1922.

"CHAMBER PLAN." (number four of a set of four sheets; number
inscribed on verso), unsigned. Dated on verso: February 17, 1842.
Ink, watercolor, and graphite emendations on wove paper;
12⅛ × 8½". Gift of W. B. Clarke, 1922. This drawing was not
included in the exhibition.

COTTAGE VILLA
FOR
A. CLARKE, Esq.
HAWLEY. ST.   W.F.PRATT. Arch.

Elevation of "COTTAGE VILLA / FOR / A. CLARKE. ESQ /
HAWLEY. ST." (number one of a set of four sheets; number
inscribed on verso), undated. Signed: "W. F. Pratt. Arch.ᵗ"
Ink and watercolor on wove paper; 9 × 12". Gift of W. B.
Clarke, 1922.

"SIDE ELEVATION / OF / COTTAGE VILLA." (number two of
a set of four sheets; number inscribed on verso), undated.
Signed: "W. F. Pratt. Arch^t." Ink and watercolor on wove paper;
8½ × 12". Gift of W. B. Clarke, 1922.

Joseph C. Wells (1814–1860)

Henry C. Bowen House, Roseland Cottage,
Route 169, Woodstock, Connecticut, c.1846

Roseland Cottage, overlooking the traditional town common in Wood-stock, Connecticut, presents a striking sight. The bright pink Gothic Revival cottage was built in 1846 as a summer house for Henry Chandler Bowen (1813–1896) and his family. Bowen was a nineteenth-century success story, a man who left his native Woodstock to seek his fortune in New York City at age twenty, opened his dry goods store five years later, married his former boss's daughter, and founded the influential Congregational newspaper, *The Independent.*

The house was designed by Joseph Collins Wells, an English architect who had recently come to New York. According to a notice of his death published in *The Crayon*, Wells "easily found discriminating patrons, for whom he erected residences remarkable for domestic conveniences and good taste . . . which led to his employment on commissions of greater importance." Indeed, Roseland Cottage was such a residence, and Henry Bowen that type of patron. Bowen hired Wells in 1850 to design his four-story Silk Warehouse, the "marble stores" on Broadway, noted in *The Crayon* as one of the architect's contributions to the city's "architectural adornment." He was no doubt also responsible for Wells's commission for the Plymouth Church in Brooklyn, of which Bowen was a founder and to which he brought Henry Ward Beecher. Wells went on to design many public buildings and private residences, and was one of the thirteen architects who founded the American Institute of Architects in 1857.

Sometime between 4 July 1845, when Bowen purchased the land, and 13 October 1845, when he signed a contract with two local builders, Wells completed a sheet of drawings with floor plans and front and side elevations of the commodious "cottage" in full-blown Gothic style, the style later popularized by Andrew Jackson Downing. He also drew up detailed specifications for the carpentry and the masonry to accompany the contract. The house and barn were to cost $4,700 and be completed by 1 August 1846. Innovations included a bathroom on the first floor of the house and a bowling alley attached to the barn.

At some point, Wells presented the Bowens with a house portrait (no doubt a skill he learned as part of his English training), which they had framed in an elaborate carved frame. It shows the house with the barn in the background as they would appear when finished, complete with the Gothic fence in front and a lattice enclosure for the rose garden after which the house was named.

The records Henry Bowen kept offer an interesting glimpse into the challenges of building a modern house in the country in the mid-nine-teenth century, as well as the costs involved. Within a month of signing the contract, the Woodstock builders, Samuel Underwood and Lewis Chamberlain, apparently after studying the plans and specifications, realized they were over their heads and informed Bowen they were "unable to fulfil [sic] the contract." Citing "destruction" and "ruin," they turned the job down a second time, and Bowen found another local builder Edward Eaton, who completed the project by early 1847. Eaton, too, had concerns about some of the work, once telling Bowen it would be cheaper to have the diamond-paned window sash made in New York, "as our country sashmakers are not acquainted with that kind of work."

Expenses, including construction costs, furniture, wallpaper, roses, and trees, summarized in an account under "Dwelling House & Barn &c Woodstock Conn.," total $19,936.44. Hundreds of receipts provide greater detail for laborers' wages and board, the cost of lumber and supplies, and transportation of materials shipped from New York by water, rail, and ox cart to the site. Bowen paid Wells $530.84 on 21 November 1846.

Historic New England purchased Roseland Cottage from Bowen's descendants in 1970, with the assistance of the Connecticut Historical Commission. At the same time, a descendant donated Wells's drawings and many of the original furnishings made by Brooklyn, New York, cabinetmaker Thomas Brooks in the Gothic style to complement the architecture. RCN

Roseland Cottage in the late nineteenth century.

Presentation perspective of the Bowen house,
Roseland Cottage, in original frame, undated and
unsigned. Black and blue ink and watercolor on wove
paper; 13¾ × 21". Gift of Margaret Carson Holt, 1970.

Charles Roath (c. 1800 – c. 1849)

Unidentified Townhouses and Store, 1846

What little we know about Charles Roath shows him to have evolved, like many men of his generation, from carpenter to architect. Asher Benjamin and Edward Shaw experienced a similar transformation, although in Roath's case the leap seems to have occurred almost overnight. From 1830 to 1834, he is listed in Boston city directories as a stair builder; in 1835, he changed his title to architect and presumably never looked back. His local career, although apparently brief, was very active. According to building contracts recorded by Suffolk County, in the decade 1835 to 1846, some sixty townhouses, many in groups of from two to ten, and a German Lutheran Church, at Suffolk and Waltham streets in the city, were to be erected according to "plans drawn by Charles Roath of Boston, Architect." In one year alone, 1845 to 1846, Roath designed ten houses in Dover Street, nine in Oswego Street, South Cove, and seven more in Albany, Harvard, and Hudson streets. He practiced out of a drafting room at 23 Joy's Building during the 1840s, and then—despite what seems to have been a growing practice—vanishes from the known record.

This elevation, ink and watercolor on wove paper, is standard for the draftsmanship of the period. It shows a pair of unidentified and unlocated brick and stone townhouses, presumably for Boston, perhaps never erected. The unit to the right incorporates a ground-level storefront of granite posts and lintels, a ubiquitous feature of the nineteenth-century Boston Granite style of commercial architecture. The brick load-bearing walls and wooden spans are otherwise unremarkable, and they required relatively minimal graphics beyond the arrangement of rooms and façade details. The rectangular first-floor plan contains an off-center entry that leads to a rear ell with a washroom, and upstairs to the parlor, dining room, and kitchen. It can be assumed that the design, like the drawings, was a standard one and varied little from many of the other houses Roath sprinkled across the growing city. JFO'G

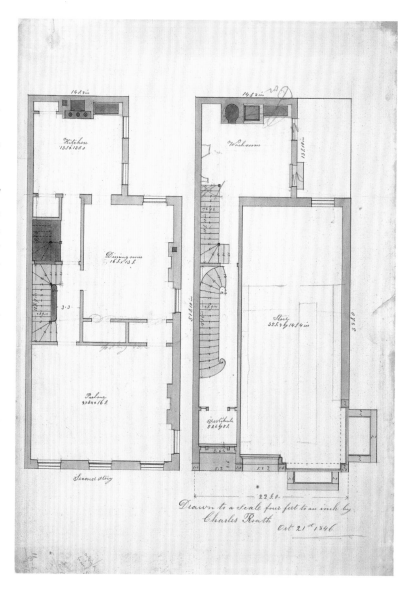

Floor plans for an unidentified townhouse and store.
Signed and dated: "Drawn to a scale four feet to an inch by /
Charles Roath / Oct 21st 1846." Ink and watercolor on wove
(Whatman) paper; 19½ × 13½". Provenance unknown.
This drawing was not included in the exhibition.

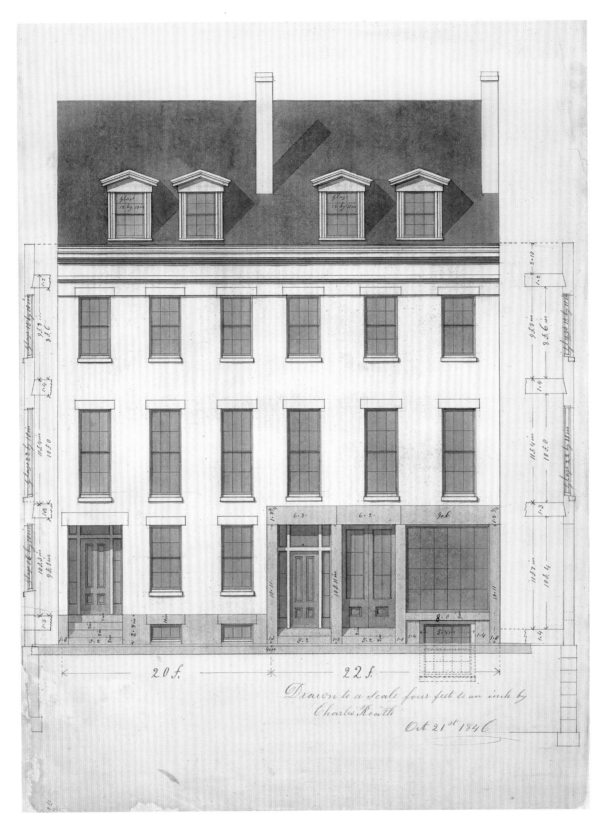

Elevation of unidentified joined townhouses, one with shop front, and front wall sections. Signed and dated: "Drawn to a scale four feet to an inch by / Charles Roath / Oct 21st 1846." Ink, graphite, and watercolor on wove paper; 19½ × 13½". Provenance unknown.

Gervase Wheeler (1823/25–1889)

Unidentified Italianate Villa, c. 1850

"Sketch for East Elevation" (one of a set of four sheets),
undated. Signed: "Gervase Wheeler Architect."
Ink, watercolor, and graphite on wove paper; 19 × 26¾".
Library and Archives purchase, 1961.

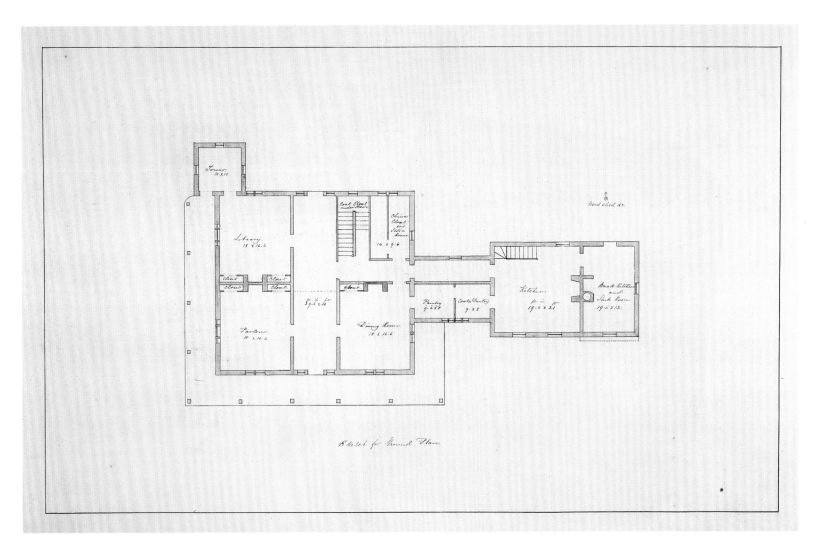

"Sketch for Ground Plan" (one of a set of four sheets),
undated and unsigned. Ink, watercolor, and graphite
on wove paper; 19 × 27 3/16". Library and Archives
purchase, 1961.

Gervase Wheeler (1823/25–1889)
Unidentified Italianate Villa, c. 1850

Gervase Wheeler, an English-born architect who trained with R. C. Carpenter in London, practiced in this country from 1847 to the first days of 1860, working in Maine, Connecticut, Philadelphia, and New York, and briefly in association with Richard Upjohn and Henry Austin. During his stay, he published a number of articles and two influential books on domestic architecture, *Rural Homes* (1851) and *Homes for the People* (1855), that rivaled the now more famous publications of Andrew Jackson Downing.

The plan for this villa combines a balanced central-hall block with asymmetrical additions containing a tower and the service wing. The elevation shows an extended two-story residence of boxy shapes with trabeated and half-circular windows, a veranda, three-story tower, or campanile, and standing-seam metal roof. It follows the mode of villa design then associated with the Italian countryside, a mode fashionable in the United States from the mid-1830s through the 1850s, and hence to be found coming frequently from the architectural drafting rooms of the period. The fashion originated in England much earlier but was given impetus here by several American publications, foremost among them Andrew Jackson Downing's *Cottage Residences* (1842), which was quickly followed by designs for towered villas published by a host of other architects. Wheeler himself included such houses in both his American publications. Downing, in his *The Architecture of Country Houses* (1850), wrote that such an Italianate villa is "remarkable for expressing the elegant culture and variety of accomplishment of the retired citizen or man of the world . . . [and is] very significant of the multiform tastes, habits, and wants of modern civilization." These villas combine classical details with an irregular or picturesque silhouette thought suitable in the Romantic era for a suburban or rural site. The upper reaches of the tower provide a place for viewing the surrounding vistas or, as one English writer put it, a lookout and refuge from unwanted guests. Wheeler shows an exterior of clapboards over a lumber frame, but such houses were also realized with brownstone, brick, or stucco exteriors. JFO'G

Joseph Hayward (1810–1880)

Oakes Ames House (not built),
North Easton, Massachusetts, c. 1850

Joseph Hayward was a life-long carpenter who lived in the Brockton-Bridgewater area south of Boston and obviously somewhere acquired rudimentary skills as a drafter. Oakes Ames (1804–1873), manufacturer and politician, was the son of Oliver Ames (1779–1863), who established a shovel factory at North Easton, near Brockton, in the early nineteenth century. Oakes and his brother, Oliver II, took over the business in 1844, and after its expansion during the Civil War, became major clients of H. H. Richardson, who designed five buildings for the town. Later Ames family homes still dot the landscape, and Richardson's works form a major pilgrimage objective for students of American architecture. This house would have stood in sharp contrast to the master's work.

By mid-century, Oakes Ames would have been in a position to order a design for a large home from Hayward, although the initiative appears to have been Hayward's, judging by the inscription on the drawing of the south elevation (see page 73), which proudly points out its originality. Technically typical of the time, the drawings show a naively conceived castellated Italianate pile with two main towers, corner turrets, pepper-grinder chimneys, and segmental and half-round arched window openings. This is a naive rendition of a mansion house design popular in the period. The graphics have a folk art quality, especially in the startling colors and the flat, decorative depiction of the landscape at the east elevation. Despite this patch of acid greenery, the building is isolated from any suggestion of ambience, a fact that separates it from the Romantic integration of architecture and landscape espoused by A. J. Downing in this era. The house apparently was never built, although Oliver had a house designed by Bostonian George Snell erected in North Easton in 1862. No other graphite work by Hayward has yet come to light. JFO'G

View from the East.

Elevation of the "View from the East" of the Oakes Ames house, undated and unsigned. Brown ink and ink and/or watercolor washes on wove paper; 13¼ × 19". Library and Archives purchase, 1988.

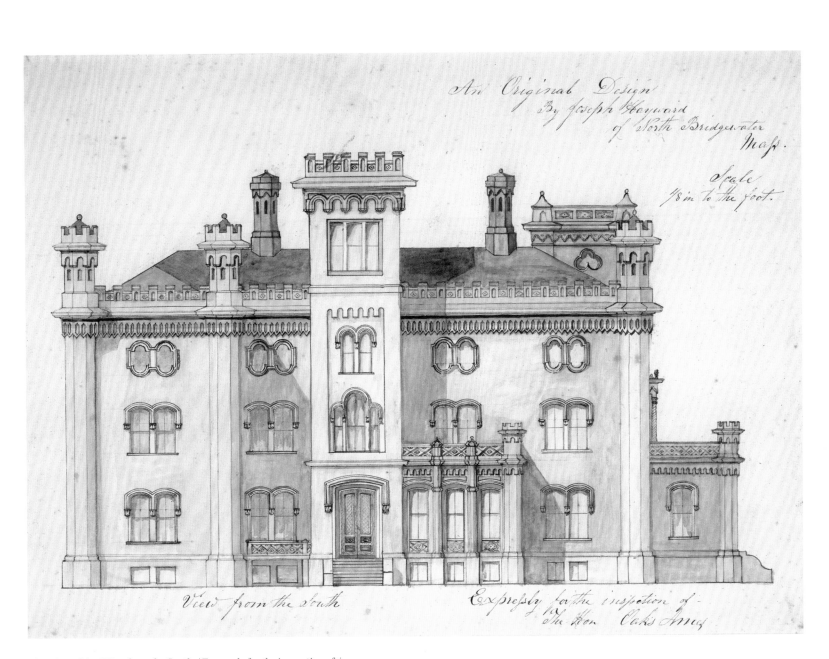

An Original Design
By Joseph Hayward
of North Bridgewater
Mass.

Scale
⅛ in. to the foot.

View from the South

Expressly for the inspection of
The Hon Oakes Ames

Elevation of the "View from the South / Expressly for the inspection of / The Hon Oakes Ames," undated. Signed: "An Original Design / By Joseph Hayward / of North Bridgewater / Mass." Brown ink, ink and/or watercolor washes, and graphite underdrawing on wove (J Whatman Turkey Mill) paper; 13¼ × 19¼". Library and Archives purchase, 1988.

Alexander R. Esty (1826–1881)

Unidentified Italianate House, c. 1855

As popularized in the 1850s and 1860s, the Italianate style of architecture found more favor with house builders than the Gothic Revival or other exotic historical styles. This was especially true in eastern New England. The Italianate style lent itself more readily to the traditional two-story symmetrical house form that appealed to the innate conservatism of many New Englanders. These designs could be given a picturesque air, particularly by the addition of cupolas or towers, while retaining a link to the classical revival styles of the early nineteenth century, which used the same classical vocabulary well known to builders.

This elevation for an unidentified project represents a conservative response to changing architectural fashions. An arcaded entrance portico with a balustrade provides a clear link to Italian Renaissance villas, as does the exterior stucco that probably was intended to cover a house built of wood or brick. The addition of a cupola in the center of the roof provided an economical alternative to the engaged tower more commonly associated with the style. Esty provided his own distinctive embellishment by including round-headed attic windows that break the typically straight eave line of the cornice supported on brackets.

A native of Framingham, Massachusetts, Alexander Esty trained under Boston architects Richard Bond and Gridley J. F. Bryant in the 1840s, when picturesque romantic styles were first becoming popular. Esty is best known today for several Gothic Revival-style churches and institutional buildings, many of stone construction. These commissions reflect an expertise in the English Gothic Revival, but it is probable that these high-profile ecclesiastical and public commissions led to residential projects as well. Esty's drawing for this unidentified house has much in common with another of his designs, the Billings house, which was built on Central Street in Framingham in 1852. The polished drawing, done in pen and ink and watercolor, supports the belief that there may be many handsome undocumented examples of Esty's residential work in eastern New England. RGR

The Billings house in Framingham, Massachusetts, in the late nineteenth century. Its design bears a strong similarity to the drawing depicted here.

Elevation of the "Front View of Dwelling" (one of a set of twenty-three sheets, originally bound), undated. Signed: "Alexander R. Esty Arch[t] / N[o] 2 Change Avenue / Boston." Ink, ink and/or watercolor washes, and graphite underdrawing and emendations on wove (J Whatman Turkey Mill) paper; 23 7/16 × 17 13/16". Provenance unknown.

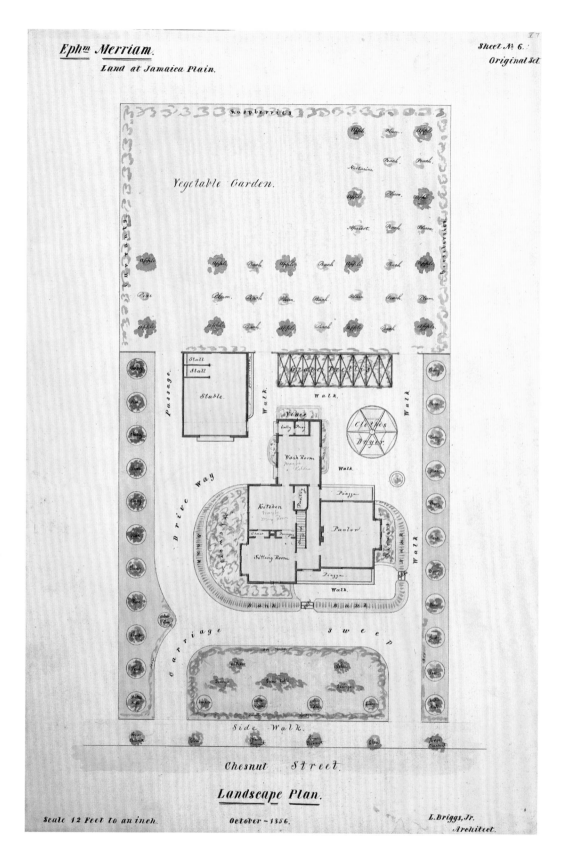

"Eph^m Merriam. / Land at Jamaica Plain. / Landscape Plan."
("Sheet N° 6. [of nine sheets; number one now missing] / Original Set.").
Signed: "L. Briggs, Jr. / Architect." Dated: "October – 1856." Black
and brown ink, watercolor, and graphite underdrawing and notations
on wove paper; 19½ × 13". Gift of Elizabeth Huebener, 1937.

Luther Briggs, Jr. (1822–1905)

Ephraim Merriam House,
Chestnut Avenue, Jamaica Plain, Boston, 1856–57

Luther Briggs, Jr., trained as an architect with Gridley J. F. Bryant and his uncle-in-law, Alexander Parris, two men known for their large urban masonry buildings. However, Briggs lived in Dorchester, Massachusetts, and his suburban architecture was influenced by the picturesque styles and ornamental landscape designs featured in the books of Andrew Jackson Downing.[1] For Ephraim Merriam, Briggs designed an Italianate-style house on Chestnut Avenue (identified as Chestnut Street on the drawing) in Jamaica Plain, then a fashionable suburban community. Following Downing's advice, Briggs prepared a landscape plan in which the front portion of the lot was devoted to lawns, shrubbery, and flower gardens laid out in an ornamental fashion and integral with the design and placement of the house. The rear third of the lot, out of view from the street, was reserved for a vegetable garden and fruit trees and bushes. Although the Merriam house survives, the original lot has been subdivided, eliminating any possibility of restoring the original landscape plan. RGR

Stores and Tenements for Matthew Bartlett (built?),
Broad and Belmont Streets, Boston, 1856

Matthew Bartlett operated the Boston Steam Bakery at 226 Broad Street, Boston. The design for stores and tenements at Broad and Belmont streets in the Fort Hill neighborhood may not have been built. Bartlett sold the property in 1857, and the Fort Hill neighborhood was later leveled in a nineteenth-century urban renewal project. In keeping with the waterfront neighborhood (the site was adjacent to a large multistory sailors' retirement home), the building as designed featured typical storefronts and a plain façade with a simple Italianate cornice. The plan shows tenement rooms above the storefronts and in a separate five-story block linked by a one-story connector. Although the apartments were small— one living room 14½ by 14½ feet and one bedroom 10½ by 14½ feet, with no plumbing or kitchen facilities—the amount of light created by having two separate blocks must have been a major improvement over typical waterfront tenement housing. RGR

Ephraim Merriam house in 2007.

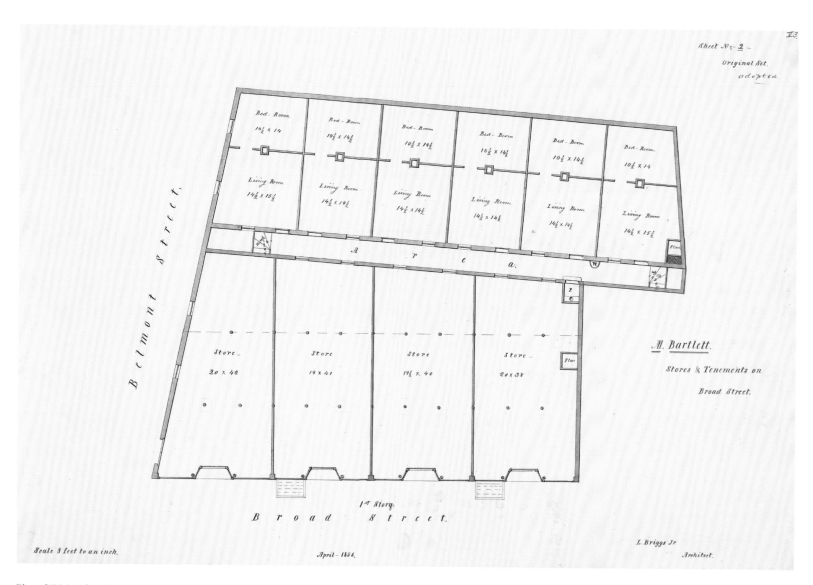

Plan of "M. Bartlett. / Stores & Tenements on / Broad Street. /
1st Story." ("Sheet Nº - 2 - [of six sheets] / Original Set. / adopted").
Signed: "L. Briggs Jr / Architect." Dated: "April – 1856." Black ink,
watercolor, graphite, and graphite underdrawing on wove paper;
12¹³⁄₁₆ × 19¼". Gift of Elizabeth Huebener, 1937.

Elevations of "M. Bartlett, / Stores & Tenements, on, / Broad
Street. / Elevation on Broad Street. / Elevations on Belmont
Street." ("Sheet Nº. 1 [of six sheets] / Original Set / adopted").
Signed: "L. Briggs Jr / Architect. / 27 Joy's Building / Boston."
Dated: "April – 1856." Black and red ink, watercolor, and graphite
on wove paper; 19¼ × 12¾". Gift of Elizabeth Huebener, 1937.

Original Set
not given

M. Bartlett,

Stores & Tenements, on,

Broad Street.

Elevation on Broad Street.

Elevations on Belmont Street.

Scale 8 feet to an inch.

April - 1856.

L. Briggs Jr Architect.

27 Joy's Building

Boston.

Luther Briggs, Jr. (1822–1905)

James F. Bigelow House, Park Street,
East Abington (now Rockland), Massachusetts, 1857–58

Luther Briggs, Jr's., debt to Andrew Jackson Downing is evident in the series of façade elevations developed for James Bigelow. He offered the Rockland shoe manufacturer no fewer than five alternate schemes (of which two are shown) for his new house. Bigelow evidently was open to a variety of historical styles for exterior treatments. The Gothic Revival-style solution offered a crenellated tower with quatrefoil windows, vergeboard in the gable ends, and lancet arched windows. The design in the "Rhenish Picturesque Style" is essentially Romanesque in derivation, a style popularized in Germany as "Rundbogistil," or round-arched style.

Although of wood construction, these designs called for a large amount of fussy and intricate ornamental trim on the exterior that would have been custom fabricated. The full-scale window detail sheet indicates the architect prepared extensive drawings to ensure that work was custom-made and the carpenters were not given a free hand to interpret his intentions.

The plan also provides the comforts expected in a modern upper-middle-class home at mid-century. Sitting room, dining room, and parlor are the large ground-floor rooms, each with a fireplace and ample natural lighting. The kitchen wing includes locations for the sink, cooking range, and set kettle, along with alcoves for a china closet and a pantry. In the rear is a separate washroom with boiler for clothes. While there is an attached exterior privy, the owners probably had second-floor water closets.

The cost may have dictated the final solution, as the Gothic Revival-style design that was selected had less expensive embellishments. The house still stands, although significantly altered. An early illustration (see page 83) of the completed design reveals there was, like the Merriam house (see pages 76–77), a landscape design to set off the picturesque character of the house. RGR

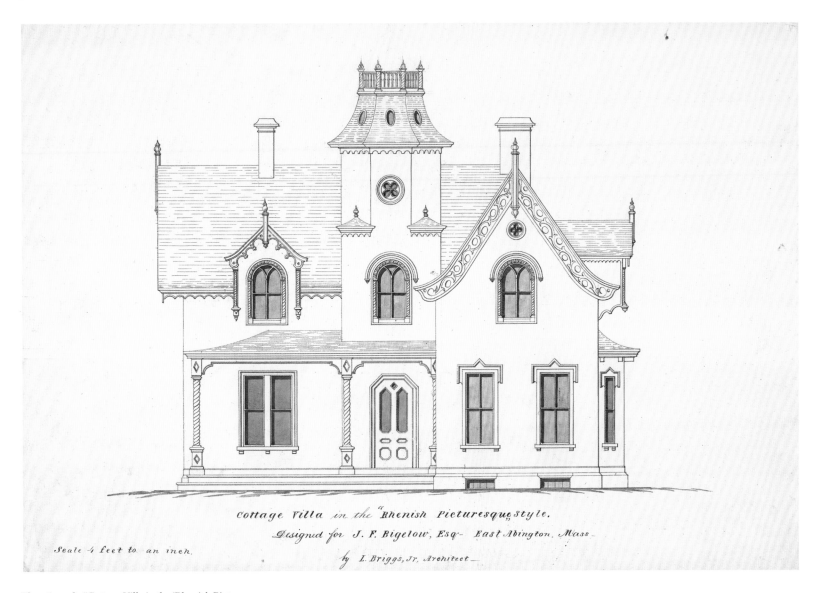

Cottage Villa in the "Rhenish Picturesque" style.

Designed for J. F. Bigelow, Esq- East Abington, Mass.

by L. Briggs, Jr, Architect-

Scale 4 feet to an inch.

Elevation of a "Cottage Villa in the 'Rhenish Picturesque, Style." (one of a set of nineteen sheets; one now missing), undated. Signed: "Designed for J. F. Bigelow, Esq – East Abington, Mass / by L. Briggs, Jr. Architect." Brown and black ink, brown ink washes, and graphite underdrawing and emendations on wove paper; 13⅜ × 19⅜". Gift of Elizabeth Huebener, 1937.

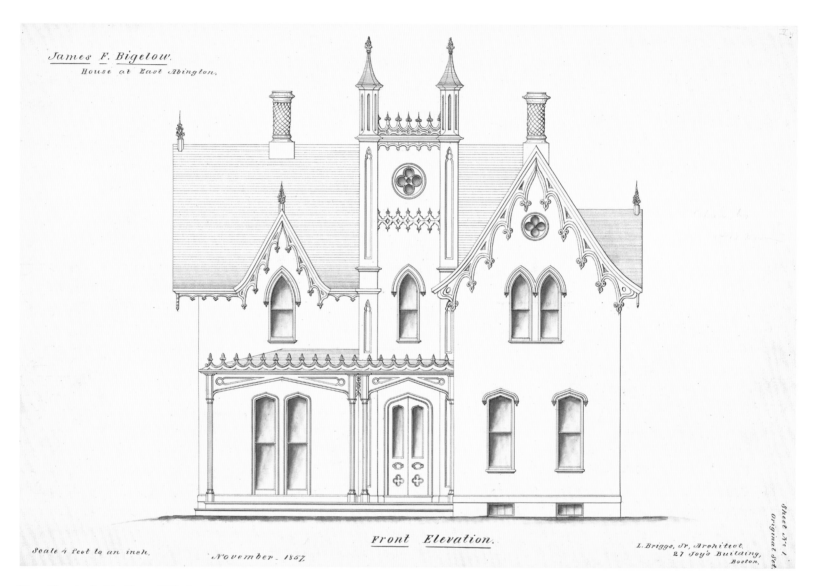

James F. Bigelow.
House at East Abington.

Front Elevation.

Scale 4 feet to an inch.   November – 1857.   L. Briggs, Jr, Architect.
27 Joy's Building,
Boston.

Sheet Nᵒ 1.
Original Set.

"Front Elevation." of the "James F. Bigelow. / House at
East Abington." ("Sheet Nᵒ 1 [of nineteen sheets; one now
missing] / Original Set."). Signed: "L. Briggs, Jr, Architect. /
27 Joy's Building, / Boston." Dated: "November – 1857." Faint
graphite inscription on front reads: "Copied by A. B. Norton
[?] or Nash [?]." Black and blue ink, watercolor and/or ink
washes, and graphite underdrawing and emendations on wove
paper; 13¾ × 19". Gift of Elizabeth Huebener, 1937.

RESIDENCE OF J. F. BIGELOW, EAST ABINGTON.

Illustration of the J. F. Bigelow house, 1866.

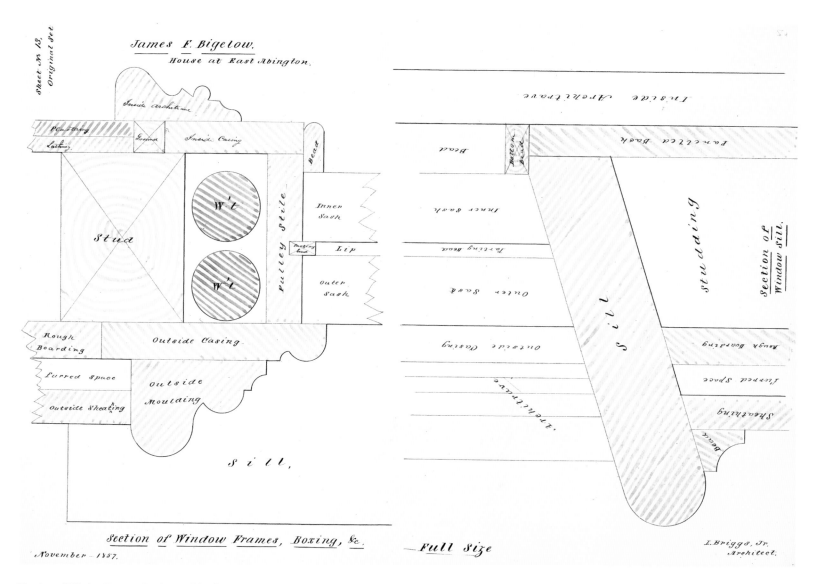

"Section of Window Frames, Boxing, &c." for the "James F. Bigelow. / House at East Abington." ("Sheet Nº 13, [of nineteen sheets; one now missing] / Original Set"). Signed: "L. Briggs, Jr. / Architect." Dated: "November – 1857." Black ink, watercolor, and graphite underdrawing; 12¾ × 19". Gift of Elizabeth Huebener, 1937.

Plan of the "Principal Story" of the "James F. Bigelow / House at East Abington." ("Sheet Nº 4 [of nineteen sheets; one now missing] / Original Set"). Signed: "L. Briggs. Jr, / Architect." Dated: "October 1857." Black ink, watercolor, and graphite underdrawing; 19 × 12¾". Gift of Elizabeth Huebener, 1937.

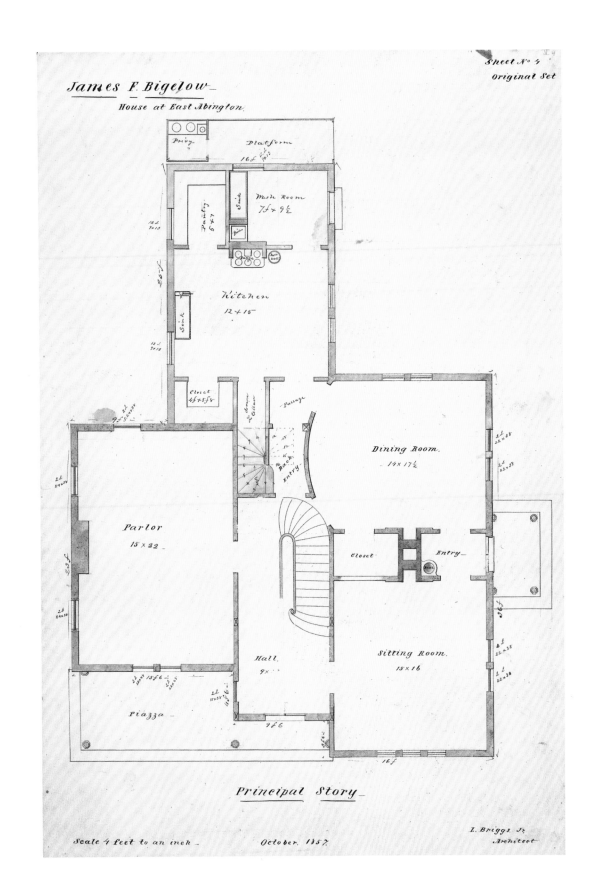

James F. Bigelow

House at East Abington.

Privy

Platform
16f

Wash Room
7½ x 9½

Pantry
6 x 7

Sink

Kitchen
12 + 15

Sink

Closet
4½ x 5½

Passage

Dining Room.
14 x 17½

Back
Entry

Parlor
15 x 22

Closet   Entry

Hall.
9 x

Sitting Room.
15 x 16

Piazza

9 f 6

16 f

Principal Story.

Scale 4 feet to an inch.   October. 1857.

L. Briggs, Jr.
Architect

85

Luther Briggs, Jr. (1822–1905)

P. D. Wallis House, Chester Square,
(now Massachusetts Avenue), Boston, 1858

Luther Briggs, Jr., designed rowhouses in the newly developed South End neighborhood of Boston, where the French Mansard style predominated. The house for builder P. D. Wallis was acquired by Francis Dane and is now the headquarters of the South End Historical Society. It is one of the rowhouses that fronted what was a large oval green called Chester Square. Although the square has since been bisected by Massachusetts Avenue, the surrounding houses and outer sections of the green survive.

As was characteristic of the South End neighborhood, pressed-brick façades with bowfronted bays and Mansard roofs provided a uniform vocabulary for many of the houses. Absolute uniformity was avoided when individual houses were custom designed, as opposed to rows of dwellings erected by one developer. For the Wallis house, Briggs employed Italianate-style windows and doors with trim carved in brownstone. Brownstone also was used for the ashlar stone basement level. The elevation drawing called for iron balconies on both the first and second floors, but it appears that, as built, only the first floor had the longer windows. The attic-story plan shows a billiard room and three bedrooms in the Mansard roof.

The use of custom-designed entrances with ornamental staircases was a way of distinguishing one rowhouse from another. For the Wallis house, Briggs also provided a detail sheet of the elaborate cast-iron newel post and handrail. Unfortunately, this feature has not survived. RGR

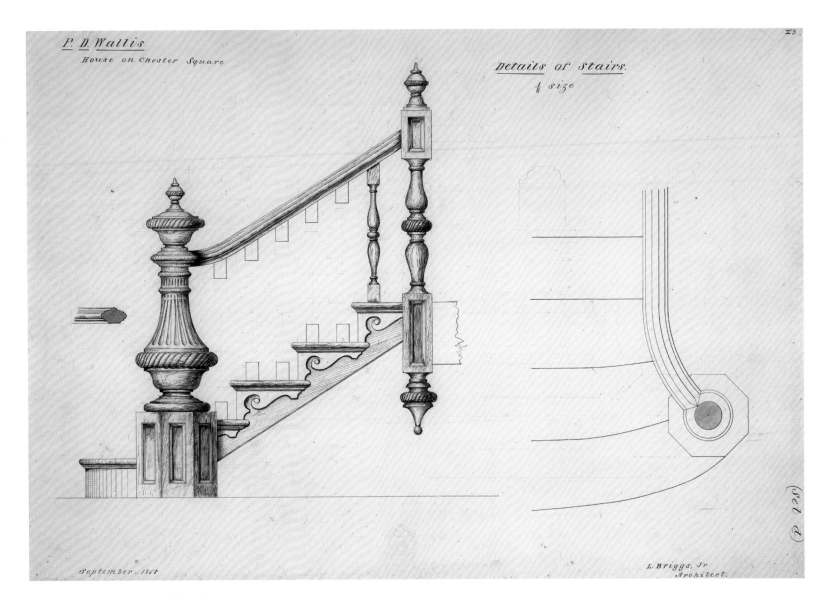

"Details of Stairs." for the "P. D. Wallis. / House on
Chester Square" (one of four sheets). Signed: "L. Briggs,
Jr / Architect." Dated: "September – 1858." Brown ink,
watercolor and/or ink washes, and graphite underdrawing and emendations on wove (J Whatman) paper;
13¼ × 19¼". Gift of Elizabeth Huebener, 1937.

P. D. Wallis house about 1984.

Plan of the "Attic Story" and the "Front Elevation." of the
"P. D. Wallis. / House on Chester Square / (as originally
intended)" (one of four sheets). Signed: "L. Briggs, Jr. /
Architect." Dated: "June 1858." Black ink, watercolor
and/or ink washes, and graphite underdrawing on wove
(J Whatman Turkey Mill with partial date of 1856 ?)
paper; 19¾ × 13⅜". Gift of Elizabeth Huebener, 1937.

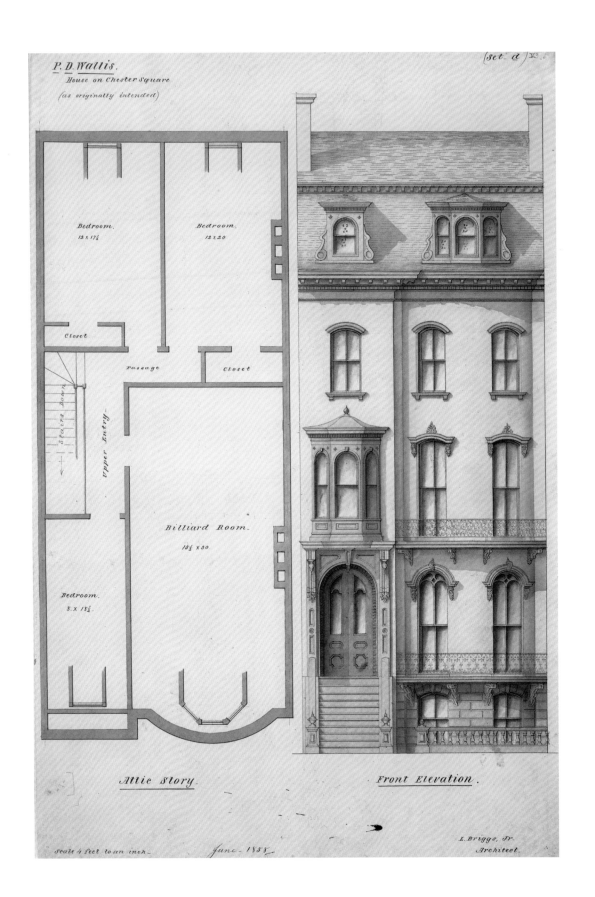

P. D. Wallis.
House on Chester Square
(as originally intended)

(Set. A.)

Bedroom.
12 x 17½

Bedroom.
12 x 20

Closet

Passage   Closet

Upper Entry.

Stairs down

Billiard Room.
18½ x 30

Bedroom.
8 x 18½

Attic Story.

Front Elevation.

Scale 4 feet to an inch.   June. 1858.

L. Briggs, Jr.
Architect.

Luther Briggs, Jr. (1822–1905)

Ell Addition to the House of H. Emerson (built ?),
Harrison Square, Clam Point, Dorchester,
Boston, Massachusetts, 1860

Harrison Square was a neighborhood of Dorchester, now known as Clam Point. During the mid-nineteenth century, this area provided a semi-rural refuge well outside the city limits. Although now more densely developed and in close proximity to a major highway, Clam Point's historic charms are still evident in the quality of the surviving early nineteenth-century architecture.

The small addition that Luther Briggs, Jr., designed for the Emerson house (which has not been located) consisted of a three-story wing added to an existing ell. Built at a lower grade, the ground floor was essentially a basement room for "Fuel &c," while above was the "Gardener's Room" and above that a bedroom, probably also for the gardener. The plans for living quarters for a gardener and the very elaborate Gothic Revival-style fretwork on the rear elevation suggest that Emerson planned a large designed garden that required a resident employee. Indeed, the design for the birdhouse, probably fabricated of cast iron, is an exceptionally ornate and lavish one for a piece of garden architecture. Perhaps the Gothic Revival-style fretwork was meant to terminate the view from a formal garden bordered by ornamental hedges or flower beds. RGR

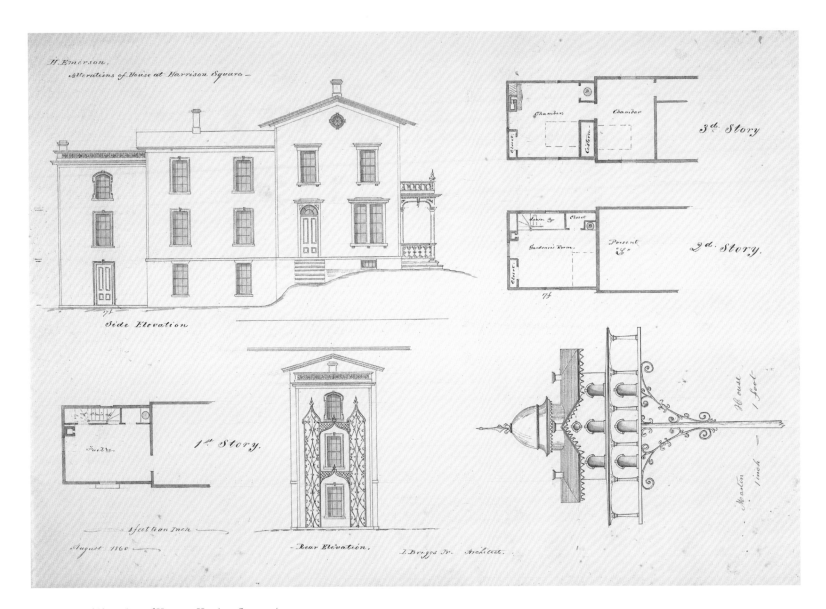

"H. Emerson. / Alterations of House at Harrison Square. /
Side Elevation / 3rd Story / 2nd Story. / Martin House /
Rear Elevation. / 1st Story." Signed: "L. Briggs Jr. Architect."
Dated: "August 1860." Black ink, ink and/or watercolor
washes, and graphite underdrawing on wove (J Whatman
1859) paper; 13 × 19¾". Gift of Elizabeth Huebener, 1937.

Nathaniel J. Bradlee (1829–1888)

Unidentified Townhouse, 1858

Nathaniel J. Bradlee trained in the office of George M. Dexter and acquired that firm upon his mentor's retirement. A very successful architect, Bradlee was well known in his own day for his services as an engineer in expanding the Boston Waterworks at Chestnut Hill, as well as for his activities as a businessman and candidate for mayor of Boston. At the time of his death, his office had taken on Walter T. Winslow and George H. Wetherell as partners, and those men continued the firm into the twentieth century.

These drawings for an unidentified townhouse represent the early phase of Bradlee's career as he began to establish a reputation designing townhouses for Boston's rapidly growing neighborhoods in the years leading up to the Civil War. The young architect's design accommodates the slope of the street, which was probably on Boston's Beacon Hill. Bradlee's design—Victorian in a neighborhood of Federal-period townhouses—displays two very modern features. The first is the Mansard roof, a style that had been introduced into the city ten years earlier by a French architect named Jean Lemoulnier. By 1858, the date of this drawing, the fashionable French Second Empire style had begun to capture the public's imagination and achieved widespread popularity by the end of the decade. The earliest known examples of the Mansard roof appeared on freestanding houses designed for suburban settings. By contrast, the Bradlee design, also a freestanding house, was evidently intended for an urban site.

The second modern treatment appears in the exterior ornament, particularly for the windows and doors. Bradlee's crisp rendering techniques strongly suggest that the material was to be cast iron rather than sandstone. The intricacy of the floral detailing would have been very expensive for hand-carved masonry, whereas cast iron could have provided a much more economical solution. The use of cast iron applied directly to the exterior of a building (as opposed to balcony and fence railing) also would have been uncommon in 1858. This combination of Mansard roof and cast-iron ornament offered a stylistically modern and progressive reworking of the traditional Boston bowfront townhouse. RGR

"Front Elevation" of an unidentified townhouse. Signed: "Nath¹ J. Bradlee, Arch¹." Dated: "Boston, Nov. 29. 1858." Black ink, watercolor and/or ink washes, and graphite underdrawing on wove paper; 12⅝ × 9⅝". Bequest of Dorothy S. F. M. Codman, 1969.

Attic Story. 8'-6"

Third Story. 9'-0"

Second Story. 10'-0"

First Story. 11'-0"

Basement. 8 ft.

35'-3"

Front Elevation.

Nathl J. Bradlee. Arch^t
Boston. Nov. 29. 1858.

Scale 15in = 1 Ft.

93

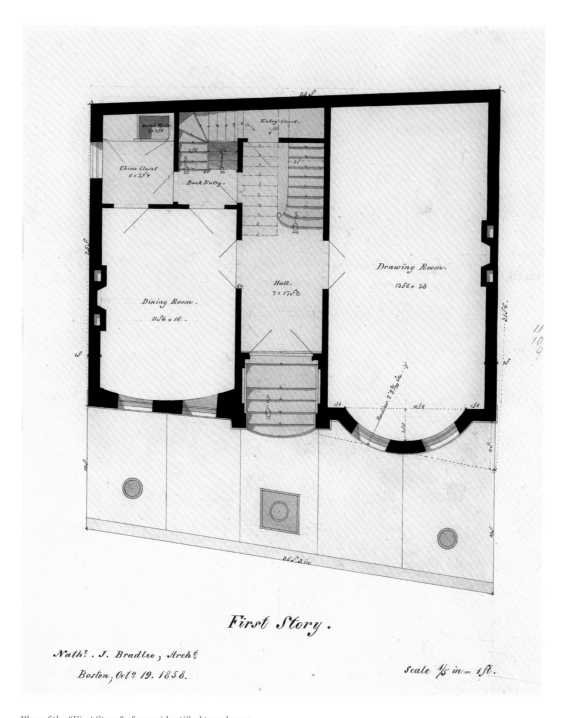

First Story.

Nathl. J. Bradlee, Arch^t.
Boston, Oct^o 19. 1858.

scale 1/8 in = 1 ft.

Plan of the "First Story" of an unidentified townhouse.
Signed: "Nathl. J. Bradlee, Arch^t." Dated: "Boston, Oct^o 19.
1858." Red and black ink, watercolor and/or ink washes,
and graphite underdrawing on wove paper; 12⅝ × 9⅝".
Bequest of Dorothy S. F. M. Codman, 1969.

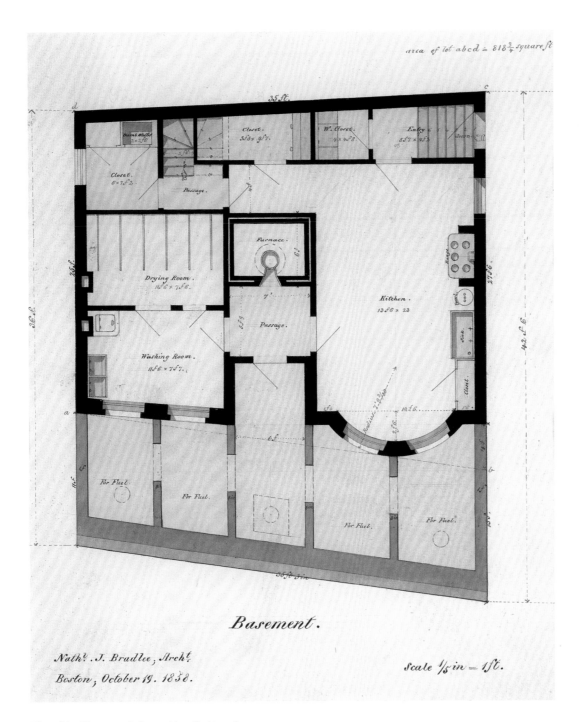

area of lot abcd = 818¾ square ft

Furnace.

Drying Room.

Kitchen.

Passage.

Washing Room.

For Fuel.
For Fuel.
For Fuel.
For Fuel.

Closet.
Passage.
Closet.
W. Closet.
Entry

Basement.

Nath⁺. J. Bradlee, Arch⁺.
Boston, October 19. 1858.

Scale ⅕ in = 1ft.

Plan of the "Basement" of an unidentified townhouse.
Signed: "Nath¹. J. Bradlee, Arch¹." Dated: "Boston,
October 19. 1858." Red and black ink, watercolor and/or
ink washes, and graphite underdrawing on wove paper;
12⅝ × 9⅝". Bequest of Dorothy S. F. M. Codman, 1969.

Henry M. Francis (1836–1908)

Student Drawing, 1860

In 1860, no college or university in this country offered training in architecture. (The first academic architectural program, at MIT, opened its doors in 1868.) Aspirants typically paid established architects to teach them the profession until they had skills enough to work as draftsmen or establish their own practices. At the age of twenty-three, Henry Francis entered the office of one of Boston's leading architects, Alexander R. Esty, who had himself trained under Richard Bond and then worked for Gridley J. F. Bryant (see pages 74–75). Francis had previously studied at Groton Academy, near his native Lunenburg, Massachusetts, and his relatively late entry into the profession may have reflected a career change, or a previous lack of personal funds. In any case, this rare student drawing from an architect's office illustrates the type of skills to be gained from a master. Francis went on to have a long career, working often in the Richardsonian Romanesque style. At his death, his two sons inherited the firm.

Esty is best known for his many Boston-area churches in the Gothic Revival-style, and Francis's large drawing exhibits a very polished interpretation of that style. In ink and watercolor, it presents a brick and (probably intended as cast) stone Tudor front with shadows struck at forty-five degrees, assuming the sun to be to the upper left. This remained for many generations an approved drafting procedure. The drip moldings over openings, (cast) brackets, and carved wooden doors are all typical elements of the style, and Francis also shows alternate treatments of the windows: interior wood blinds versus curtains on the ground floor, oriel versus faux balcony on the upper. Such an accomplished drawing could be, in actual practice, presented to a client for discussion. It might then be scribbled over and a new one prepared. RGR and JFO'G

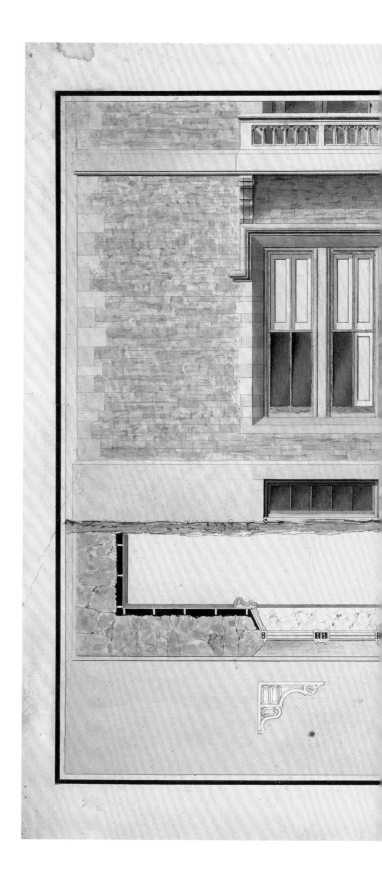

Elevation (one of a set of two sheets). Signed and dated: "H M Francis Architecture Student / with A R Estey [sic] Change Av. / Boston 1860." Ink, watercolor, and graphite on wove paper; 16¾ × 27¾". Library and Archives purchase, 1989.

Henry M. Francis (1836–1908)

Charles F. Harding House (built?),
Fitchburg, Massachusetts, 1880s

Henry Francis worked for Alexander Esty from 1859 to 1861, and later trained with George M. Harding in Portland, Maine, and George Meacham in Boston, before establishing his own practice in 1868. Settling in Fitchburg, Massachusetts, near where he grew up, Francis quickly became the preeminent architect in this small, prosperous industrial city.[1] One of Fitchburg's leading citizens was Charles Harding, for whom Francis designed at least two houses on Atlantic Avenue in the 1880s. This drawing is similar to the Queen Anne-style house Harding built at 26 Atlantic Avenue, but it is not clear whether this design was revised for that location, and it is not known if it was constructed. This drawing was probably part of a portfolio, or may have been intended to be published in the new Boston architectural journal, *The American Architect and Building News*. Clearly, the focus was to be on the options for floor plans, with a color perspective view to suggest what the house might look like, depending upon the finishes selected. As with the houses Harding built on Atlantic Avenue, the design is for a double house that is intended to look like a single-family home. This popular solution ensured the house would be compatible on a street of predominantly single-family homes. RGR

Plans for first and second floors and exterior perspective for a "Design of House / for / Chas. F. Harding Esq," undated. Signed: "H M / Francis / Architect." Graphite, red pencil, watercolor, ink, and graphite emendations on wove paper; 15½ × 14¾". Library and Archives purchase, 1989.

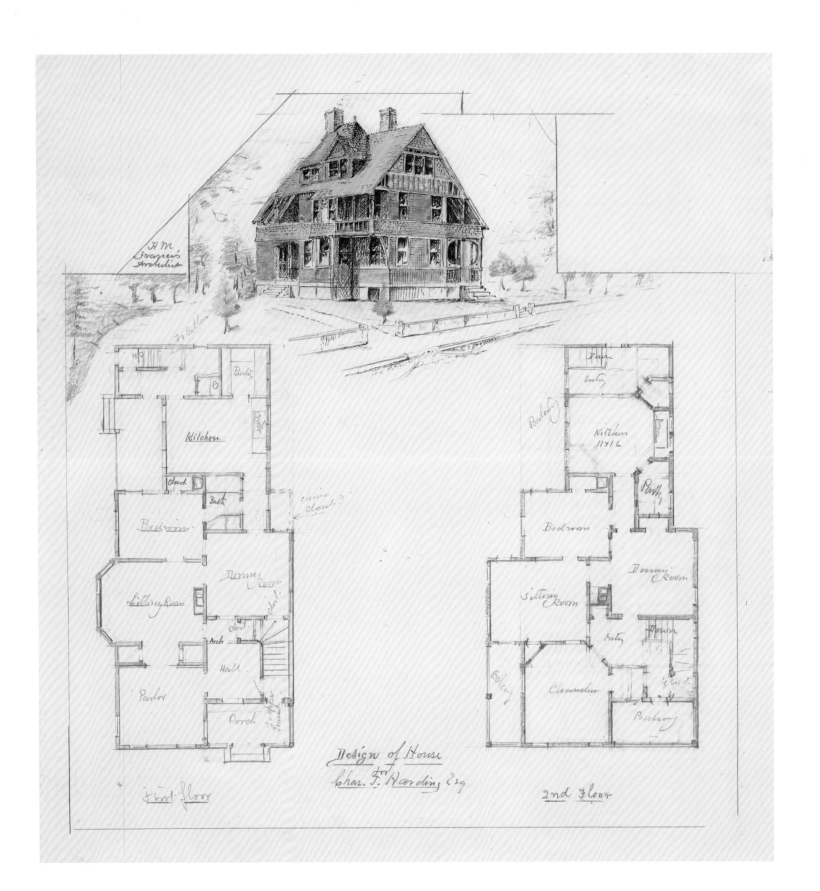

Design of House
for
Chas. F. Harding Esq

First Floor   2nd Floor

John Hubbard Sturgis (1834–1888)

Measured Drawings of the Hancock House,
Beacon Street, Boston, c. 1863 (demolished)

"HANCOCK HOUSE BOSTON / South Elevation."
(one of a set of seven sheets), unsigned and undated.
Black ink, watercolor, and graphite emendations on
wove (J Whatman Turkey Mill) paper; 14¾ × 20½".
Library and Archives purchase, 1965.

"Staircase in Hancock House / from actual measures" /
"Elevation Hall Window Hancock House" / "Plan of
Hall Window" (one of a set of seven sheets), undated.
Signed: "J H S [?]." Black ink and graphite on wove paper;
14¾ × 20½". Library and Archives purchase, 1965.

John Hubbard Sturgis (1834–1888)
Measured Drawings of the Hancock House

The drawings of the Hancock House, unlike nearly all the other plans, elevations, and details in this catalogue, were produced long after its construction, in fact, approximately 126 years later. They are seminal documents in the history of the Colonial Revival and in the practice of historic preservation in the United States.

In 1737, Boston merchant and entrepreneur Thomas Hancock (1703–1764) built a grand house on Beacon Hill, overlooking the Boston Common. The house was constructed of Braintree, Massachusetts, granite, with doors and window surrounds and corner quoins of Connecticut sandstone, and was embellished on the interior with elaborate carved woodwork, imported wallpaper, and fireplace tiles.

Thomas's nephew, John Hancock (1737–1793), signer of the Declaration of Independence, inherited Thomas's fortune and house. Following the Revolution, John was elected the first governor of Massachusetts. He died at the age of fifty-six, while serving his second gubernatorial term. It was his intention to leave the house and the grounds to the Commonwealth of Massachusetts, to be used possibly as a governor's mansion. However, his desire was not clearly outlined in a legal document, and the house remained in the possession of the Hancock family for the next seventy years. During that time, it became increasingly revered as a relic, partly because of its architecture, but even more because of its historical association.

In 1859, the family offered to sell the house and grounds to the Commonwealth for $100,000. During the next few years, with the Civil War raging, the Massachusetts legislature failed to take definitive action on the family's offer. So, in 1863, the Hancock heirs sold the estate to other parties. As the May 12, *Boston Evening Journal* reported, the Hancock Mansion and estate "now belong to James M. Beebe and Gardner Brewer . . . who will immediately proceed to erect two first-class dwelling houses . . ." (see pages 106–7). "The old dwelling," the article noted, "so long one of the places in our midst consecrated to the memory of the 'times which tried men's souls,' is to be pulled down." Thus began one of the earliest battles for historic preservation.

Within days of the announced sale, the city of Boston formed a committee "to consider the expediency of any measures for the preservation of the Hancock House." As it turned out, Brewer and Beebe had spent $125,000 to purchase only the land upon which the house stood. The Hancock heirs retained ownership of the house and its contents, which they proceeded to offer as a gift to the city to be "preserved as a memento of our colonial and revolutionary history." For a time, it seemed as if the city, working with the state, would be able to forge a plan to preserve the house. On 1 June 1863, several Boston papers reported that the house would be carefully disassembled and reconstructed on a vacant lot in the Back Bay. There it would serve as "a museum of antiquities open to the public forever."

In an effort to keep the house in its original location, Thomas Oliver Hazard Perry Burnham, a publisher and antiquarian book dealer, printed a large broadside in bright red ink, which appealed to the new owners to give up their plans to build on the site. Architect Arthur Gilman published a long article about the house in the June issue of *The Atlantic Monthly*, in which he wrote, "It stands, in fact, a solitary monumental pillar in the stream of time—a link to connect the present with the eventful past." In the end, neither the city and state's proposal nor Burnham's appeal nor Gilman's article had any effect. On 15 June, a Boston paper reported that the house would be sold at auction, piece by piece.

In response to the impending demolition of what had become an iconic building, a young architect named John Hubbard Sturgis measured the house and made a set of drawings to scale. They are considered to be the earliest measured drawings to record an American domestic building. Sturgis, who may have done the drawings at Gilman's suggestion, had received his training in England under artist James K. Colling; he would have been familiar with the measured drawings of historic buildings by Colling and others. Later, Sturgis would incorporate elements of the Hancock House in some of his domestic designs during his partnership with Charles Brigham.[1]

In the 1880s and 1890s, other architects found inspiration in the Hancock House's classic proportions and began to incorporate details from it and other colonial buildings into their designs for new private residences and public buildings. LC and RCN

The Hancock House about 1863.

Unidentified Library, c. 1865

This richly colored and finely detailed elevation of the fireplace wall of a library dates to the mid-1860s, when the Renaissance Revival style was popular for both elegant townhouses and substantial country villas. Its large size may indicate that it was intended as a presentation piece. Neither the architect nor the client is known.

The arrangement of low bookcases placed on either side of an elaborate mantelpiece surmounted by a large mirror was fairly conventional at the time; the same elements with different detailing can be seen in several late nineteenth-century photographs of libraries in Boston houses, including the James M. Beebe house, one of the twin townhouses built on the site of the recently demolished Hancock House (see pages 106–7). Often the low bookcases continued around the entire room.

The proposed room was to be 25 feet wide and 13 feet 7 inches high to the bottom of the egg-and-dart cornice, which was presumably to be made of molded plaster. The escutcheons and the arched tops of the doors indicate they were to be glazed to protect the books within. The colorful bindings may have been intended as a foil to the otherwise somber color scheme often suggested for the walls, drapery, and carpet of libraries at the time, or they may have been included merely to add additional color to the presentation. The gas wall brackets on either side of the mirror probably would match a chandelier in the center of the room.

Busts of authors, including Shakespeare (looking a bit scornful) and Byron, sit atop the bookcases. One wonders if they were already owned by the client, or if the architect was suggesting they be acquired as appropriate decoration. One also wonders if the architect was suggesting that existing paintings be reframed with matching frames to create a balanced arrangement.

The notations on the drawing appear to be in two different hands. "4' Plate" (written upside down in the middle of the mirror and indicating the width of the mirror plate needed), the scale, and the measurement inside the fireplace are in ink, and are probably the hand of the architect. The pencil inscriptions may have been added by the client. Most are measurements, but the comment under the side view of the chimney breast could be read as a directive: "shelf of mantel/not deep enough."

About a decade after this drawing was made, Charles Wyllys Elliott, manager of the Household Art Company in Boston, published *The Book of American Interiors*. Elliott focused primarily on two rooms of the house, the dining room and the library, which he stated "has come to be *the* room of the house." After discussing the architecture, decoration, furniture, paintings, and books in a library with the same layout, designed by Ware and Van Brunt for George B. Chase of Boston, he gives his thoughts on what a library should be: "Such a room is not merely the place to receive and preserve those books which record the lives and thoughts of other men and women. It should be the most interesting, stimulating, and useful room of the house. Here the family should gather in the evening for talk, for work, for reading; here should come friendly people; here should wide, open hospitable bookcases offer and tempt all comers by books placed within their reach."

One assumes the library proposed in this drawing turned out to be such a room. It is hoped that someday its architect and those who enjoyed it will be identified. RCN

Library in the George B. Chase house,
234 Beacon Street, Boston, about 1876.

Library in the James M. Beebe house, 30 Beacon Street,
Boston, in the late nineteenth century.

Elevation of an unidentified library, unsigned
and undated. Watercolor, graphite, and graphite
notations and emendations on wove paper;
30 × 43½". Library and Archives purchase, 1973.

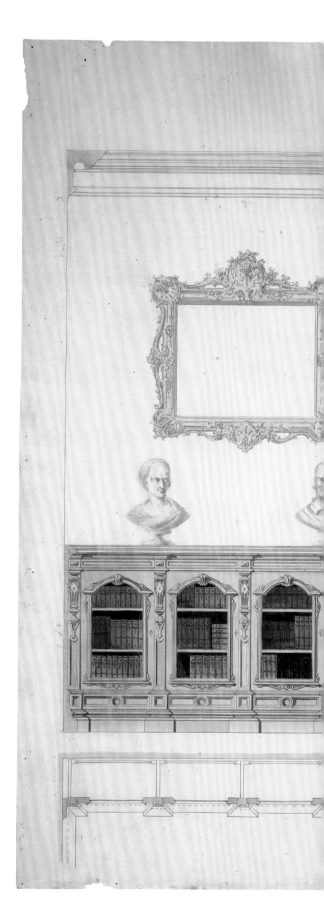

Scale 1½" = 1 foot

Gridley J. F. Bryant (1816–1899)

*James M. Beebe and Gardner Brewer Townhouses,
Boston, 1864–65 (demolished)*

In addition to being one of the most prolific Boston architects of the nineteenth century, Gridley J. F. Bryant was also an indefatigable self-promoter. Throughout his long career, he never missed an opportunity to publicize his work, both in the popular press and via the medium of printed lithographs of proposed and completed projects. This pair of townhouses, completed in 1864 for two prominent Boston merchants, was designed in a highly sophisticated interpretation of contemporary French Renaissance Revival architecture of the Paris of Napoleon III. This was the style of the earliest Back Bay houses, and Beebe and Brewer matched the chutzpah of developers of our own day by acquiring a site on Beacon Street next to the Massachusetts State House, forcing the demolition of the historic Hancock House (see pages 100–102), and constructing showy dwellings quite different from the surrounding architecture. In contrast to the unadorned brick of the Federal- and Greek Revival-style houses on Beacon Hill, the Beebe-Brewer houses employed an ornate façade in brown Portland sandstone. The basement and first floor of ashlar blocks support upper floors with quoins, paneling, and window trim.

The townhouses were contemporary with the new Boston City Hall in the same style by Bryant and his frequent collaborator Arthur Gilman. In fact, Arthur Gilman was the artistic force during Bryant's French Second Empire period, and he was very likely principal designer of this project. As this is not a construction drawing, the names of both architects do not appear. Bryant generally handled construction supervision and, since Gilman had moved to New York City in 1865, he may have felt justified in using only his name. Nonetheless, he skirted even the loose ethical standards of his day by not including Gilman as an associate architect. RGR

The Beebe-Brewer townhouses about 1869.

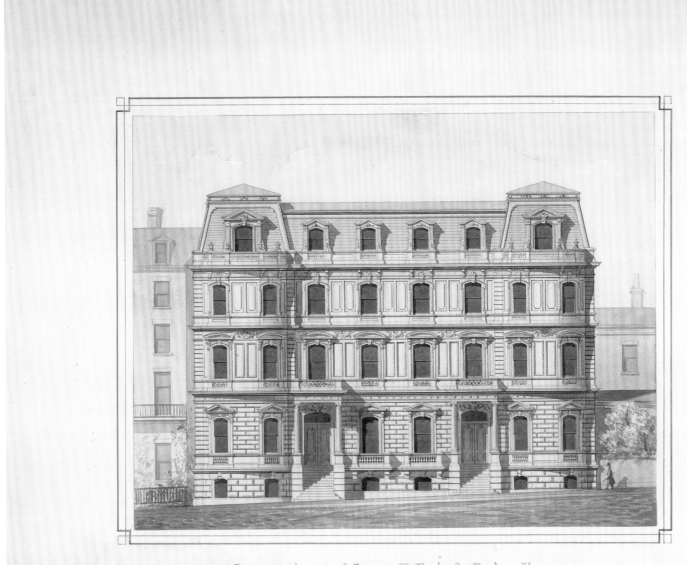

Town residences of James M. Beebe & Gardner Brewer
covering the John Hancock estate on
BEACON STREET, BOSTON, MASS.
G. J. F. Bryant, Arch't.

Presentation elevation of "Town residences of James M. Beebe &
Gardner Brewer / covering the John Hancock estate on / BEACON
STREET, BOSTON, MASS." (on presentation mount), undated.
Signed: "G. J. F. Bryant, Arch't." (on presentation mount).
Graphite, ink, and watercolor on wove paper; 11½ × 14⅞".
Gift of Nancy and Bill Osgood, 1995.

Gridley J. F. Bryant (1816–1899)

Thomas Wigglesworth House,
Old Neck Road, Manchester, Massachusetts, 1889

Gridley J. F. Bryant began his career as an independent architect in 1837, and continued to design as late as 1892. The summer cottage for Thomas Wigglesworth in Manchester is one of his last documented projects, and the last for which drawings survive. As with most mainstream architects, Bryant changed with the times and adopted new styles. His Wigglesworth cottage employs a mixture of the Queen Anne and English Colonial Revival styles, then typical of much of the architecture being built. The ocean façade, with its large veranda, opens up into a kind of attached circular gazebo at one end. This was standard for large summer homes, as was a large bay window for the dining room at the other end of the façade. The gambrel roof, a popular English Colonial Revival-style motif, is used as a decorative embellishment in much the same way as the Mansard roof had been used earlier. This was quite different from the approach of Bryant's leading younger contemporaries, who incorporated the roof with the walls to suggest a picturesque organic architecture.

Bryant's traditional approach to design is also evident in the elevation of the framing plan (see frontispiece). Contrary to the trends in the late nineteenth century to build using smaller dimensional framing members (a transition to the balloon frame), Bryant carefully delineated a plan with closely spaced, large-sized framing members intended to withstand the severest weather conditions. RGR

Thomas Wigglesworth house in 1981.

Elevation of "OCEAN FRONT" of house for "MR. THOMAS
WIGGLESWORTH / Manchester Mass." (one of a set of fourteen
sheets). Signed: "G. J. F. BRYANT / Archt." Dated: "Boston
Feby 1889." Black ink and graphite on starch-coated fabric;
20½ × 24". Gift of Rebecca Gardner Campbell, 1996.

Edward Dow (1820–1894)

Walter Aiken House, Franklin,
New Hampshire, c. 1868 (destroyed by fire)

Like many architects who practiced in the 1800s, Edward Dow began his career as a builder. His father and grandfather were skilled craftsmen, and several members of Dow's family, living at Newport and Croydon, New Hampshire, were employed in the building trades. Although the source of Dow's architectural training is unknown, this and other known drawings show that he was a meticulous draftsman. But no other known drawing by Dow includes the carefully studied shadow effects and varied tonalities of this masterful rendering, which is reminiscent of the shaded elevation drawings that were common in the earlier decades of the century.

Edward Dow was born in Lemington, Vermont, but his family moved to Croydon in his early boyhood, and to Newport when he was sixteen. He learned carpentry from his father and attended Kimball Union Academy in Plainfield, New Hampshire. Dow first worked as a contractor and builder in Fall River, Massachusetts, reportedly studying architecture in Boston. He moved to Concord, New Hampshire, around 1845, continuing in business as a carpenter, but by 1854 had established himself as an architect.

After service as a sharpshooter in the Civil War, Dow affiliated with partners who shared his knowledge of building construction. His first major partner was Giles Wheeler (1834–1915), an experienced carpenter and builder who joined Dow's architectural practice in 1873 and left in 1885. Dow's last partner, with whom he affiliated in 1890, was James E. Randlett (1846–1909), who had worked as a carpenter and cabinetmaker.

In practice alone or with his partners, Dow designed many private residences and a number of important public buildings. Among the New Hampshire commissions of the Dow office were St. Paul's Episcopal Church (1859) in Concord; Penacook Academy building (1866) in Boscawen; Kent Wing (1867), New Hampshire Asylum, in Concord; Culver Hall (1871) at Dartmouth College; town halls in Charlestown (1872) and Newport (1873); a new state prison (1878) in Concord; the Merrimack County Almshouse (1878) in Boscawen; and the Memorial Arch (1883) in Tilton. From 1864 to 1866, Dow also served as supervising architect for the enlargement of the New Hampshire State House under Gridley J. F. Bryant of Boston. At the end of his career, Dow and partner James Randlett designed Thompson Hall (1892), the first building of the College of Agriculture and the Mechanic Arts in Durham, New Hampshire.

The Aiken house was the residence of the leading inventor and industrialist of Franklin, New Hampshire. Walter Aiken (1831–1893) was the son of a machinist and inventor who moved to Franklin in 1838. Inheriting his father's mechanical aptitude, Aiken invented one of the first American knitting machines and registered more than forty patents, making the Winnipesaukee River valley a center of knitting machine production and of hosiery manufacturing. Aiken was largely responsible for developing the mechanical aspects of the Mount Washington Cog Railway.

Aiken's house of circa 1868, sited on a bluff overlooking Franklin village, cost $50,000, and was considered to be one of the finest dwellings in New Hampshire. It burned in February 1877. Aiken rebuilt it in brick on the old foundations, replicating the essential design of the wooden predecessor. After passing to Aiken's son James, the brick house became the Franklin Hospital in 1907. It no longer stands.

Architect Dow clearly followed the precepts of Andrew Jackson Downing in designing this and other Italianate villas for prominent clients. Both Dow and Aiken may have been mindful of Downing's assertion that "there are men of imagination—men whose ambition and energy will give them no peace within the mere bounds of rationality. These are the men for picturesque villas. . . . It is for such that the architect may safely introduce the tower and the campanile—any and every feature that indicates originality, boldness, energy, and variety of character." JLG

The Walter Aiken house of about 1877–78, which was built to
replace the dwelling depicted in Edward Dow's drawing.
The photograph dates to about 1895.

Elevation, undated and unsigned. Contemporary paper
label on back of original frame reads: "Elevation of House
For Walter Aiken Esq / Edward Dow Archt." Ink and
watercolor and ink washes on heavy wove paper; 16 × 20".
Library and Archives purchase, 2007.

Peabody and Stearns (1870–1917)

Robert Swain Peabody (1845–1917)
John Goddard Stearns (1843–1917)

William Sumner Appleton, Sr., House,
Holbrook Hall, Newton, Massachusetts, 1875 (demolished)

Robert Swain Peabody and John Goddard Stearns, Jr., formed their partnership in 1870. Peabody was the artist-architect, an 1866 graduate of Harvard who later studied at the Ecole des Beaux-Arts in Paris. Stearns was the engineer, an 1863 graduate of the Lawrence Scientific School at Harvard, and an experienced draftsman and designer. Several employees of the firm reported that Peabody worked with the clients and did at least the rough designs for most projects, while Stearns ensured that the commissions were completed on time and on budget. This successful relationship lasted for an almost unprecedented forty-seven years, until the deaths of both partners in fall 1917.

The Appleton house was constructed in the Oak Hill area of Newton Centre. The seventeen sheets in the collection are among the earliest existing residential drawings for the firm and clearly illustrate their developing expertise in the design of a proper yet comfortable country estate. Appleton and his wife, Edith Stuart Appleton (parents of William Sumner Appleton, Jr., founder of the Society for the Preservation of New England Antiquities, now Historic New England), built their country estate on 340 acres. The house was designed in the popular Stick Style, which featured wood construction with amounts of applied wooden detailing to barge boards, dormers, and porch enclosures—a style described by one critic of the period as the product of the "gnawing tooth of the jig-saw" which "grievously tormented all manner of woodwork." It was saved from boxy boredom by the octagonal tower room that burst out on the front veranda from the dining room, plentiful roof dormers, and the billiard room to the rear of the house, with its charming raised roof supported by clerestory windows—a detail perhaps unique in Peabody and Stearns's designs.

The Appleton property fronted on the Charles River, and the house was situated to take advantage of the views and breezes that the site provided. Large verandas on the front (north) and rear (south) elevations were connected by the large transitional Queen Anne living hall that ran through the center of the house. All the main rooms (morning room, library, parlor, dining room, study) opened off this living hall, which thus provided the main axis and organizational feature of the floor plan. French windows opened several of these principal rooms onto the verandas and provided views of the river and the surrounding landscape in addition to natural air conditioning. AR

W. S. Appleton, Sr., house in the 1880s.

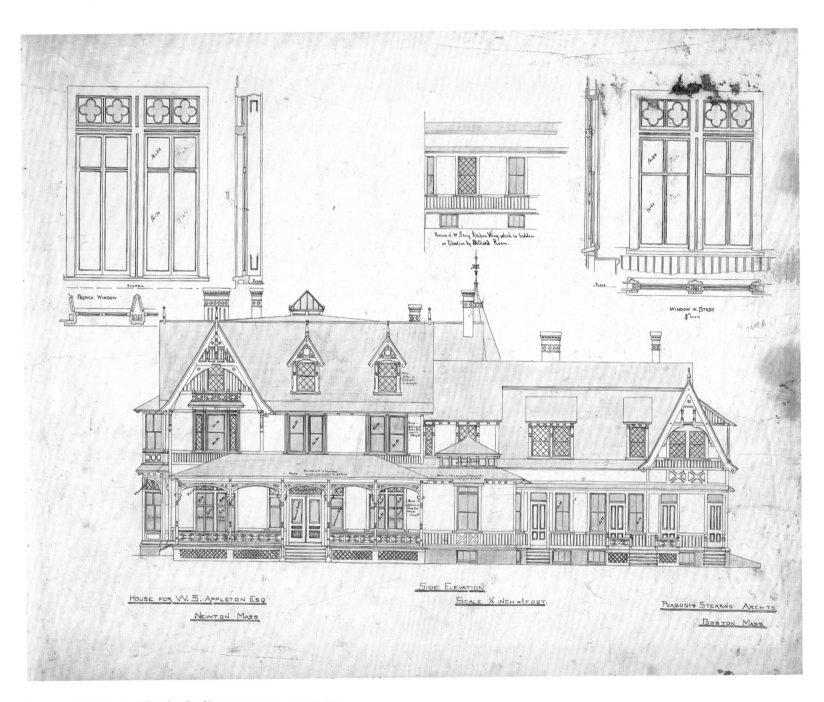

"SIDE ELEVATION" and window details of "HOUSE FOR W. S. APPLETON ESQ / NEWTON MASS" (one of a set of seventeen sheets), undated. Signed: "PEABODY STEARNS ARCHTS / BOSTON MASS." Black ink and watercolor on starch-coated fabric; 29 × 36". Gift of William Sumner Appleton, Jr.

McKim, Mead and White (1879–1910 and beyond)

Charles Follen McKim (1847–1909)
William Rutherford Mead (1846–1928)
Stanford White (1853–1906)

William Watts Sherman House,
Shepard Street, Newport, Rhode Island, 1881

By the 1880s, the New York firm of McKim, Mead and White was among the most important architectural offices in the country. Charles McKim studied at the Ecole des Beaux-Arts in Paris, then joined the firm of Gambrill and Richardson in New York until 1872. Stanford White worked in that office from 1870 to 1878, then traveled. William Rutherford Mead, an Amherst College graduate, worked for Russell Sturgis in New York, and then gradually joined McKim in partnership. White entered their office on his return from Europe. Early work by the firm in the residential Shingle Style preceded a host of large classical public buildings throughout the country.

The seminal William Watts Sherman house was designed in the Gambrill and Richardson office in 1874. It has been hailed as a major step in H. H. Richardson's career, signaling his turn away from the typical house design of the time to his more personal, controlled forms. Although Richardson conceived the designs that came from his office, he communicated them to his drafters in thumbnail sketches. The better-known drawings for the Sherman house have always been assigned by historians to White, and, since the interiors were left incomplete when the house was first occupied in 1876, Richardson later recommended that White finish them. Alterations and additions were made to the interior in 1881. These pencil sketches would seem to be in-house studies for that work. Since almost all the drawings from the Richardson office are housed at Harvard's Houghton Library, and the major cache of McKim, Mead and White drawings is at the New-York Historical Society, Historic New England is most fortunate to have this study. JFO'G

W. W. Sherman house about 1880.

Interior elevations and reflected ceiling plan for "Second
Story Hall for W. W. Sherman Esq." (one of a group of seven
sheets), undated and unsigned. Graphite on wove paper;
18 × 29½". Gift of Jim Righter, 2002.

John M. Allen (1842–1912)

Rev. John C. Brooks Cottage,
Corner of Allen and Water Streets,
Marion, Massachusetts, 1882

John M. Allen, native and life-long resident of Marion, Massachusetts, a coastal summer community south of Boston, occupied an office in the city for a number of years. He studied at the Lawrence Scientific School at Harvard, then worked in the office of Ware and Van Brunt. On his own, he designed commercial buildings in Boston and elsewhere, and a number of residences in Marion.

The Rev. John C. Brooks was an Episcopal minister and the brother of famed Phillips Brooks, rector of Gambrill and Richardson's Trinity Church on Copley Square, Boston, and a clergyman of renown in his own right. He came to Marion at least as early as 1879. His cottage on the corner of Allen and Water streets had as near neighbor H. H. Richardson's summer house designed the previous year for Brooks's former classmate, the Rev. Percy Browne.

In general form, Brooks's house owed much to the local vernacular. Allen's workmanlike presentation shows a relatively compact Shingle Style cottage on the edge of Buzzards Bay. The transom screen of the entrance porch may be a lingering Queen Anne touch or a reference to the ramma of Japanese architecture. A photograph dated 1885 shows, among other differences, that the shed-roofed porch beneath the gable, left without a railing in the drawing, had by then acquired both railing and ramma. The fan-shaped frame through which we view the scene is surely meant to allude to Asian inspiration. The inscription "Built in ..." suggests that this is an after-the-fact drawing and may have been a gift to the owner from the architect. JFO'G

Rev. John C. Brooks cottage in 1885.

The Brooks cottage in 1898.

Perspective, identified, signed, and dated: "Cottage of Rev.
John C. Brooks, in Marion, Mass. / built in Spring & Summer
of 1882 – John M. Allen Architect," and "J. M. Allen, Ach't."
(the second signature perhaps intended to clearly identify
the delineator). Black and brown ink and watercolor on wove
paper; 8½ × 14" (irregular). Gift of Christopher Monkhouse
in honor of his three co-authors of the exhibition and the
catalogue: James F. O'Gorman, Roger G. Reed, and Earle G.
Shettleworth, Jr., 2009.

John Calvin Stevens (1855–1940)

Joseph A. King Cottage,
Great Diamond Island, Casco Bay, Maine, 1888

Like so many picturesque locations on the Maine coast, Casco Bay experienced the development of flourishing summer colonies after the Civil War. Four major resort communities were established there in the 1880s: Little Diamond Island (1882), Great Diamond Island (1882), Cushing's Island (1883), and Delano Park, Cape Elizabeth (1885). While some families settling in these new retreats were "from away," most were prosperous local middle- and upper-middle-class businessmen and professionals with wives and children seeking a seasonal escape from the heat of the Portland peninsula.

Many of these men commissioned their city's up-and-coming architect John Calvin Stevens to design a fashionable Shingle Style cottage, which was economical to build due to its relatively modest scale, clean vernacular lines, local materials, exposed framing, and open interior plan. As Stevens's partner, Albert Winslow Cobb, wrote in 1889 in their book *Examples of American Domestic Architecture*:

> To design structures of a somewhat transitory character is no ignoble task for the architect. If it be even a mere shell of a wooden summer cottage that he is called upon to contrive, he need not despise the work: he may well give his best thought to making the house graceful, to grouping its rooms effectively and conveniently, and to inventing bits of pretty detail here and there ...

Such was the case with the Great Diamond Island summer home that John Calvin Stevens planned for Joseph A. King, a Portland hardware merchant, in February and March 1888, as recorded in the architect's daybook for that year. On 16 February 1888, Stevens made these two pen and ink drawings for King. One is a composite, showing the side eleva-

tion of a proposed gambrel-roofed cottage, elaborated with a sketch of the "Corner of Piazza" in the upper left and a three-quarter view of the house in the upper right. An accompanying sheet delineated a first floor comprised of a sitting room positioned to capture the ocean view, a dining room, and kitchen; and a second floor with three chambers and two bedrooms. These simple, skillfully sketched presentation drawings were the means by which Stevens communicated his concept of the new cottage to his client. Once he received King's approval, the architect worked with two of his draftsmen to create a set of construction drawings for the builder, which would include floor and framing plans as well as elevations and selected details.

By 1890, Joseph King had built this cottage essentially as John Calvin Stevens had designed it. A later owner, Fred H. Palmer, a Portland department store owner, called Stevens back in 1920 to suggest some additions which were not implemented by the client or the next owner, Farrington H. Whipple. Despite Albert Winslow Cobb's admonition on the ephemeral nature of such frame summer homes, that "it is in many respects best that the structure endure not much more than a century," the King cottage remains in use today as a treasured landmark on Great Diamond Island. EGSJr

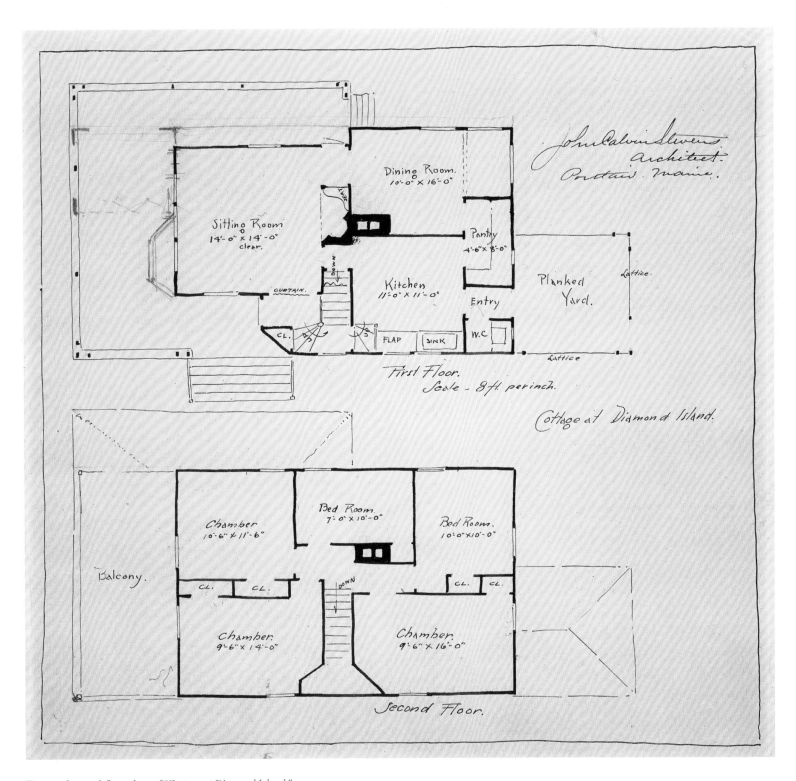

First- and second-floor plans of "Cottage at Diamond Island,"
undated. Signed: "John Calvin Stevens. / Architect. / Portland Maine."
Black ink, graphite, and graphite emendations on wove paper;
9 × 9⅜". Gift of Earle G. Shettleworth, Jr., 2006.

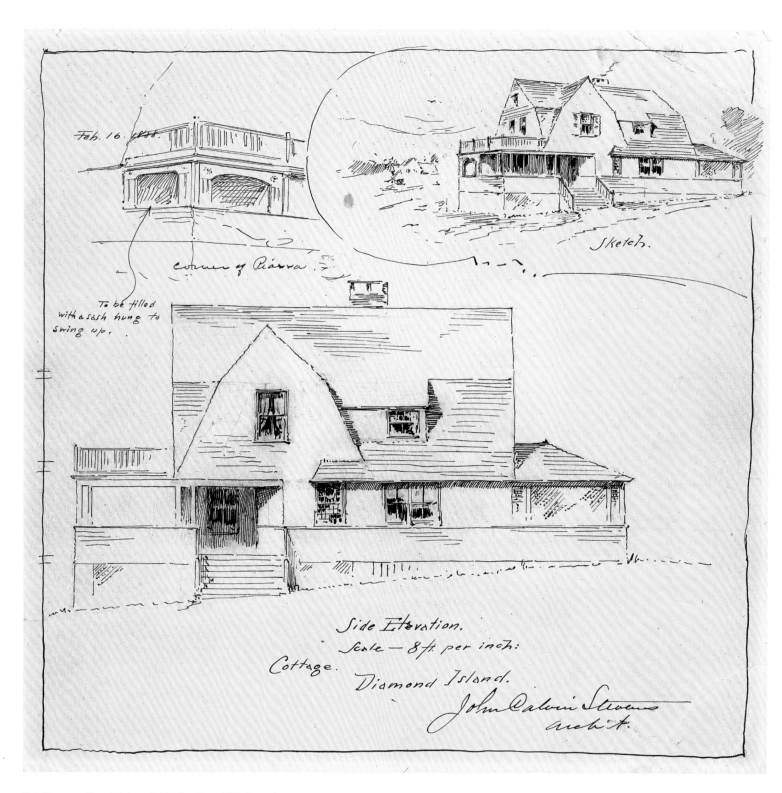

Detail, perspective sketch, and side elevation of "Cottage. /
Diamond Island." Signed: "John Calvin Stevens / Arch't." Dated:
"Feb 16. 1888." Black ink, graphite, and graphite emendations on
wove paper; 9 × 9⅜". Gift of Earle G. Shettleworth, Jr., 2006.

J. A. King cottage (left) in the 1890s.

Arthur Little (1852–1925)

Addition to the George R. Emmerton House,
Essex Street, Salem, Massachusetts, 1885

Arthur Little studied architecture at MIT in the early 1870s (although he never earned a degree), and trained as a draftsman and apprentice in the Peabody and Stearns office in Boston. In 1877, he authored the pioneering *Early New England Interiors,* a series of romantic sketches of colonial houses he had made during excursions through the New England countryside. By 1879, he had his own office, and his first house, Cliffs of 1879, in Manchester-by-the-Sea, Massachusetts, was in a fully developed English Colonial Revival idiom. In the early 1880s, he made a name for himself with a series of dramatically innovative shingled summer houses in Swampscott, Massachusetts, on Little's Point, for family members, and in Marblehead and Manchester on Boston's North Shore.

In 1885, George and Lennie Emmerton commissioned Little to alter and expand their 1818 brick Federal mansion on Essex Street in Salem. The Emmertons had deep pockets: Lennie was a descendant of Captain John Bertram, a privateer and ship owner.

Despite the indicated measurements, this side elevation of the house is not a working drawing, but a conceptual rendering to highlight Little's additions and to distinguish them from the body of the original house. Embellishing the new rear ell, whose fenestration is at least an homage to 1818, are a polygonal second-floor oriel and a two-story colonnade derived from a number of Salem houses of the same period. Applied to the body of the house is a new side entrance and porte cochere. These, with their ashlar surrounds and crowning swan-neck pediment, are adapted from the central door and window elements of Boston's John Hancock House, demolished in 1863, but perhaps known to Little through the measured drawings of it made by John Hubbard Sturgis (see pages 100–102). They have been so pulled and stretched out of scale as to be surreally unrecognizable, and they dominate the original house, which is shown in a flat, ghostly gray to contrast with the robust, full-blooded qualities of Little's alterations. The whole is tied together by the use of the same material—brick—and decorative elements like balustrading, but it is at best an uneasy marriage, the felony compounded by the first-floor

windows flanking the porte cochere, direct cribs from Richard Norman Shaw's Swan house, London, of 1875. (They reappear in Little's remodeled façade of 75 Beacon Street, Boston, of the same year.) The purpose of these juxtaposed elements is to play with scale, to shock, to leave behind the realm of safety for a new way of seeing. The house survives without significant alterations.

Four years later, Little used these same elements—polygonal bay, oval windows, swan-neck pediment, and two-story colonnade—on his J. A. Thorpe house at 168 Brattle Street in Cambridge. There, the uneasiness of scale has been replaced by a smooth transition from one part to another, the whole wrapped in a uniform clapboard skin, forecasting the academicism that would come to dominate the firm composed of Arthur Little and Herbert W. C. Browne after 1890. SAD

G. R. Emmerton house in the 1890s.

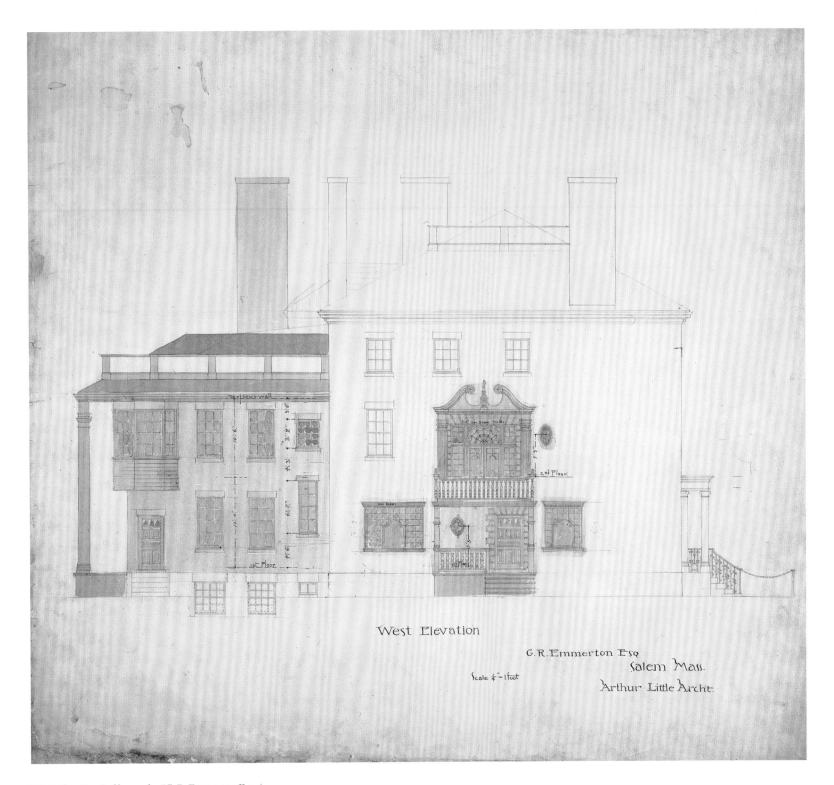

West Elevation

G. R. Emmerton Esq

Salem Mass.

Scale ¼"=1foot

Arthur Little Archt.

"West Elevation," of house for "G. R. Emmerton Esq /
Salem Mass." (one of twenty-six sheets), undated. Signed:
"Arthur Little Archt." Black and red ink, graphite, watercolor,
and graphite emendations on wove paper; 24½ × 26".
Gift of Herbert W. C. Browne, 1939.

Little and Browne (1890 – c. 1939)

Arthur Little (1852–1925)
Herbert W. C. Browne (1860–1946)

Henry Clay Frick Estate, Eagle Rock, Prides Crossing, Beverly, Massachusetts, 1902–05 (demolished)

After his break with Andrew Carnegie, Henry Clay Frick began to extricate himself from Pittsburgh and Clayton, his home there. He leased the William H. Vanderbilt house, 640 Fifth Avenue in New York, and a series of summer rentals on Boston's North Shore to house his ever growing art collection. One rental, the Robert Stow Bradley house at Prides Crossing, was designed and built in 1896 by the Boston firm of Little and Browne.

Around the turn of the twentieth century, Prides Crossing, long an all-Boston resort community, came increasingly to be dominated by captains of industry from outside the area, many of whom turned to Little and Browne for their houses. Thus, when Frick determined to buy land and build there, he, too, turned to the firm to execute his ideas.

In 1902, Frick bought a parcel of fifty seaward-facing acres on Hale Street, which he named Eagle Rock, and requested a brick and limestone Georgian manor house. He was a demanding patron. Arthur Little, who appears to have been the principal architect on the job, was bombarded with letters indicating that no detail or expense was too small to escape Frick's notice. Little was reminded to keep everything as simple as possible, a seeming contradiction for so grand a house, but no doubt a predictable reaction in 1902 to the High Victorian excesses of Clayton and 640 Fifth Avenue.

The firm also was contracted to lay out and landscape the estate. From Hale Street, where the Eagle Rock property was bordered by a $100,000 fence, a driveway curved up the hill and passed through wrought-iron gates into a graveled courtyard before the great house. The other three sides of the court were defined by a boundary of brick piers topped with stone balls and panels of wrought iron into which electric lamp standards were incorporated. The gateposts themselves were crowned with swagged urns, from a neoclassical repertoire much beloved by Little and Browne, but somewhat at odds with the baroque exuberance of the ironwork. This drawing of the entrance gate to the courtyard is clearly a working drawing done to scale, rather dry and academic, reflecting the firm's increasing commitment after 1890 to classical European styles.

The Frick job was the biggest and most expensive that Little and Browne ever executed, and the 1902–05 house the grandest ever built on the North Shore, costing $604,116. The grounds absorbed another $321,517. Outbuildings included a $50,000 stable, an automobile and power house, a gardener's cottage, a vast range of greenhouses, and a shed to house Frick's private railway car.

Henry Clay Frick died in 1919, and his wife, Adelaide, in 1931. Their daughter, Helen Clay Frick, inherited the property. She had part of the house demolished in 1937 and, in 1970, the remainder. Architectural and decorative elements—paneling, chimneypieces, etc.—were saved and transferred to Pittsburgh for incorporation in a new art museum Helen Frick was building. The brick piers and wrought-iron panels were also sent there, to be used in the museum's parking lot. A smaller Georgian-style house, reusing other decorative elements from the Little and Browne house, was built on the Prides Crossing site for a family member. SAD

Henry Clay Frick estate about 1905.

Plan and elevation of "INCH SCALE DRAWING OF FORE / COURT FENCE AND GATES FROM / MAIN AVENUE HOUSE FOR / H C FRICK ESQ AT PRIDES MASS" (one of a group of 389 sheets). Signed: "Little & Browne Architects / 70 Kilby St Boston Mass." Dated and initialed: "February 6, 1905 (G.P.F. & F.W.M.)" and "Revised Sept. 23, '05 / C.C.H." Red and black ink, graphite, watercolor, and graphite notations and emendations on starch-coated fabric; 28 × 36". Gift of Herbert W. C. Browne, 1939.

Little and Browne (1890 – c. 1939)

Arthur Little (1852–1925)
Herbert W. C. Browne (1860–1946)

Addition to the William S. and John T. Spaulding House,
Sunset Rock, Prides Crossing, Beverly, Massachusetts,
1907–09 (demolished)

One of the great lost houses of Boston's North Shore, Sunset Rock commanded a promontory fifty feet above the Atlantic at Prides Crossing. Brothers William Stuart Spaulding (1865–1937) and John Taylor Spaulding (1870–1947), heirs to a sugar-trust fortune, bought the old Paine estate in 1897 and leveled its house. They hired the firm of F. L. and J. C. Olmsted to lay out the roads, but Herbert Browne designed the Jacobethan-style house and gardens. Each summer, guests strolled along the seaside terraces and viewed the brothers' steam yacht, *Isis*, anchored below.

Emerging from dense woods, visitors would first glimpse Sunset Rock from the perspective of this drawing. They would come to the small paved forecourt, walled in by the broad Weymouth granite façade and its long parapeted cross-gables. Entering the house through an octagonal vestibule, they would cross a narrow gallery and proceed into the loggia, with Pompeian designs on its high vaulted ceiling and sweeping views of the Atlantic on three sides. Elegant staircases led down to the terraces. Sunset Rock was widely covered in the architectural and shelter magazines; Harold Eberlein declared it the epitome of the "Formal American Country House . . . a conspicuous justification of the policy of having the architect not only design and supervise the erection of the house, but create the setting as well."

The Spauldings spent winters in their parents' corner townhouse at 99 Beacon Street in Boston, overlooking both the Public Garden and the Charles River. The Brownes were neighbors; Thomas Browne bought 98 Beacon in 1881 and hired son Herbert to remodel it. In 1894, the Spauldings asked Herbert Browne to remodel 99 Beacon, and—between 1897 and 1934—to design, decorate, expand, and repair Sunset Rock, and even to furnish the yacht.

Found crumpled in a Herbert Browne scrapbook, this fragile yellowed drawing shows a 1907–09 addition of symmetrical wings. The design was a challenge, given the constricted ledge and the wings' divergent purposes of service spaces (left) and Great Room (right). Symmetry triumphs over interior flow, as guests had to cross the Billiard Room to enter the Great Room. Penciled sketching atop this finished draft illustrates the depth of the left cross-gable and the oval sweep of the forecourt, as if Browne were explaining the volumes to the Spauldings. He also added another planter (in different ink) and erased and relocated the drawing's legend. Perhaps Browne remade the drawing for a final presentation and kept this draft.

The Spauldings filled 99 Beacon and Sunset Rock with art, beginning with Edo woodblock prints purchased in Japan in 1909. They built fireproof vaults at each house for the prints, and when they made their seasonal moves, they sent their favorite prints ahead by van, accompanied by a butler wielding a fire extinguisher. By 1912, they were buying prints from other collectors, including Frank Lloyd Wright, and, in 1913, they bankrolled Wright's trip to Japan. Wright returned with $125,000 in rare prints and, in 1914, presented the brothers with a sleek Modernist design for a gallery room, featuring slanted wall panels to display prints. One of Wright's great unbuilt designs, the gallery footprint matched the Great Room at Sunset Rock.

Shortly after John's death, both houses were demolished. Sunset Rock was replaced by a brick ranch house suitable for year-round living. On Beacon Street, the entrance to the Arthur Fiedler footbridge occupies the site of the Spaulding and Browne houses. But great treasures do survive. The Spauldings left to the Museum of Fine Arts in Boston not only Japanese prints, but also John's collection of early modern art. Herbert Browne restored the Harrison Gray Otis House for William Sumner Appleton and donated Little and Browne's account books, drawings, and photographs to Historic New England. TO

W. S. and J. T. Spaulding house in 1899, before the addition.

House of Messrs. W. S. & J. T. Spaulding
showing addition of two wings
& the original house
Little & Browne Archts
July 1909

Perspective of "House of Messrs. W. S. & J. T. Spaulding / showing
addition of two wings / to the original house." Signed and dated
in Herbert Browne's hand: "Little & Browne Archts / July 1909."
Black ink, watercolor, and graphite underdrawing and emendations
on tracing paper; 8⅞ × 14⅛". Gift of Herbert W. C. Browne, 1939.

James A. Clough (1850–1917)

Building for Michael H. Baker,
High Street, Holyoke, Massachusetts, 1886

In the late nineteenth century, prosperous mill towns like Holyoke typically featured a central business district in close proximity to large mill buildings along the river. Rows of commercial buildings with ground-floor shops had upper floors suitable for a variety of uses, such as an expansion of the business to the second floor, office space for professionals, or apartments for people of moderate means. By the late nineteenth century, when mill owners rarely provided housing for their workers, buildings such as the Baker building offered an alternative to large-scale tenement housing.

Architect James A. Clough was one of the leading designers during the period of Holyoke's major industrial prosperity. Clough was born in Chicopee, Massachusetts, and came to Holyoke in 1870 to work as a carpenter. Sometime between 1880 and 1884, when he was first listed in the local directory as an architect, he attended art and architecture courses at MIT. (His obituary noted that he was "a student of art rather than a mechanical drafter.") Clough's major work in Holyoke included the Holyoke Public Library.[1]

Michael H. Baker had this building erected in 1886 for his stove and furnace business. The upper floors were rented out as three apartments. According to the 1888 city directory, the occupants (only adult males were listed) were Vincent C. Canova, an employee at William Skinner & Sons, silk manufacturers; Edwin T. Ferris, an employee at the Massachusetts Screw Company; and Anthony More, who worked at the National Blank Book Company.[2]

The design for the Baker building shows the influence of the Richardsonian Romanesque style. The use of rough quarry-faced stone trim and the broad arches on the second floor are evidence of the client's desire for a stylish building set apart from its immediate neighbors in the brick row. The arches and paired windows on the second floor may indicate that the floor above the street level was a continuation of Baker's business, rather than part of the apartment units, but no floor plans survive to document this use. RGR

Michael H. Baker building, second from right, about 1890.

Front Elevation of a Brick Block
Mr. M. H. Baker
James A. Clough Archt.

Jacob Luippold (c. 1846–1917)

Philip Albret House, Folsom Street,
Dorchester, Boston, Massachusetts, 1888

The Jacob Luippold collection of architectural drawings at Historic New England represents the work of a German immigrant who found a prosperous clientele in his own ethnic community in Roxbury and Jamaica Plain, Massachusetts. The very existence—and survival—of these drawings of vernacular buildings is extremely rare. Luippold's designs reflect his aspirations to provide the most modern American architectural fashions to clients who were largely working and middle class.

Born in Württemberg, Germany, in about 1846, Luippold immigrated to America in 1866, after he had come of age. According to the 1870 Federal census and Boston city directories, Luippold first worked as a carpenter. His future wife, Barbara, arrived in this country in 1871, and the two were married a year later.[1]

The drawing for the Albret house is an example of a carpenter proposing attractive architectural designs for prospective clients. The house was built in 1888, but Jacob Luippold was not listed as an architect in the Boston city directories until 1892. That same year, he took on John Martin Luippold (1873–1970), probably his nephew, as a draftsman. John Martin was born in Greenfield, Massachusetts, the son of a quarry worker. He lived with Jacob, and the city directory records that, in 1893, he worked for a year as a draftsman in the Devonshire Street office of an unknown architect. John Martin ended his long career as a draftsman for the United Fruit Company.

The front elevation for the Albret house shows the influence of the Queen Anne style in the massing and complex roof treatment, as well as in the decorative shingles on the bay window. Luippold used the design for the bay window on his own house at 89 Mozart Street in Jamaica Plain (see page 38). His house is smaller, with a gable roof, yet both feature Italianate-style brackets of the kind Luippold would have crafted as a young carpenter. RGR

Philip Albret house in 2007.

Elevation of "Front View for Ph. Albret," undated.
Signed: "Drawn by Jacob Luippold." Black and red ink,
watercolor, and graphite emendations on wove paper;
14½ × 11". Library and Archives purchase, 1986.

Jacob Luippold (c. 1846–1917)

Unidentified Building with Store and Apartments, c. 1900

The majority of buildings designed by Jacob Luippold were multifamily structures, particularly three-deckers, a building type that predominated in Jamaica Plain and Roxbury, Massachusetts, in the late nineteenth century. As is the case here, there was often a store on the ground floor. This drawing for a two-family house and store is characteristic of Luippold's efforts to provide rather ornate architectural embellishments for a kind of building not normally associated with such expensive refinements. Although the drawing is not dated, it probably was executed around 1900. By then an assured architect, Luippold shows his mastery of intricate English Colonial Revival-style ornamental trim. It is drawn in a free style that demonstrates the architect's particular affinity for the latest architectural fashions. While the building has not been identified, a double house and store at 66 Boylston Street, Jamaica Plain, Massachusetts, dated 1896, survives with similar English Colonial Revival detailing. RGR

"FRONT ELEVATION" of an unidentified building, unsigned.
Stamped: "JACOB LUIPPOLD, / ARCHITECT, / 89 MOZART
STREET, / JAMAICA PLAIN." Graphite and watercolor on
wove paper; 13½ × 11". Library and Archives purchase, 1986.

Ogden Codman, Jr. (1863–1951)

Paneled Room in The Grange, the Codman House,
Codman Road, Lincoln, Massachusetts, 1890s

In 1969, Historic New England acquired The Grange, the Codman family property in Lincoln, Massachusetts, a bequest from Dorothy S. F. M. Codman, the last surviving member of the family that had been associated with the estate for five generations.

The Codmans were prodigious record keepers. Their archive, one of Historic New England's most extensive, spans the years 1759 to the 1960s, filling one hundred linear feet of shelf space. From Ogden Codman, Jr., the eldest son and child of Ogden Codman and Sarah Fletcher Bradlee, the organization ultimately received more than 1,700 architectural drawings, sketches, and watercolor renderings, a material legacy of his architectural career, as part of the bequest of his younger sister, Dorothy. Ogden was the only member of his generation to have entered a profession and to have established himself away from the family and his native surroundings. As an architect and decorator, Codman earned a considerable reputation among the cultured and social circles of Boston, Newport, and New York, where he was known for his elegant interpretations of the eighteenth-century neoclassical and English Colonial Revival styles. His active career lasted approximately thirty years, beginning in 1891, when he opened his first office in Boston, until 1920, when he closed his New York office and moved to France for the rest of his life.

For Ogden, The Grange not only was the country seat where he had spent many of his childhood years, but it also represented much of what the Codman family stood for and why it was to be revered. Unfortunately, the Codmans' loss of much of their fortune in the Great Boston Fire of 1872 resulted in a self-imposed exile to France until 1884. Under the guidance of his uncle, architect John Hubbard Sturgis, Ogden returned to America and enrolled in the school of architecture at the School of Technology, now the Massachusetts Institute of Technology during the year 1883–84. More important for Codman's future architectural career was the influence that his uncle, a partner in the architectural firm of Sturgis and Brigham, exerted in passing on the value of making measured drawings of old buildings. Sturgis had learned of this approach during his years in England and was one of the earliest proponents in America for this method of studying historic buildings (see pages 100–102).

From the 1880s until the early 1900s, Codman studied The Grange in great detail and "restored" several rooms of the house to their earlier eighteenth-century style. Historic New England's collection preserves all Codman's drawings of The Grange, including those showing the house as he found it and those resulting from his researches into its appearance after the remodeling of the late 1790s. Years later, he described his attachment to The Grange: "My father's country house . . . was thoroughly of the eighteenth century. When I left Boston, it made a restrained and simple background, and during the eight years I passed in Europe . . . I think the aforesaid background prevented me from being carried away by eccentricities that otherwise might have proved too seductive."[1] The Grange provided a touchstone of taste for Ogden throughout his life.

This drawing of the paneled room at The Grange is especially significant, not only as it records one of the few, perhaps the only, unaltered spaces dating to the original c. 1740 Chambers Russell mansion altered by John Codman in 1797, but because it is probably one of the few that was drawn by Codman himself. His hand identified the room in the lower right-hand corner: "The Grange, Panelled Room, SE, Ground Floor, 1730." In the classical style with pilasters and well-defined moldings, this elevation shows the principles of design that Codman would adhere to so conscientiously in his own work: proportion, symmetry, and the use of an order in the treatment of the wall. PCM

Paneled room, The Grange, the Codman house, about 1893 to 1897.

Interior elevation of "The Grange / Pannelled Room / SE. Ground floor 1730," undated and unsigned. Black ink and graphite on wove (Whatman 1884) paper; 13¼ × 20". Bequest of Dorothy S. F. M. Codman, 1969.

Ogden Codman, Jr. (1863–1951)

Unidentified Interior, 1890s

For his early commissions for interiors, Codman provided clients with meticulous watercolor elevations to suggest several options for the treatment of walls, curtains, and furniture design. Although renderings of this sort were customary among European decorating firms, American firms did not produce drawings of this quality, or at least they have not survived. Such drawings were done to show clients that Codman could carry out interiors with the same finesse as the best French firms. It is unlikely that he executed any of the actual drawings himself; and he remarked years later that he had employed students from the Ecole des Beaux-Arts to create the drawings for the Cornelius Vanderbilt commission to decorate the second and third floors of The Breakers. Although the unidentified elevation may possibly relate to The Breakers, the deep cove is unlike any of its completed rooms.

The Breakers commission in 1894 to 1895, however, was Codman's most important one to date, and he fully credited Edith Wharton for bringing it about. Among Codman's papers at Historic New England are numerous letters from Wharton during this period. As his constant advisor, she wrote to him in May 1897, that "it was perhaps poor policy in the beginning to overwhelm your clients by the number of your water colour designs but you are now firmly enough established to be less lavish in this respect."[1]

Codman took her advice, as after the turn of the century, he virtually ceased to provide his clients with anything more than schematic drawings in ink on linen. He and Wharton had, of course, worked very closely during these years collaborating on their seminal work, *The Decoration of Houses*, still considered a bible for the revival of classical taste in interior decoration.

Codman's former draftsman, Emery Roth, a young Hungarian immigrant, described Codman's method of designing an elevation such as this, clearly comprised of well-known classical references. Codman would choose a design he considered suitable for adaptation from his extensive collection of eighteenth- and nineteenth-century architectural books, from such noted French masters as Jacques-François Blondel, Daniel Marot, or C. A. d'Aviler. He would then have elements of the design reproduced as faithfully as conditions permitted for the specific room.

There are no indications on this drawing of the source for the classical details or of the delineator. Most of the interior renderings from Codman's office were given to The Metropolitan Museum of Art when he closed his office in 1920, but a few such as this found their way to the Codman archives at Historic New England. PCM

Elevation, undated and unsigned. Ink, graphite, and watercolor on tracing paper; 14½ × 23⅛". Bequest of Dorothy S. F. M. Codman, 1969.

Ogden Codman, Jr. (1863–1951)

Martha Codman House, Berkeley Villa,
Bellevue Avenue, Newport, Rhode Island, 1910

Berkeley Villa was designed in 1910 for Martha Catherine Codman, Ogden Codman's wealthy unmarried cousin, who summered in Newport for many years. Located at the head of Bellevue Avenue, the house replaced an earlier Victorian structure that Martha had purchased in 1897 from John G. Weaver. Berkeley Villa is one of Codman's most successful country houses and shows his particular ability to synthesize American and English eighteenth-century sources. He placed the house on the extreme northwest corner of the property to allow for a large walled formal garden to the south, as well as to shield the occupants from the hotel that stood next door. It was the second house that Codman had designed for his cousin; the previous one, in Washington, D.C., had been built two years earlier. The exterior of Berkeley Villa was based on three houses from the Boston area that Codman had measured and drawn years before, while the interior was drawn primarily from English sources. It was his extensive knowledge of eighteenth-century architecture that allowed him to marry such differing sources so successfully. For the exterior, the Shirley-Eustis house in Roxbury, Massachusetts (attributed to Peter Harrison, 1746), inspired the story heights, roofline, and dormers; the Perez Morton house, also in Roxbury (Charles Bulfinch, 1796), was the inspiration for the octagonal bay with the second-story loggia; not visible in the drawings was a third Boston source, the Eben Crafts house, which inspired the double columns around the doorway (Peter Banner, 1805). Consistent with his prejudice against the inappropriately oversized "cottages" that lined Bellevue Avenue, Codman designed a composite "colonial" that was more in keeping with Newport's eighteenth-century tradition. The phrase scientific eclecticism aptly describes Codman's precise manner of combining earlier architectural models.

While understatement was appropriate for the exterior, however, the interior had to provide a suitably elegant ambience for a rich single woman from a distinguished New England family which included the great China Trade merchant Elias Haskett Derby. The arrangement and design for a large circular domed hall with a spiral staircase ascending on the left appears to have been taken from a scheme by James Paine, for Wardour Hall, published in his 1767 book, *Plans, Elevations, and Sections of Noblemen's and Gentlemen's Houses*. The detailing of the dome, as illustrated in the drawing of the hall, is derived from the stair hall at Home

house by Robert Adam (1777). Another model that Codman mentioned was the circular stair hall of John McComb, Jr., and Joseph François Mangin's New York City Hall. On the right at Berkeley Villa, the three principal rooms—library, drawing, and dining—were arranged en filade looking into the garden. What distinguished Codman's design was his adjustment of these various sources to the proportions of the house. While the hall space is eminently grand, it is not overpowering, with all decorative details handled in the traditional classical manner. The close relationship between the architect and his client enabled Codman to oversee all aspects of the interior design and decoration. Codman wrote: "when I only did decoration in houses built by other architects, I had to correct so many bad mistakes that . . . I learned to plan houses with rooms that lent themselves to decoration."[1] The scale drawings illustrated here were probably done by Codman's head draftsman, Charles Wulff, who managed all aspects of the business from his arrival in 1910 until the office closed in 1920. However, all decisions, down to the smallest details, for choice of materials and designs for both interiors and exteriors, were made exclusively by Codman.

We know much about Codman's philosophy of design and his knowledge of colonial buildings from his extensive correspondence with family and fellow architect friends. One of his most frequent correspondents with whom he exchanged architectural nuggets was Fiske Kimball, in letters dating from 1917 to 1938. It is not surprising, therefore, that Ogden recommended Kimball to Martha Codman as an appropriate architect for the addition of a teahouse to the property in 1926. Kimball, a scholar of the architect Samuel McIntire, knew that a replication of McIntire's teahouse done for Elias Haskett Derby was the perfect complement for his client's "colonial" house, and was appropriate in light of her ancestry.

Berkeley Villa was occupied by its mistress every summer until her death in 1948, but after 1938, she shared responsibilities with Maxim Karolik, a Russian tenor thirty years her junior, whom she married, much to the shock of other members of the summer colony. However, this union and their mutual interest in American decorative arts, many pieces of which she had inherited, resulted in the formation of three major collections of American art, which were given by Martha and Maxim Karolik to the Museum of Fine Arts, Boston. PCM

"ONE QUARTER PLAN OF / 2ND STORY. HALL." and "SECTION." for the "RESIDENCE. NEWPORT RI. / FOR MISS M. CODMAN" (one of a set of forty-eight sheets), undated. Signed: "OGDEN CODMAN ARCH'T. 571 5TH AVE. N.Y.C." Graphite on tracing paper; 30 × 17". Bequest of Dorothy S. F. M. Codman, 1969.

SKYLIGHT.

SECTION.

ONE QUARTER PLAN OF
2ND STORY HALL.

SCALE ½"=1'-0"

RESIDENCE NEWPORT R.I.
FOR MISS M. COMAN.

OGDEN COMAN ARCH'T.
571 5TH AVE. N.Y.C.

Martha Codman house about 1948.

Martha Codman house about 1948.

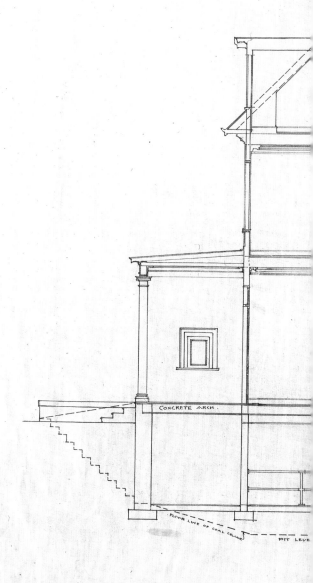

RESIDENCE FOR MISS.M.CODMAN.
NEWPORT.R.I.

"LONGITUDINAL SECTION" for "RESIDENCE FOR MISS M. CODMAN. /
NEWPORT, R. I." (one of a set of forty-eight sheets), undated. Signed:
"OGDEN CODMAN ARCH'T. / WINDSOR ARCADE N.Y.C." Black and
red ink and graphite underdrawing on starch-coated fabric; 19 × 30".
Bequest of Dorothy S. F. M. Codman, 1969.

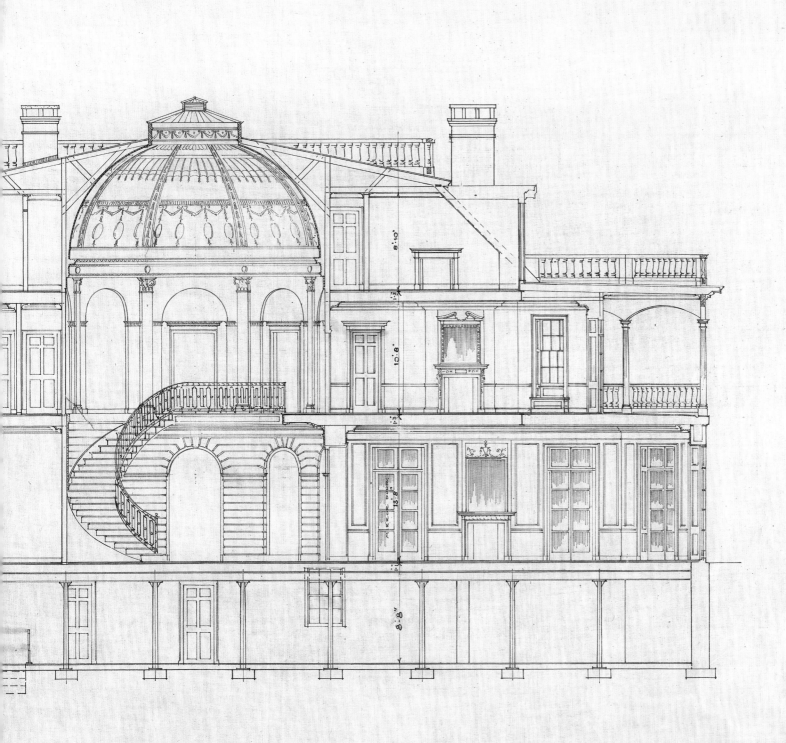

LONGITUDINAL SECTION
SCALE ¼ INCH = 1'0"

OGDEN CODMAN ARCH'T.
WINDSOR ARCADE N.Y.C.

William F. Goodwin (1861–?)

Frederick W. Paine House, Dudley Street,
Brookline, Massachusetts, 1892

Brookline is a residential suburb of Boston, which resisted annexation efforts by its larger neighbor; this helped preserve its character as a town of predominantly single-family homes. Frederick W. Paine, a Boston banker, selected a site that exemplified Brookline's well-known suburban amenities. Located on Heath Hill, the house overlooks the Brookline Reservoir, Fisher Hill, and Boylston Street. Boylston Street provided direct access to Boston and, in the 1890s, when this house was built, plans were before town meeting to establish a streetcar line there. Behind Paine's house stands the home and office of Frederick Law Olmsted and his sons. Paine selected the Olmsted firm to prepare landscape plans for this residence.[1]

William F. Goodwin's design is for a house in the English Colonial Revival style that would be compatible with its neighbors in appearance, scale, and materials. The design featured an abundance of windows, especially bays and oriels, providing testimony to the importance of views from within the house to the landscaped acre-and-a-half lot. Curiously, the architect's pen and ink sketch conveys a more modest suburban house on a relatively level lot and does not fully portray the house's vertical proportions. The multiple gambrel roofs provide a full third story of bedrooms. Barely visible in the drawing is the large oriel window to the right of the entrance portico, and what cannot be seen is the enclosed porch on the opposite end of the house.

William F. Goodwin probably trained with his father, an architect and engineer in Portland, Maine, before moving to Boston in 1882.[2] He hired out as a draftsman for several years before briefly relocating to Los Angeles. Returning to Boston, he worked as an architect from about 1889 until 1905, when he and his wife moved to an unknown location.[3] Although Paine hired Goodwin in 1896 to design a Shingle Style house next door at 54 Dudley Street, he selected another architect to enlarge his own house in 1901.[4] Still standing, the Paine house was extensively remodeled at the end of the twentieth century. RGR

F. W. Paine house in the early twentieth century, after expansion.

"Perspective Sketch of House For / F W Paine Esq / Dudley
Street / Brookline Mass." Signed: "Wᵐ F Goodwin Architect
Chadwick Bl'dg Boston Mass." Initialed: "ʀɴw[?]" Dated:
"Dec 22 '92." Black ink on wove paper; 12⅛ × 17⁷⁄₁₆".
Gift of the Estate of Stephen Wheatland, 1987.

Longfellow, Alden and Harlow (1886–1896)

Alexander Wadsworth Longfellow, Jr. (1854–1934)
Frank Ellis Alden (1859–1908)
Alfred Branch Harlow (1857–1927)

James A. Noyes House,
Highland Street, Cambridge, Massachusetts, 1893–94

Alexander Longfellow, the firm's chief designer, graduated from Harvard, studied at MIT and the Ecole des Beaux-Arts in Paris, worked in the studio of Henry Hobson Richardson, then formed a decade-long partnership (1886–96) with Alden and Harlow in Boston and Pittsburgh. The Noyes house was perhaps the finest of a series of large gambrel-roof, English Colonial Revival designs turned out by the office. These were "New England images," according to Margaret Henderson Floyd, created by recasting the Richardsonian Shingle Style into classical domestic forms derived from the eighteenth century. The core of this boxy plan is the central hall that leads to a rear stair and is flanked by chimney stacks dividing front and rear rooms, but Longfellow avoided the implied symmetry with a dining room bay that bulges toward the front, another bay that curves out from the back parlor, and a kitchen complex that breaks out of the basic rectangle to the rear. The same dynamic interplay of symmetry-asymmetry occurs on the front elevation, where the rigid balance of the overhanging second floor and line of dormers in the dominating gambrel is upset by that bulging dining room bay. The result is an inspired reworking of the basic elements of colonial Georgian architecture.

Presentation drawings such as these became common with the general availability of tracing paper after the Civil War. These are part of a series of schemes, each captured in pencil and washes in the hands of an adroit draftsman such as Longfellow, and easily traced, altered, and retraced following the observations, probably recording a conversation between client and architect, jotted on them. JFO'G

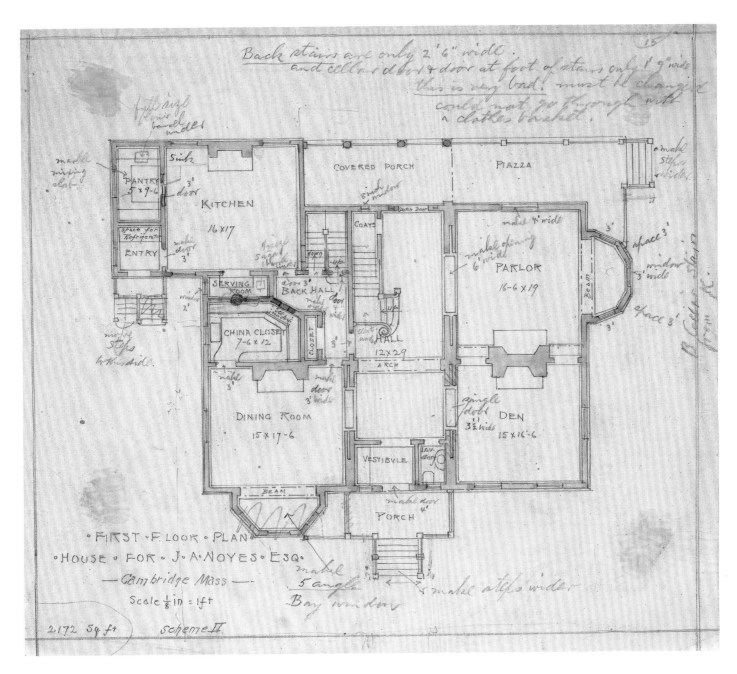

Back stairs are only 2'6" wide.
and cellar door & door at foot of stairs only 1'9" wide
this is very bad! must be changed
could not go through with
a clothes basket.

COVERED PORCH

PIAZZA

PANTRY
5 x 9-6

sink

KITCHEN
16 x 17

ENTRY

space for
refrigerator

SERVING
ROOM

BACK HALL

CHINA CLOSET
7-6 x 12

COATS

Dutch Door

PARLOR
16-6 x 19

DINING ROOM
15 x 17-6

HALL
12 x 29

ARCH

DEN
15 x 16'-6

BEAM

VESTIBULE

LAV.
stairs

PORCH

Bay window

· FIRST · FLOOR · PLAN ·
· HOUSE · FOR · J · A · NOYES · ESQ ·
— Cambridge Mass —
Scale ⅛ in = 1 ft

2172 Sq ft   scheme II

"FIRST FLOOR PLAN / HOUSE FOR J A NOYES ESQ / Cambridge
Mass / Scheme II" (one of a group of seventy-four drawings),
undated and unsigned. Graphite, watercolor, orange pencil/
crayon, and graphite emendations on tracing paper; 9¾ × 11⅛".
Gift of Penelope B. Noyes, c. 1960.

J. A. Noyes house in 1903.

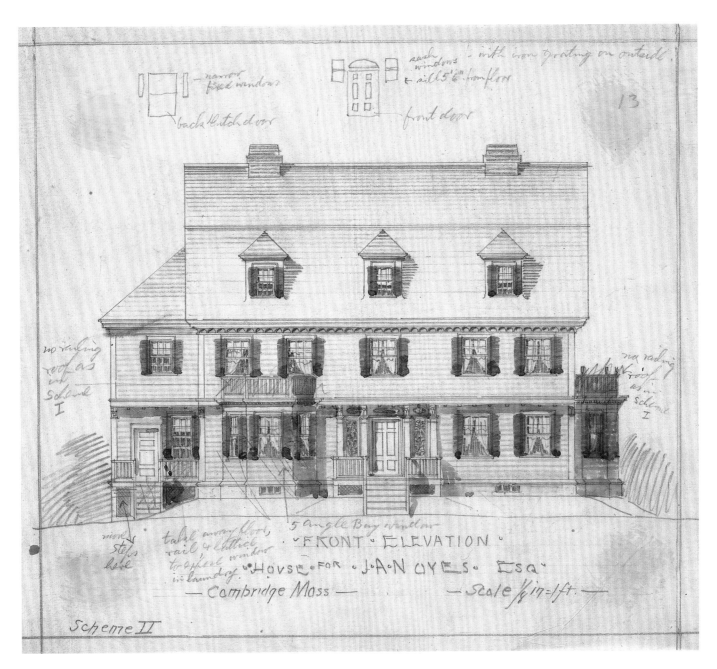

"FRONT ELEVATION / HOUSE FOR J A NOYES ESQ / Cambridge
Mass / Scheme II" (one of a group of seventy-four drawings),
undated and unsigned. Graphite, watercolor, orange pencil/crayon,
and graphite emendations on tracing paper; 9⅞ × 11". Gift of
Penelope B. Noyes, c. 1960.

Samuel Rantin and Son (c. 1895 – c. 1917)

Samuel Rantin (c. 1847–1929)
Samuel J. Rantin (1875–1960)

John McCarthy and William Kallady House,
Calumet Street, Roxbury, Boston, Massachusetts, 1897

Samuel Rantin and Son, Architects, was one of the most prolific firms to specialize in the ubiquitous Boston three-decker house. The drawings for the McCarthy-Kallady house are typical of the three-decker genre in general and the Rantin firm's work in particular.

Samuel Rantin was an Irish immigrant. He began as a carpenter and is first listed in the Boston city directories under that trade in 1881. After an absence from the directory listings in 1891 and 1892, Rantin reappears in 1893 as an architect. His son, Samuel J. Rantin, apparently trained in the office of architects Walker and Kimball before joining his father in about 1895. Samuel Rantin and Son was most prolific during the years 1895 to 1910. The firm ended around 1917, when father and son apparently parted company. Samuel J. Rantin was later a banker in Roxbury.[1]

The fact that the drawing is labeled "No. 7" suggests it represented a portfolio of designs. Notwithstanding the economical nature of the drawings, color is added to suggest the final appearance of the completed building. Architectural ornamentation is minimal, reflecting the modest investment capabilities of the owners: for example, the porch railings are square balusters, and decorative shingles are used only on the gable ends. The front elevation includes a section showing the construction of one corner of the building from foundation to roof. The elevations provide only minimal dimensions; however written specifications may have provided additional details.

According to a real estate magazine, John McCarthy and William Kallady contracted with Samuel Rantin and Son to build two $4,000 three-family houses at 152 and 154 Calumet Street in 1897.[2] Calumet Street, located on Parker Hill in Roxbury, was once a fashionable suburban neighborhood. By the late nineteenth century, after Roxbury was annexed by the city of Boston, Parker Hill became heavily developed as a working-class neighborhood of multifamily homes. John McCarthy, who lived in one of the units at 154 Calumet, was a fireman. William Kallady lived in number 152. The two men had been neighbors elsewhere in Boston before erecting these two buildings. Both houses have been somewhat altered, but the original designs for the porches differed; this drawing is for number 154.

The Rantin design represents a very typical three-family house of the period. Each unit has a parlor, kitchen and pantry, two bedrooms, and a full bathroom. Each apartment has a back porch and back hall leading to the side entrance. Constructed with "open plumbing," these houses could be built rapidly, with heating and plumbing added later. RGR

McCarthy and Kallady houses in 2007.

"FRONT ELEVATION" and wall section of "HOUSE FOR M[ESS].
J. McCARTHY AND W. KALLADY / N[o]– 7 – JAN. – 26 – 1897. /
CALUMET ST., ROXBURY, MASS." (one of a set of nine drawings).
Stamped: "RETURN TO / SAMUEL RANTIN & SON, / ARCHITECTS /
1117 Columbus Ave. / Boston, – Mass."; embossed with seal.
Black, red, and orange ink and graphite on starch-coated fabric;
20⅞ × 11". Library and Archives purchase, 1992.

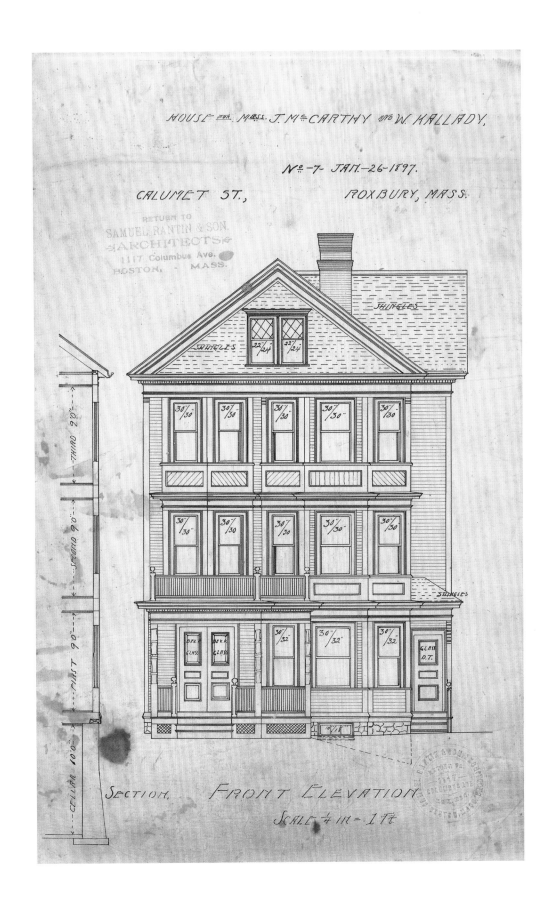

HOUSE FOR MESSS. J. MCCARTHY AND W. HALLADY.

Nº -7- JAN.-26-1897.

CALUMET ST.,   ROXBURY, MASS.

SHINGLES

SHINGLES

SHINGLES

SECTION.   FRONT ELEVATION

SCALE ¼ IN = 1 FT.

149

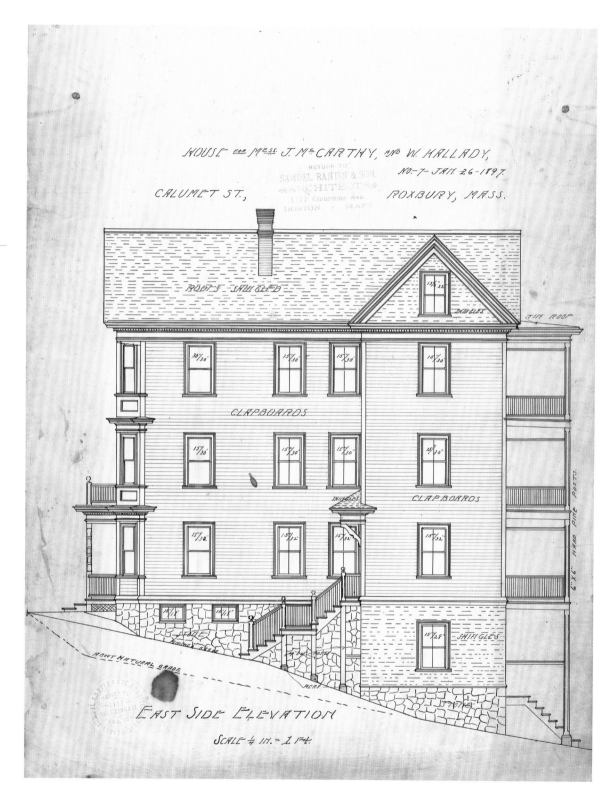

"EAST SIDE ELEVATION" of "HOUSE FOR M^ESS. J. McCARTHY,
AND W. KALLADY / NO. – 7 – JAN. – 26 – 1897. / CALUMET ST.,
ROXBURY, MASS." (one of a set of nine drawings). Stamped:
"RETURN TO / SAMUEL RANTIN & SON, / ARCHITECTS /
1117 Columbus Ave. / Boston, – Mass."; embossed with seal.
Black, red, and orange ink and graphite on starch-coated
fabric; 20¾ × 16¼". Library and Archives purchase, 1992.

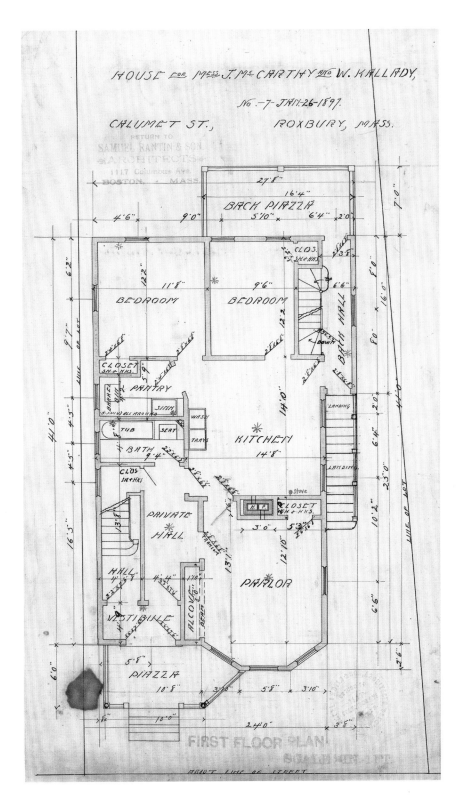

"FIRST FLOOR PLAN" of "HOUSE FOR M[ESS]. J. McCARTHY AND
W. KALLADY / NO. – 7 – JAN. – 26 – 1897. / CALUMET ST., ROXBURY,
MASS." (one of a set of nine drawings). Stamped: "RETURN TO
SAMUEL RANTIN & SON, / ARCHITECTS / 1117 Columbus Ave. /
Boston, – Mass."; embossed with seal. Black and red ink, graphite
underdrawing, and watercolor on starch-coated fabric; 21⅛ × 11".
Library and Archives purchase, 1992.

Charles A. Platt (1861–1933) and Thomas A. Fox (1864–1946)

Harriet Crowninshield Coolidge House,
Old Harrisville Road, Dublin, New Hampshire, 1900

The second of the five houses designed by Charles A. Platt for the Dublin, New Hampshire, summer colony, the Harriet Crowninshield Coolidge house typifies this group. A flush-boarded, two-and-a-half story hip-roofed mass with projecting pergolas on the western and southern sides, the building resembles the formula for summer house architecture that Platt had developed in the 1890s for friends in the art colony at Cornish, New Hampshire, where he summered from 1889 until his death in 1933. In Dublin, Platt's five houses between 1898 and 1908 included one for Mr. and Mrs. Francis Jencks, Platt's sister and her husband, and a second for Mr. Jencks's sister and brother-in-law. The personal and professional connections between artists and other members of the Cornish and Dublin colonies were very close.

Harriet Coolidge (1871–1905) was the daughter of General Casper Coolidge, one of the founders of the Dublin colony. A Bostonian who married Isaac Norris in the same year the house was built, she may have invited Thomas A. Fox, a Boston architect, to collaborate on the project because Platt had no formal preparation as an architect. Platt trained as an etcher and painter, first at the National Academy of Design and the Art Students League in New York City and then at the Académie Julian in Paris. After being invited to join friends in Cornish, Platt began to experiment with architecture and garden design for himself and others. In 1895, he accepted his first non-Cornish commission for a house and garden near Boston, the home of his second wife, Eleanor Hardy Bunker, the widow of the painter Dennis Miller Bunker. (For information on Thomas A. Fox, who later practiced with Edwards J. Gale, see the two entries on an apartment building and a country house in Plymouth, Massachusetts, in this catalogue [pages 154–57].) Among Fox and Gale's few surviving buildings in the Boston area are several structures at Weld, the Larz Anderson estate in Brookline, Massachusetts, where Charles Platt designed the Italian-inspired gardens in 1902. Platt and Fox never collaborated again.

The watercolor perspective view of the Coolidge house as drawn and signed by Charles A. Platt relates to two other watercolor drawings from this early period of his career—an elevation for the Misses Edith and Grace Lawrence house (1896) and a plot plan for the Hermitage, the home and studio of the sculptor Herbert Adams (1903), both in Plainfield, New Hampshire, adjacent to Cornish. The Coolidge house drawing is more of an artist's rendering than a perspective drawing by a trained architect.

Like Cornish, Dublin attracted artists, musicians, and professionals in several fields, urbanites fleeing the heat of the city, who came, frequently from Boston, to enjoy Dublin Lake, Mount Monadnock, and the camaraderie of like-minded individuals. Platt's houses in both communities were intended to speak to the current fascination with the gardens and architecture of Renaissance Italy, seen in the symmetry, axial organization, and loggias of the Coolidge house, and which Platt had popularized in his book, *Italian Gardens* (1894). KNM

Harriet Crowninshield Coolidge house in 2007.

"Sketch of West Elevation of / House for Mrs. Harriet
C. Coolidge at Dublin N. H." Signed: "Charles A. Platt /
Thomas A. Fox / architects." Graphite, black ink, and
watercolor on tracing paper; 13¼ × 24⅛". Gift of
Samuel D. Perry and Alice deV. Perry, 2004.

Fox and Gale (c. 1891–c. 1932)

Thomas A. Fox (1864–1946)
Edwards J. Gale (c. 1868–1949)

Unidentified Apartment Building, c. 1900

By the beginning of the twentieth century, apartment living was a well-established housing option in Boston and its inner suburbs for people from across the social spectrum. *The American Architect and Building News* even asserted that among Bostonians the "apartment, or 'French flat'" had gained acceptance "long before it occurred to the New Yorkers that fashionable people could live in anything but a separate dwelling-house . . ." It is unknown if the red brick apartment block with light stone or terra-cotta trim shown in delineator J. C. Clapp, Jr.'s, attractive rendering for architects Fox and Gale was ever built. But similar structures erected near the turn of the past century still stand in places like the Beacon Street corridor in Brookline, Massachusetts, and the nearby Charlesgate–Fenway area of Boston. A building strikingly similar to the one shown here is Arthur Bowditch's 1901–02 Carlton Hotel at 1138 Boylston Street, now part of the Berklee College of Music.[1]

Clapp's rendering shows two elevations of a block-wide property with three frontages on public streets. The third, unseen, public façade around the corner is most probably a mirror image of the twin-bayed elevation at left. The center section of the building's right-hand elevation has been recessed to create a light court open to the street on all but the ground floor, creating a footprint that appears to be a variant of the "dumbbell" footprint infamous from its association with New York City tenement houses, but which was also used for higher-end multiunit buildings. (In subsequent years, an apartment plan featuring a full-fledged garden courtyard open to the street would become locally popular: many examples of buildings featuring this scheme can be found in Brookline and Cambridge, Massachusetts.) Stylistically, Fox and Gale's building is a late-Victorian version of the Georgian Revival, which drew its inspiration from the red brick, classically ornamented high-style architecture of late seventeenth- and early eighteenth-century England, a mode that appeared in simplified form in colonial America.

Only a few works by Fox and Gale, a Boston firm in business from about 1891 to the early 1930s, are currently known, and the firm's history remains somewhat obscure. Thomas A. Fox and Edwards J. Gale graduated from MIT in the late 1880s; a third designer, fellow alumnus Alexander S. Jenney, was briefly a firm affiliate at the turn of the century. Fox and Gale's earliest attributed building, the Rockingham County Probate and Deeds Office in Exeter, New Hampshire (1892), uses a Georgian Revival idiom that bears some kinship with the building shown here. Another early commission, designed under the name Fox, Jenney, and Gale, was a small public library for the upscale Boston suburb of Weston, Massachusetts (1899–1900). Later the firm designed the Copley Square subway kiosk located adjacent to McKim, Mead and White's great Boston Public Library building, a belle-époque confection, which in terms of sheer volume of users must be the firm's most popular surviving building.[2]

If Fox and Gale had a specialty, however, it appears to have been the laying out of country house grounds in the Italianizing manner promoted by Charles A. Platt, with whom Fox collaborated on the Harriet Coolidge house in Dublin, New Hampshire (see pages 152–53). Platt's aesthetic seems to have made a major impact on the firm. Among the turn-of-the-century estates for which the firm designed landscape features and related structures were Larz and Isabel Anderson's Brookline estate, Weld, which had an Italian garden by Platt; Highlands, the William H. Gratwick estate in Livingston County, New York; and the expansive Charles A. Stone summer retreat in Plymouth, Massachusetts, for which they also designed the main house. Fox and Gale's work for Stone is discussed on pages 156–57.[3] DCCJr

Perspective of an unidentified apartment building,
undated. Signed by delineator: "JC Clapp Jr." Watercolor
and graphite on paper-faced four-ply board; 24⅛ × 30¹⁄₁₆".
Gift of Samuel D. Perry and Alice deV. Perry, 2004.

Fox and Gale (c. 1891–c. 1932)

Thomas A. Fox (1864–1946)
Edwards J. Gale (c. 1868–1949)

Charles A. Stone House, The Terraces,
Rocky Point, Plymouth, Massachusetts, c. 1903
(demolished)

Thomas A. Fox and Edwards J. Gale's design for Charles A. Stone's summer retreat, like Harriet Coolidge's house in New Hampshire (see pages 152–53), is English Colonial Revival in spirit but hardly archaeological in detail. With their low hip roofs, overhanging eves, appended pergolas, and distinctive grouping of second-story windows, the two houses are close siblings, if not quite twins. The Coolidge commission may represent firm principal Fox's only collaboration with Charles A. Platt, but the latter's design aesthetic apparently made a lasting impression.

The Coolidge house drawing only hints at its surroundings, but delineator J. C. Clapp, Jr.'s, bird's-eye view of the Stone house shows how fully Fox and Gale had absorbed Charles Platt's Italian Renaissance-inspired landscape style as well. At a time when classical architecture in all its many manifestations—not least its colonial American offshoot—was enjoying a resurgence, such formal landscapes provided fashionable and aesthetically appropriate settings for builders of country houses. The Italian landscape aesthetic achieved an apotheosis of sorts on the house's oceanfront side (not pictured), where no fewer than seven terraces cascaded down the hillside from mansion to swimming pool.

Born in Newton, Massachusetts, in 1867, Charles A. Stone was an MIT-trained engineer and co-founder of Stone and Webster, a firm that grew to become one of the twentieth century's greatest civil and electrical engineering concerns. During its hundred-plus years of operation, Stone and Webster designed and built a vast range of projects encompassing from hydro to nuclear power generation plants, manufacturing complexes, MIT's Cambridge campus, and a giant World War I shipyard.

Stone began purchasing land in the Warren Cove/Rocky Point area of Plymouth in the late 1890s, and by 1910 had amassed some four to five hundred acres overlooking Plymouth Bay. The main house appears to have been ready for the 1903 summer season, although work on the extensive property may have continued for several years thereafter. The completed compound must have been a stunning place indeed, a spread fully capable of hosting the four hundred Stone and Webster employees who descended upon it in July 1910 for a company outing. In addition to the main house, with its suite of formal entertaining spaces, ten bedrooms, six baths and servants' wing, the estate included a one-hundred-foot-long swimming pool, two tennis courts, a nine-room guest cottage, a stable complex, a greenhouse, a playhouse, and other outbuildings.[1]

While Stone came to own retreats in Long Island, Virginia, and New Hampshire, the Plymouth estate was still in his hands at the time of his death in 1941. The property was placed on the market sometime in the 1940s and was subdivided by the end of the decade, with the main house and most of its landscape features subsequently being demolished, although sections of the estate's granite walls and some outbuildings remain. Since the early 1970s, Pilgrim Station, a nuclear power plant built by Bechtel, a Stone and Webster competitor, has occupied land nearby.[2]

The contrast between J. C. Clapp, Jr.'s, impressionistic image of the Stone house and his rendering of Fox and Gale's turn-of-the-century apartment building (see pages 154–55) exemplifies the contemporary evolution of fashions of architectural illustration. A review of a 1904 Boston Architectural Club exhibition evokes the newer style in its assessment of Clapp's entry to that show:

> the birds-eye view of a house and garden at Weston . . . has given pleasure to all who saw it. No [black-and-white] illustration can convey the delicate harmony of clear cool grays and greens that make of the house and its setting a creature of the imagination rather than an aggregate of sticks and stones and earth. Mr. Clapp will go far because he knows where to stop.[3]

John Cotton Clapp, Jr. (1870–1930), was the son of a Dorchester, Massachusetts, printer and publisher. While represented here solely in the capacity of delineator, Clapp was in fact listed as an architect in Boston city directories from about 1897 to 1901 and again from 1910 to 1916. (During the latter period both Clapp and Fox and Gale rented offices at 3 Park Street, Boston.) While it is currently unknown which if any of Clapp's designs were built, let alone survive, it is worth noting that his submission to a 1905 *Ladies' Home Journal* small house design competition was judged second to successful North Shore architect William G. Rantoul. John Clapp was also an early member of, and donor to, Historic New England).[4] DCCJr

C. A. Stone house in the early twentieth century.

Perspective of the Charles A. Stone house, undated.
Signed by delineator: "JC Clapp Jr." Watercolor
and graphite on tracing paper; 18¾ × 34½". Gift of
Samuel D. Perry and Alice deV. Perry, 2004.

Edward Pearce Casey (1864–1940)

Hildreth K. Bloodgood House, Stone Manor Drive,
New Marlborough, Massachusetts, c. 1906–07

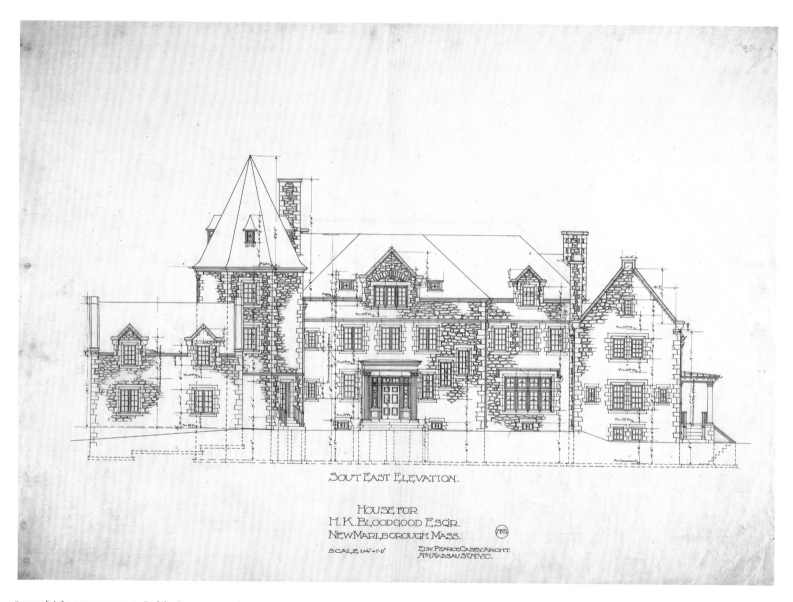

"SOUT [sic] EAST ELEVATION" of the "HOUSE FOR / H. K. BLOODGOOD
ESQR. / NEW MARLBOROUGH MASS. / Nº 5" (one of a set of twelve sheets),
undated. Signed: "EDW. PEARCE CASEY ARCHT. / Nº 1 NASSAU ST. N.Y.C."
Black and red ink and graphite underdrawing on starch-coated fabric;
30 × 41½". Gift of Mrs. Edward Pearce Casey, 1941.

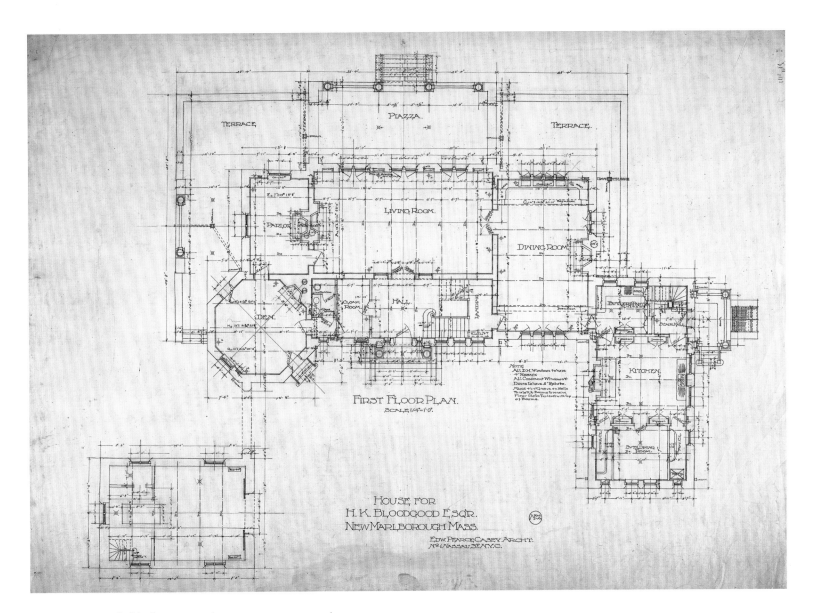

"FIRST FLOOR PLAN" of the "HOUSE FOR / H. K. BLOODGOOD ESQR. /
NEW MARLBOROUGH MASS. / Nº 2" (one of a set of twelve sheets), undated. Signed: "EDW. PEARCE CASEY ARCHT. / Nº 1 NASSAU ST. N.Y.C."
Black and red ink and graphite underdrawing on starch-coated fabric;
29¾ × 41". Gift of Mrs. Edward Pearce Casey, 1941.

Edward Pearce Casey (1864–1940)
Hildreth K. Bloodgood House

The fashion for building large country estates in remote locations was not uncommon in the late nineteenth century. Men of wealth typically sought out country locations to provide an outlet for their hobbies and engaged architects to design these private retreats from the business world. Hildreth K. Bloodgood's passion was raising cocker spaniels in what he called the Mepal Kennels; he also raised Hackney horses and ponies. His fashionable New York architect, Edward P. Casey, was his wife's nephew.

Casey attended the Ecole des Beaux-Arts in Paris. His career received a major boost when his father, Thomas Lincoln Casey, a brigadier-general and Chief of Engineers in the U. S. Army Corps of Engineers, secured for him the position of architect to complete work on the new Library of Congress building in Washington.[1] The Bloodgood mansion was constructed of ashlar stone in a style that drew inspiration from British Colonial architecture of the eighteenth century in New York and Canada, rather than European precedents suggestive of royalty.[2]

The house is sited on a hill with a cleared vista northwest toward the Taconic Range. The main entrance, on the southeast façade, features a simple Tuscan portico, echoing the traditional front porch of a summer cottage, rather than a porte cochere. The plan also is reminiscent of a large summer cottage: the entrance hall has the stairway placed to one side so as not to spoil the view through the large living room to the Taconic hills beyond. A parlor is placed to one side of the living room, while a hexagonal den occupies the base of the tower. On the other side is a dining room, also with views, and a projecting kitchen wing. Two terraces and a piazza run along the entire expanse of the northeast façade, facing the view. The Bloodgood house has managed to survive the historically brief fashion for large country estates through serial reincarnation—first as a private school, then as an inn, and today as a spa. RGR

H. K. Bloodgood house in the 1930s.

160

A. H. Davenport and Company (active 1880–1908 and beyond)

Unidentified Interior, Early Twentieth Century

The blue and gray dining room elevation depicted in this undated drawing conveys a cheerful, bright, and comparatively modern interior, with long, low banquettes upholstered in deep royal blue and set beneath tall casements hung with curtains and valances in the same rich blue. Pots glowing with blooming plants line the window sills and overlook a garden of shrubbery. The window seats flank a broad fireplace embellished with blue and white tile, the focal point for a varied collection of blue and white china arrayed along the mantel and in the glazed cupboard above the hearth. A decorative floral wallpaper border in subdued grays runs along the ceiling. The pale gray woodwork and deep blue upholstery echo the colors of the china and tile. The scene evokes a sense of prosperous suburban comfort and hospitality: the formality and restraint of the tight blue upholstery, smooth drapes, and flat valances contrasting with the casual asymmetry of flowers and pots and the mantel's informal display of vases, plates, jars, and teapots.

In this drawing, as in the other interior drawing from A. H. Davenport and Company in this catalogue (see pages 164–65), the intent is not to sell the firm's furniture, but its decorating skills. In this instance, the scene is not an evocation of the past but an invitation to modern living. By the early twentieth century, collecting blue and white china was a passion some thirty to forty years old. One English collector, writing in 1891, ascribed the origins of the Aesthetic Movement's "Blue Mania," as he called it, to Charles Augustus Howell, a friend of John Ruskin, Dante Gabriel Rossetti, and James McNeil Whistler, who through Howell's connoisseurship of the china were "inoculated" with a fascination for old blue and white china.[1] The appeal of the colorful antiques remained strong, and in the Davenport interior, it underlies the entire decorative scheme. In the bits of old china, in the assorted pots, in the handcrafted Spanish baroque tile panels of the fireplace, and in the sunburst rays of the iron fireback, one also catches glimpses of the Aesthetic sensibility, here translated into an upper-middle-class domesticity.

Rendering interiors demanded skillful draftsmanship to capture not just the architectural components but also the room's decor, with its variety of objects and accessories, their individual colors, surfaces, and textures, and the presence of light and shadow from multiple sources. The elevation drawing of the blue and gray dining room encapsulates this challenge, with an underlying drawing in graphite overlaid in pen and ink and then richly washed in watercolor.

Determining the date of the drawing is somewhat problematic: the drawing is stamped with a company address at 55 Washington Street, Boston, but at least until 1908, when the executors of Albert H. Davenport (1845–1906) sold the company, the firm occupied an 1878 showroom and factory at 96–98 Washington Street. Following the sale, the company lost its foremost designer, Francis Henry Bacon (1856–1940), an MIT-trained architect, draftsman, and classical archaeologist who left to found his own furniture firm (the F. H. Bacon Decorative and Furniture Company), but it continued under the same name and under its managing director, Edwin Ford, a civil engineer by training and from 1883 to 1893 the owner of Ford and Brooks, an ecclesiastical art company.

By 1911, when Ford was listed as the firm's general manager, the company had moved from downtown Boston to 574 Boylston Street in the Back Bay. In 1914, A. H. Davenport merged with Irving and Casson, another prominent Boston furniture manufacturer specializing in architectural woodwork, and thereafter occupied various locations on Boylston Street, where the latter firm had operated from the late 1880s. Thus, it seems possible that the drawing was produced at some point between 1908 and 1911, when A. H. Davenport and Company perhaps relocated under new leadership.

Drawings such as this were part of an extensive library and archive established in the Davenport Company merger with Irving and Casson. The library was described in a 1917 publication: "composed of three hundred books and hundreds of clippings, [it] covers the fields of interior decorating, architecture and furniture" and was intended "for the use of employee and the public." The entry added: "A useful scrap-book is kept in loose leaf form. Cuts of furniture of different periods and styles are clipped from various sources and arranged in the folio. Thus furniture, tapestries and other decorations for all uses are easily available."[2] The company librarian was Miss Ruth V. Cook, who went on to a long and valuable career as the librarian of the Harvard School of Architecture (Graduate School of Design) from 1919 to 1956. SZ

DINING ROOM IN BLUE AND GRAY

SCALE 3/4" = 1 FOOT

Elevation of "DINING ROOM IN BLUE AND GRAY,"
undated. Stamped: "RETURN TO / A. H. DAVENPORT CO. /
55 WASHINGTON ST. / BOSTON, MASS." Ink, watercolor,
and graphite underdrawing on textured wove watercolor
paper; 9¼ × 17¼". Library and Archives purchase, 1994.

A. H. Davenport and Company (active 1880–1908 and beyond)

Unidentified Room Model, Early Twentieth Century

At the turn of the twentieth century, A. H. Davenport and Company, of Boston and East Cambridge, Massachusetts, was one of the foremost commercial decorating companies in the country, supplying both retail and custom furniture and furnishings designed and manufactured as well as imported by the firm. An 1880 description of the company's five-story Boston showrooms and factories "cordially" welcomed "the occupants of the humble cottage and the stately mansions" to take in the displays of furniture, carpeting, draperies, and wallpapers for every taste and price, but memorably to be captivated by the best that the company's craftsmen and designers could produce, luxury whose "gorgeous vista reminds one of some enchanted fairy scene . . . almost too beautiful for earth."[1]

In plan and elevation, the drawing depicts a sumptuous late-Georgian interior. The four sides fold up to create a three-dimensional miniature room, illustrating not only the company's prowess in the design and execution of architectural millwork, but also a compelling marketing tool for its decorating services. Furnished with a rich Oriental carpet, heavy green silk brocade draperies, gilded Chippendale pier glasses, and charmingly realized fantasy portraits, the drawing promotes a way of living, not, in this case in furniture, but in finishes and furnishings. The room is an elegantly light and formal drawing room, with pale gray marbleized fielded paneling, golden parquet floors laid in a herringbone pattern, brilliant, flame mahogany six-panel doors, carved door casings, and a heavily embellished projecting chimneypiece.

The dollhouse-like presentation, calling to mind the miniature rooms of the Thorne Collection at The Art Institute of Chicago, was perhaps not intended as a room plan for a specific client but rather as a showroom piece to demonstrate the company's decorating services. The Gillow furniture and decorating company of Lancaster, England (established around 1730), occupied a comparable niche in upper-class and aristocratic interior decoration and employed a similar "exploded room" presentation in the nineteenth century to depict its furniture in a domestic setting.[2] Where the Gillow drawings allowed the customer to select options from a range of furniture choices, the Davenport drawing showcases the expertise and craftsmanship of the company's architectural woodworkers. SZ

Model of an unidentified interior, undated and unsigned.
Watercolor and graphite on two-ply board glued to two-ply
mat board; 30¾ × 30" fully opened. Library and Archives
purchase, 1994.

Edwin J. Lewis, Jr. (1859–1937)

Unidentified Stable, c. 1905

Edwin J. Lewis, Jr., graduated from the MIT School of Architecture in 1881. After working as a draftsman for Peabody and Stearns, Lewis established his own practice in 1887. A resident of Dorchester, Massachusetts, Lewis designed a large number of buildings in that community and attained a national reputation as a designer of Unitarian churches. This drawing of the stable and the one of the garage illustrated on page 169 are part of a bound portfolio of renderings of the architect's work, most of which are not identified. This stable probably was intended for a large suburban estate. In the first decade of the twentieth century, private stables were still being built, although they would soon give way to "auto stables" for motorcars.

This building probably fronted the street, with the gated porte cochere to the right leading directly to the house (also no doubt in the Tudor Revival style). Four double doors and a walled courtyard suggest quite a large estate. The second floor probably contained storage for hay and grain as well as rooms for hired help. RGR

Front Elevation

Scale ⅛"=1'0"

"Front Elevation" of an unidentified stable, undated and
unsigned; from a bound portfolio of designs by Edwin J.
Lewis, Jr. Ink, watercolor, and graphite on wove paper;
8⅞ × 13¼". Gift of Earle G. Shettleworth, Jr., 1991.

Edwin J. Lewis, Jr. (1859–1937)

Pietro Terrile Garage,
Quincy Avenue, Winthrop, Massachusetts, c. 1907

Pietro Terrile was a prosperous grocer who built a large Tudor Revival-style house in the fashionable middle-class neighborhood of Winthrop Highlands. The Terrile house and the garage behind it still stand. A drawing for the garage survives in a portfolio of the architect's renderings. Lewis, who undoubtedly designed the house as well, was clearly promoting the concept that a garage, like a stable, should be designed to be architecturally compatible with the house. As in our own time, architects competed with kit designs for prefabricated garages. Garages (called "auto houses" or "auto stables" in the early years) were often fitted-up with maintenance features such as washers above and workpits below, as well as heating stoves. The Terrile garage had the basic features for a small garage: a concrete floor with a central drain, a workbench, and a closet for driving gear. The gable windows above the hips over the narrower end walls provide the interior with light from above. RGR

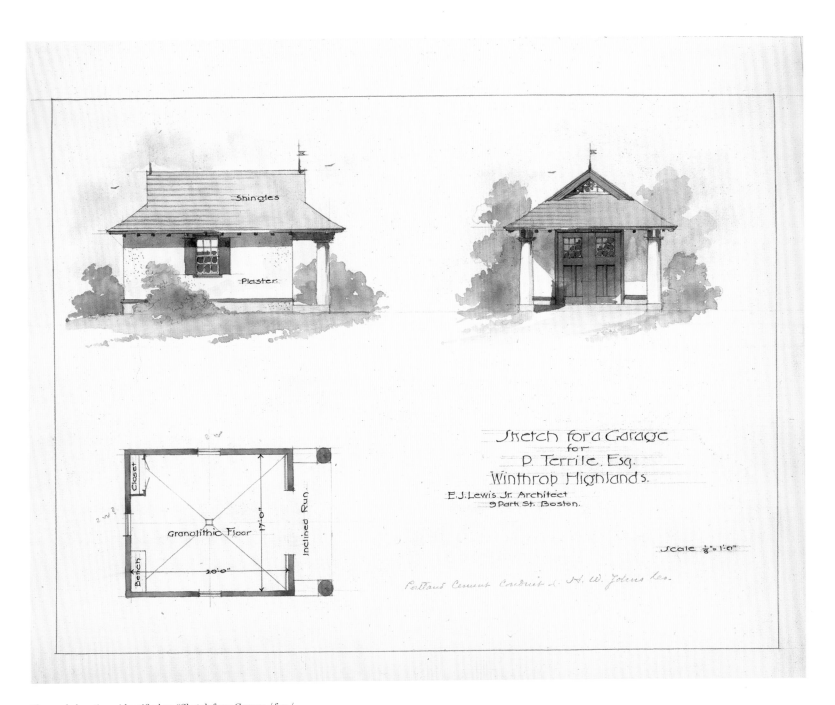

Shingles

Plaster

Closet

Granolithic Floor

Inclined Run

Bench

8'0"

2'0"

17'0"

20'0"

Sketch for a Garage
for
P. Terrile, Esq.
Winthrop Highlands.

E. J. Lewis Jr. Architect
9 Park St. Boston.

Scale ⅛"= 1'0"

Portland Cement Conduit & H. W. Johns Co.

Plan and elevations, identified as: "Sketch for a Garage / for /
P. Terrile, Esq. / Winthrop Highlands." Signed: "E. J. Lewis Jr.
Architect / 9 Park St. Boston"; from a bound portfolio of designs
by Edwin J. Lewis, Jr. Ink, watercolor, and graphite on wove
paper; 10 × 12½". Gift of Earle G. Shettleworth, Jr., 1991.

Frank Chouteau Brown (1876–1947)

Unidentified Bungalow, 1912

Frank Chouteau Brown grew up in Minneapolis, studied at the Minneapolis School of Fine Arts, and apprenticed as a draftsman in the local firm of Thomas C. Plant. In 1897, he moved to Boston and joined the office of James T. Kelley. Under his own name after 1905, Brown came to specialize in domestic architecture and the recording and restoration of colonial works. He was a "master of measured drawings," according to Charles E. Peterson, founder of the Historic American Building Survey. Brown was also an author and editor of distinction at *The Architectural Review* for thirteen years, a contributing editor at *The Architectural Record*, an editor at *Pencil Points,* an associate editor and contributor to *The White Pine Series of Architectural Monographs* on English colonial architecture, and for three years editor of *Old-Time New England.* He published a number of books and articles, including works on architectural drawing and lettering, the architectural orders, English country houses, drama and stage setting, city planning, and other subjects related to the profession.

Much of his mature architectural work demonstrated his profound knowledge of the English Colonial Revival, but in this early design Brown turned his hand to a brick version of the ubiquitous modest dwelling type of the early twentieth century, the suburban bungalow in the Arts and Crafts or Mission style. The plan is a version of the cruciform, hearth-centered Prairie House often associated with the name of Frank Lloyd Wright. The thick battered piers and chimney, broad sloping roof, and masonry give this house a more solid look than many contemporary frame bungalows. The presentation rendering is that of a gifted drafter. JFO'G

Perspective, plans, and sections of "A / BRICK COTTAGE 'BUNGALOW' / FRANK CHOUTEAU BROWN ARCHITECT 9 PARK ST. / BOSTON." Signed and dated: "Frank Chouteau Brown / Des. et Del. 1912." Black ink and graphite on tracing paper; 26 × 20 1/16". Gift of Mrs. Frank Chouteau Brown, c. 1948.

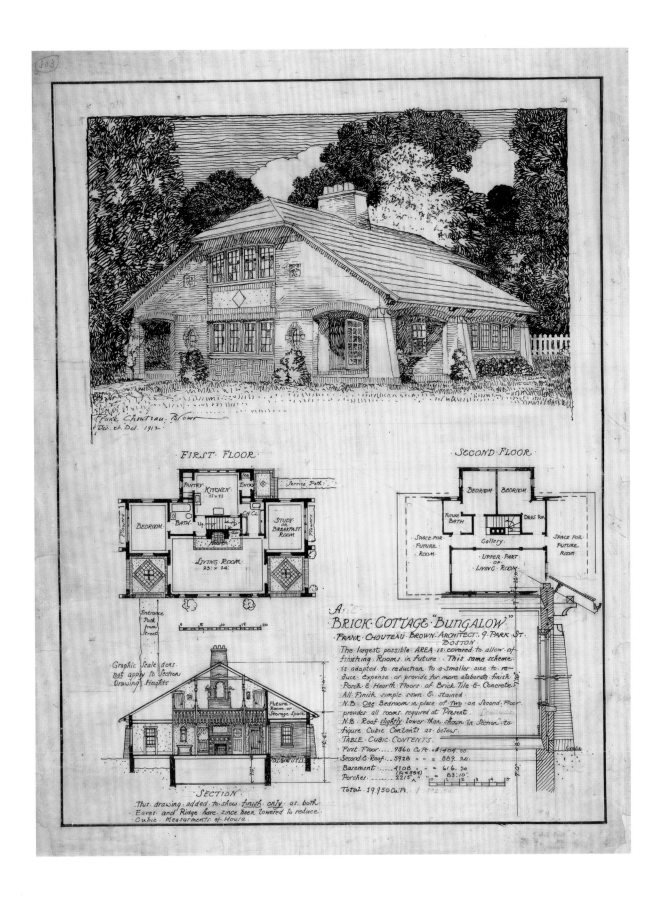

FIRST·FLOOR

SECOND·FLOOR

Frank Choutrau Brown
Des. et Del. 1912.

PANTRY KITCHEN 11 x 11 ENTRY Service Path

BEDROOM BATH Ch Cl. STUDY OR BREAKFAST ROOM

Flower Flower

LIVING·ROOM 23 x 14

BEDROOM BEDROOM

Future BATH Dres Rm

SPACE·FOR FUTURE ROOM Gallery SPACE·FOR FUTURE ROOM

UPPER·PART OF LIVING·ROOM

Entrance Path from Street

Graphic Scale does not apply to Section Drawing Heights

Future Room or Storage Space

A
BRICK·COTTAGE·"BUNGALOW"
FRANK·CHOUTEAU·BROWN·ARCHITECT·9·PARK·ST
BOSTON

The largest possible·AREA·is·covered·to·allow·of
finishing·Rooms·in·future··This·same·scheme
is·adapted·to·reduction·to·a·smaller·size·to·re-
duce·expense·or·provide·for·more·elaborate·finish
Porch·&·Hearth·Floors·of·Brick·Tile·&·Concrete
All·Finish·simple·sawn·&·stained
N.B.·One·Bedroom·in·place·of·Two·on·Second·Floor
provides·all·rooms·required·at·Present·
N.B.·Roof·slightly·lower·than·shown·in·Section·to
figure·Cubic·Contents·as·below.

TABLE·CUBIC·CONTENTS.
First·Floor.....9360 Cu.Ft. = $1404. 00
Second·&·Roof..5928 " " = 889. 20
Basement.......4108 " (½×354) = 616. 20
Porches........2215 "   83:10
Total 19,950 Cu.Ft.

SECTION.
This·drawing·added·to·show·finish·only·as·both
Eaves·and·Ridge·have·since·been·lowered·to·reduce
Cubic·Measurments·of·House.

171

Frank Chouteau Brown (1876–1947)

Thomas Dreier House, Snug Gables, Enclosing Fence,
Curtis Circle, Winchester, Massachusetts, 1924

For a picturesque site overlooking a small lake in Winchester, Frank Chouteau Brown designed a brick Tudor house for Thomas and Blanche Dreier, which was built between 1919 and 1920. In 1923, it was featured in *Country Life*. Early in his career, Dreier had worked as a printer, a reporter, and then an editor. Eventually, he launched a company in Boston, publishing house organs for businesses. When he built the Winchester house, he included a print shop in the basement, then relocated his company to his home. Years later, Dreier would publish a book about linotype. One may imagine that Brown appreciated Dreier's expertise as a printer, as the architect had published a book called *Letters and Lettering* in 1902.

In 1924, the Dreiers returned to Brown for an extensive landscaping project at their property, which would involve constructing a brick and iron fence, a fountain, terraces, and a croquet court. The drawings on the paper illustrated here were developed for use by the contractor. Notes state that stone trim and tile will be furnished by the owner, and the section in the center of the sheet provides information on plumbing for the fountain. The style of the wall is loosely Georgian, with classical detailing, while in plan, the wall defines garden spaces that are axially organized and regular. This classical approach to the garden contrasts with the medieval irregularity of the house, yet both house and garden draw upon English sources, which was typical for Brown and the Arts and Crafts ethos in Boston during this period. (In 1923, Brown published *Modern English Country Houses*.)

The fountain on the left half of the drawing was designed to overlook the croquet court and garden, whereas the decorative wall panel on the right was to face the public road. Dreier supplied tile from the Moravian Pottery and Tile Works in Doylestown, Pennsylvania, a choice that Boston architects at the time favored. The tile was sold by the Society of Arts and Crafts in their salesroom at 9 Park Street, Boston, the same building where Brown worked before relocating to Mount Vernon Square. Brass letters were affixed to the wall's cement panel, telling visitors and passersby the name of the estate, Snug Gables, the estate's date of 1920, Dreier's name, and even the name of Frank Chouteau Brown, who is credited as the architect. MM

Thomas Dreier house about 1930.

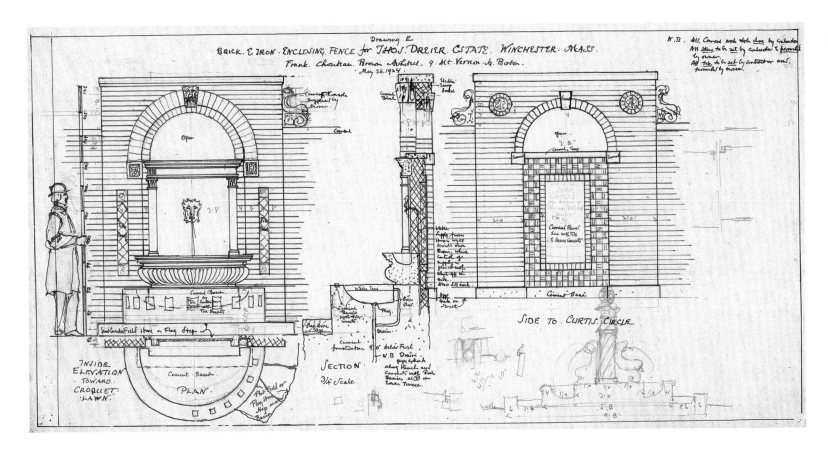

Elevations, plan, and section, identified, dated, and signed as:
"Drawing E / BRICK & IRON ENCLOSING FENCE for THOS.
DREIER ESTATE WINCHESTER MASS / Frank Chouteau Brown
Architect. 9 Mt. Vernon Sq. Boston / May 26, 1924" (one of a group
of fourteen sheets). Black and red ink and graphite emendations
and notations on tracing paper; 12⅛ × 24⅛". Gift of Mrs. Frank
Chouteau Brown, c. 1948.

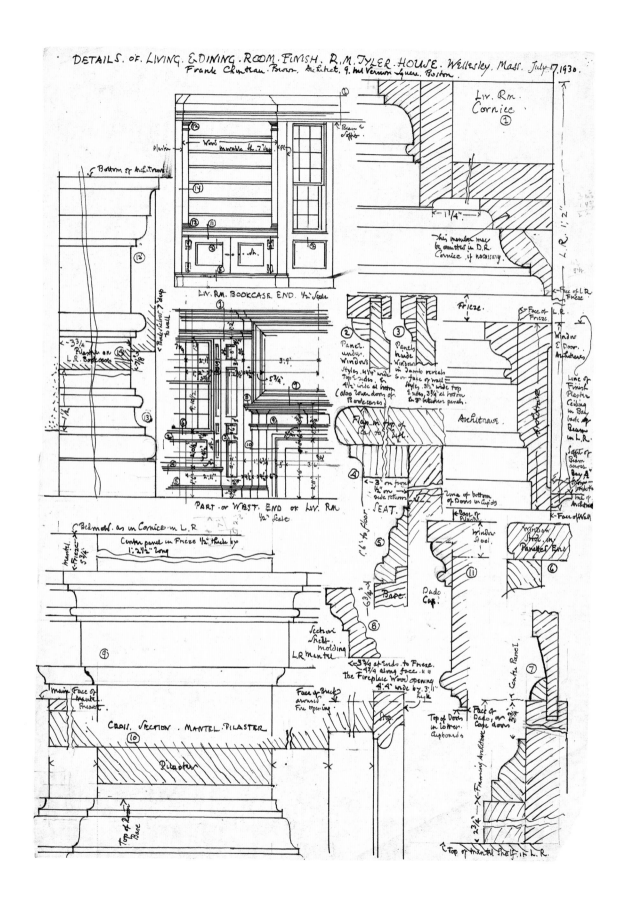

DETAILS. OF. LIVING. & DINING. ROOM. FINISH. R.M. TYLER. HOUSE. Wellesley. Mass. July 17, 1930.
Frank Chouteau Brown, Architect. 9. Mt. Vernon Square. Boston.

174

Frank Chouteau Brown (1876–1947)

R. M. Tyler House, Hundreds Road, Wellesley, Massachusetts, 1930

This drawing of finish treatments of a suburban house in the English Colonial Revival-Shingle Style demonstrates the extraordinary pains Brown took to detail the interior woodwork of the main rooms. For this working study, he delineated the profile and joinery of every molding of the fireplace frame and overmantel, window frames, built-in bookcase, and pilasters. For all of this Brown drew upon his expertise as a serious student of English and English Colonial Revival architecture. Such prescribed minute direction was a fundamental service of the accomplished architect of period homes at this time. JFO'G

Interior details, identified, dated, and signed as: "DETAILS OF LIVING & DINING ROOM FINISH R. M. TYLER HOUSE. WELLESLEY, MASS. July 17, 1930 / Frank Chouteau Brown Architect. 9 Mt Vernon Square Boston" (one of a set of twenty sheets). Black and red ink and graphite emendations on tracing paper; 20 × 14". Gift of Mrs. Frank Chouteau Brown, c. 1948.

Unidentified House on the Connecticut River, 1934

The drawings on the following page provide evidence that Brown could work in styles other than the English Colonial Revival, at least for his own amusement. There may or may not have been a client for this appropriately jaunty chateauesque stone house on the irregular banks of the Connecticut River. The drawings are certainly unresolved studies. In both sketches, Brown created a decidedly picturesque arrangement of rooms of various shapes, which rise in two floors to form an irregular silhouette, anchored by a tall chimney and a tower with a candlesnuffer roof. In one version that tower is a circular staircase; in the other variation it is an "Outlook Room," with the owner's bedroom above. In both studies, a variety of rectangular living, sleeping, and service rooms collide at odd angles with the circle. Each exterior is viewed from a different perspective and treated differently. One looks at the house from the water; the other sketch views the house from the land, but the location of the tower drifts from water to land side to remain front and center. The waterside sketch envisions a rough stone exterior with shake or slate roof and diamond pane windows. The design knowingly ignores all that has happened in the history of Modern architecture in the preceding decade. This is close to the last moment that such a statement of historical precedent could be made by a major architect—until the era of postmodern, tongue-in-cheek revivalism. JFO'G

Unidentified House, Dublin, New Hampshire, 1938

Dublin became a fashionable summer retreat for many affluent New Englanders in the early twentieth century. Unfortunately, we know neither the name of the client nor the specific location of the remodeling job illustrated on page 177. Nor does what is proposed seem reasonable. The "New Service Wing" beyond the "Old Bldg" is projected to be a gabled, one-story addition intended to contain a kitchen, pantry, and maid's room, but the adjoining room is not a dining room. This has the earmarks of some preliminary and unresolved ideas jotted down in a hurry to further the conversation about the change. As the house cannot be identified, the project may never have been executed unless in very different form. Compared to the finished 1912 perspective of the brick bungalow (see pages 170–71), Brown's later drawings are often quick, conceptual studies that present his designs with a minimum of strokes. JFO'G

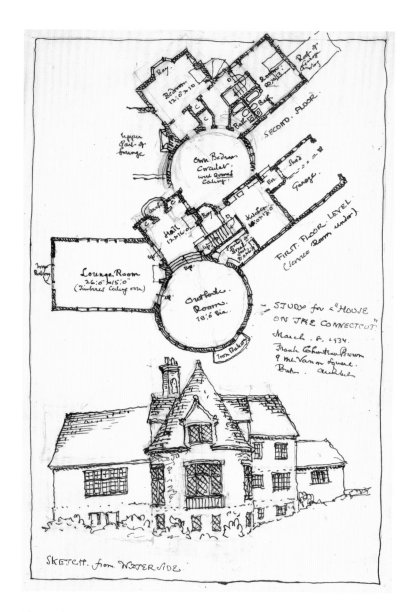

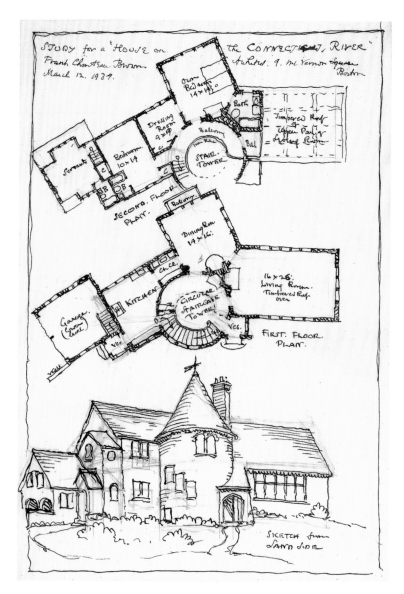

Plans and exterior perspective identified, dated, and signed as: "STUDY for a 'HOUSE / ON THE CONNECTCUT [sic]' / March 8, 1934 / Frank Chouteau Brown / 9 Mt Vernon Square / Boston / Architect / SKETCH from WATER SIDE." Black ink and graphite emendations on tracing paper; 15 × 10⅜". Gift of Mrs. Frank Chouteau Brown, c. 1948.

Plans and exterior perspective identified, dated, and signed as: "STUDY for a 'HOUSE / ON THE CONNECT[sic] RIVER' / Frank Chouteau Brown Architect. / 9. Mt Vernon Square Boston / March 12, 1934 / SKETCH from LAND SIDE." Black ink and graphite emendations on tracing paper; 15 × 10½". Gift of Mrs. Frank Chouteau Brown, c. 1948. This drawing was not included in the exhibition.

Exterior perspective and partial plan identified and signed as:
"STUDY REVISION of / HOUSE at DUBLIN N. H. / Frank Chouteau
Brown Del. et Designer." Dated: "Nov. 27, 1938." Black ink and
graphite underdrawing and emendations on tracing paper;
10 × 15". Gift of Mrs. Frank Chouteau Brown, c. 1948.

Arthur Asahel Shurcliff (né Shurtleff) (1870–1957)

Alexander Cochrane Garden, at The Hague (built?),
Hamilton, Massachusetts, c. 1915

In 1905, Alexander Cochrane (1840–1919) was a prosperous and established Boston businessman, with two architect-designed houses in Boston and Prides Crossing, Massachusetts, when he purchased an old farmhouse and fourteen acres in Hamilton, Massachusetts.[1] He owned this property, which he called The Farm or The Hague, for eight years before he called in Boston landscape architect Arthur Asahel Shurcliff in 1913.[2] Although the MIT-, Harvard-, and Olmsted-trained Shurcliff was known for his town planning and larger public commissions, through the years he continuously wove private estate design into his burgeoning practice.[3] By the time Cochrane engaged him, Shurcliff had a thorough grounding in residential design, and his reputation in the Boston area was well established.

Historic New England's Library and Archives contains several plans Shurcliff prepared for Cochrane between 1913 and 1915, including a planting plan that corresponds closely to this undated watercolor rendering of a proposed rose garden by P. O. Palmstrom. Palmstrom, a children's book illustrator, was listed in Boston city directories in the 1920s as a commercial artist located at 46 Cornhill. His drawing presents a bird's-eye view of a lush, walled, perennial garden in high summer, punctuated by columnar conifers and surrounded by evergreen shrubbery. Designed as a three-season garden, Shurcliff's plan combines a broad selection of old-fashioned and hybrid rose varieties, with "climbing roses to be trained" inside and outside the walls, and clematis and honeysuckle vines cascading over the fences.[4] Spring-blooming bulbs are under-planted amidst the roses, with numerous mid-summer perennials and fall-blooming bulbs and flowers mixed in. Low, clipped, dwarf boxwood hedges delineate the beds, with four spires of evergreen at one end of the garden, and Japanese yews and dwarf pines anchoring the steps up to the house.

While the Palmstrom painting is clearly impressionistic in nature, the basic layout corresponds closely enough to the 1915 planting plan that it seems likely that it was made at the very least in response to the Shurcliff design. Although the number of existing plans suggests that Cochrane maintained interest in pursuing improvements to his Hamilton property, in fact, it is impossible to ascertain whether or not the designs were ever executed. Subsequent drawings might have been lost; however, it is just as likely that the timing of the commission decided its fate. While the United States did not enter the First World War until 1917, by 1915 the country was feeling its effects. Most households were curtailing unnecessary expenditures, and the Hamilton house was the third and least inhabited of Cochrane's dwelling places. Completed or not, P. O. Palmstrom's luxuriant painting is an elegant reminder of Shurcliff's and Cochrane's garden scheme. EHC

Bird's-eye perspective of the Alexander Cochrane garden
(one of a group of eight drawings), undated. Signed by the
delineator on the verso: "P. O. Palmstrom / 46 Cornhill /
Boston." Watercolor and graphite on wove paper; 15 × 20½".
Gift of Earle G. Shettleworth, Jr., 1995.

Parker Morse Hooper (1877–1966)

Earle Perry Charlton House, Pond Meadow,
Prospect Avenue, Westport Point, Massachusetts, 1916–18

The architect Parker Morse Hooper is perhaps best known for the Georgian-style public library, with a rounded portico and soaring cupola, in Camden, Maine. Hooper established an architectural office in New York City in 1908, where he primarily designed Georgian- and Regency-style residences in places like Glen Cove, Long Island; Detroit, Michigan; and Washington, D. C. Having been born in Fall River, Massachusetts, he also obtained commissions there as well, including ones for the city's Highland Hospital and Nursing Home and Pond Meadow, the Westport Point, Massachusetts, summer residence for Fall River industrialist Earle Perry Charlton (1863–1930).[1]

As the owner of the Charlton (cotton) Mills in Fall River, and as a pioneer in five-and-dime stores who would eventually join forces with F. W. Woolworth, Charlton had the necessary deep pockets with which to commission a substantial ashlar and slate roofed twenty-two room home for himself, his wife, Ida, and their three children (Ruth, Virginia, and Earle, Jr.).[2] A fire in 1915 destroyed the earlier wooden cottage on his twenty-two acre Westport Point estate, thus providing the opportunity for Charlton to start afresh and take advantage of a talented architect readily familiar with the region.

Parker Morse Hooper at first envisioned the Charlton residence occupying an even larger footprint than what was actually built between 1916 and 1918. The finished structure differed from the initial presentation perspective of 1915 illustrated here, with the elimination of the northeast wing which looms so large in the middle ground of the drawing. Also, according to a family friend, Charlton's wife insisted that the architect introduce dormer windows into the hipped roof in order to make the attic more habitable. Hooper at first resisted this request for aesthetic reasons, because he did not want to interrupt the sweeping profile of the roof or the pattern of the slates.[3] But Mrs. Charlton stood her ground, and by 1916, a second perspective drawing from the northwest corner of the house clearly reveals the introduction of elliptical arched dormers, as well as the elimination of the northeast wing.[4]

In order for Hooper's clients to be able to visualize more fully what he had in mind, the architect was ably assisted by the two beautifully rendered perspectives, which were drawn by one of the foremost architectural delineators working in America in the first half of the twentieth century, Otto Eggers (1886–1953).[5] Executed for Hooper when Eggers was still doing free-lance work after training at Cooper Union, the perspectivist introduced still lifes of rocks and shrubbery into the lower left foreground in both the 1915 and 1916 presentation perspectives. This arresting ambient detail introduces an Asian note that recalls the presentation drawings of Frank Lloyd Wright, published in 1910 by Ernst Wasmuth in Berlin as a two-volume portfolio. An additional Wrightian note with Asian overtones is struck by Eggers's use of a circular cipher as his signature in the lower left corner, not unlike Wright's red chop mark.

Shortly after providing the Pond Meadow perspectives for Hooper, Eggers joined forces with John Russell Pope (1874–1937).[6] Eggers's rendering style with its "perfect balance of tonal values, elegant composition and refined pencil technique," was ideally suited for showing Pope's classical buildings—like Washington's National Gallery—to their best advantage.[7] Such highly visible commissions in turn fully exposed Eggers's talents. As an architectural delineator, in 1930 Eggers became the third recipient of the Birch Burdette Long Memorial Prize, awarded by the Architectural League of New York, for his outstanding rendering skills.[8] Eventually, Eggers would be joined by such other architectural luminaries as Hugh Ferriss and Jules Guerin, making the Long Memorial Prize the Pritzker for architectural delineation.

Hooper was justifiably proud of the Charlton commission and submitted a photograph of the Eggers rendering of Pond Meadow to the Architectural League of New York's Thirty-first Annual Exhibition in 1916, when he was in a short-lived partnership with Frank C. Farley. The photograph, mounted on stiff card, still retains the Architectural League label, which simply describes the project as a "Design for Country House."[9] CM

E. P. Charlton house in 1977.

Presentation perspective of the Earle Perry Charlton house,
in original frame. Signed with delineator Otto Eggers's circular
cipher and dated 1915. Gouache, watercolor, and graphite on board;
17½ × 34½". Gift of Christopher Monkhouse in honor of Abbott
Lowell Cummings, Lorna Condon, and Elinor Reichlin for their
steadfast stewardship of Historic New England's collection of
architectural graphics, 2009.

Halfdan M. Hanson (1884–1952)

Alterations for the John B. Drake House (built ?),
Bass Rocks, Gloucester, Massachusetts, c. 1920

At a young age, Halfdan Hanson emigrated with his family from his native Norway. He was first employed as a carpenter on summer cottages in the Gloucester area, and with the patronage of one of his employers, he enrolled in architectural courses at the International Correspondence School of Philadelphia. By 1904, he was ready to begin his career. Among his first commissions was a summer residence on Eastern Point in Gloucester for Henry Davis Sleeper, an assignment that was to bring him much other work in the future. Working closely with Sleeper over the years, Hanson designed Beauport, the Sleeper-McCann House (now a Historic New England property), executing both the initial plans and its many later alterations.

In the course of his career, Hanson designed apartment houses, theaters, a hotel, offices, and the landmark Our Lady of Good Voyage church in Gloucester, but his particular specialty was the summer house. He designed numerous residences in Gloucester and in neighboring summer communities such as Beverly, Manchester, and Magnolia, as well as in the suburban town of Newton, Massachusetts. The long list of his clients indicates that he even worked with Sleeper on projects in California for movie stars John Mack Brown and Frederic March.

The alterations Hanson proposed for the Drake residence at Bass Rocks, also on Eastern Point, a sprawling one-story-plus-roof house nestled into a spectacular site overlooking the ocean, are typical of his residential work: craftsmanship details, multi-paned casement windows opening outward to the view, and flowing shallow gable roofs. This rendering shows him to have been a gifted freehand drafter. JFO'G

Perspective of the "ALTERATIONS TO COUNTRY RESIDENCE / AT BASS ROCKS / FOR JOHN B. DRAKE ESQ" (one of a group of six drawings), undated. Signed: "H M HANSON ARCHITECT / GLOUCESTER MASS." Graphite, orange pencil, and watercolor on tracing paper; 18¾ × 37¾". Gift of Phyllis Ray, Linda Ray Brayton, and Jaqueline Ray Newton, 1983.

ALTERATIONS · TO · COUNTRY · RESIDENCE ·
· AT · BASS · ROCKS ·

· FOR · JOHN · B · DRAKE · ESQ ·

· H M HANSON · ARCHITECT ·
· GLOVCESTER · MASS ·

George F. Marlowe (1877–1955)

Houses for the Gardiner Building Association (not built),
Gardiner, Maine, 1921

The three different modest frame English Colonial Revival houses appearing in George Francis Marlowe's 1921 streetscape rendering for the Gardiner Building Association in Gardiner, Maine, are probably prototypes for a planned neighborhood of workers' homes. Such groupings of inexpensive, well-designed industrial housing in Maine go back to a row of Civil War-era, Downing-style cottages built at Cumberland Mills in Westbrook by Samuel D. Warren of Boston for his papermaking employees.

In Gardiner's case, these homes likely were intended for the families of shoemakers employed by the R. P. Hazzard Company, which had enlarged its factory for a third time in 1921. By 1926, the Hazzard Company employed 1,700 men and women who produced four hundred dozen pairs of shoes each day. Regrettably, Marlowe's attractive proposal was never realized, and Gardiner's expanding population of workers was left to find their own housing.

George F. Marlowe's three prototype houses for Gardiner bear a strong resemblance to homes designed by the Boston architectural firm of Parker, Thomas and Rice for the United States Housing Corporation's Project No. 59, a large housing development constructed on the Palmer Farm in Bath, Maine, during World War I for shipbuilders at the Bath Iron Works. Consisting of eighty dwellings in four designs, the Bath project was published in the 1919 *Report of the United States Housing Corporation* and the January 1919 issue of *The Architectural Record. The*

Architectural Record's description of Bath's new neighborhood could apply equally to Marlowe's vision for Gardiner:

> . . . a well ordered and charming New England village of attractive houses. As befits the traditions of Bath, the houses are to be of wood. Although only four types of plans are used, a skillful arrangement of porches and minor details will prevent monotony and will produce a harmonious and distinctly American appearance.

Born in London, England, George F. Marlowe moved as a child with his parents to Worcester, Massachusetts, where he received his education. He began his architectural career in two prominent Boston architectural firms: Peabody and Stearns, and Andrews, Jaques and Rantoul. From 1914 to 1931, he practiced in Boston, his most notable work being the Babson Institute in Wellesley, Massachusetts. His love of New England's colonial past is reflected in his authorship of several popular books, including *The Old Bay Path* (1942), *Coaching Roads of Old New England* (1945), and *Churches of Old New England* (1947). On two of these titles, he collaborated with the noted architectural photographer Samuel Chamberlain. EGSJr

HOUSES FOR THE GARDINER BUILDING ASSOCIATION GARDINER MAINE.

Perspective of "HOUSES FOR THE GARDINER BUILDING ASSOCIATION GARDINER MAINE." Signed: "George F. Marlowe Arch't / 5-12-21." Graphite, ink, and watercolor with fixative on paper-faced paperboard (Bainbridge illustration board no. 80); 10 × 19¾". Gift of Mr. and Mrs. Donald O. Nylander, 1995.

Arthur Todhunter Company (c. 1909 – c. 1955)

*Fireplace Design for the Shore Pavilion/Beach House
at the Benjamin DeWitt Riegel Estate, Riegel Point,
Southport, Connecticut, c. 1923*

In 1913, New York City industrialist Benjamin DeWitt Riegel (1878–1941) and his wife, Leila Edmonston Riegel (1878–1966), purchased twenty acres of land on Connecticut's Gold Coast as a country retreat. During the next several years, the Riegels transformed what had been farmland into an imposing country estate. For the design of the buildings, the Riegels hired New York City architect Henry C. Pelton (1867–1935). Pelton, an 1889 graduate of Columbia's Architectural Department in the School of Mines, is known for his design, in association with Allen and Collens of Boston, of the Riverside Church in New York. The list of his firm's commissions includes other churches, hospitals, schools, apartment buildings, townhouses, office buildings, factories, and numerous residences in southern Connecticut, especially Greenwich. For the Riegels, Pelton created a twenty-eight-room, 16,000-square-foot, Tudor Revival main house and a "shore pavilion" or beach house. That Pelton took pride in the Riegel commission is evident from a 1925 promotional publication, *Henry C. Pelton, Architect, New York City*, in which the Riegel estate is presented first among numerous other commissions.

To design the grounds of their estate, the Riegels hired landscape architect Armand R. Tibbitts (1891–1987). No expense was spared to create the remarkable landscape: twenty-two freight cars of boxwood were delivered from the South, elm trees were transplanted, and garden ornaments were imported from Europe.

Construction of the main house and the beach house began in 1922, the beach house being finished first. By May 1923, the family was ready to furnish the beach house and commissioned F. N. Dowling Company of New York to undertake the decoration. F. N. Dowling, founded in 1896, specialized in "Architectural Interiors, Period Furniture, Antiques, Panelling, Painting, Curtains." Throughout the next several years, F. N. Dowling provided all of these items and services to the Riegels, both for the estate in Southport and the New York residence. For the beach house, the company supplied curtains, furniture (antique and contemporary), rugs, lamps, and so on. It seems that Dowling went to a subcontractor, the Arthur Todhunter Company of New York, for the fireplace accessories.

Arthur Todhunter came to the United States from Britain in 1909 and established a business selling imported woodwork, hardware, and fireplace equipment. Eventually, he began to offer for sale reproduction mantels and woodwork produced in the United States. By 1918, his ads in *House and Garden* offered "Fine Reproductions," "Early English and Colonial [mantels]," and "Fireplace Accessories of Unusual and Interesting Design." His clientele for reproduction mantels grew to include architects and decorators from throughout the United States, including Little and Browne whose work is discussed elsewhere in this catalogue.

The Todhunter Company probably created the elevation of the beach house fireplace to present to the Riegels for approval. It seems clear that the Riegels accepted the design, for on 2 May 1923, Benjamin Riegel received an invoice from F. N. Dowling in the amount of $416 for: "One pair Andirons with log and spit bars; One ash curb to fit under screen; One pair tongues [sic], one brush, one fork and one shovel; One plate to hold three firetools; One wrought iron crane; One bellows; One fireback; One trivet." The items on the list match those shown in the drawing.

The Riegel/Emory Family Papers at Historic New England include hundreds of drawings and thousands of photographs and other records pertaining to the property. They document the many different contributors—architect, builder, decorator, specialist—involved in creating an estate such as the one at Riegel Point. LC

TOP: *The Riegel estate with beach house in the right foreground, about 1925.* BOTTOM: *Interior of the beach house about 1924.*

Elevation of the beach house fireplace at the Riegel estate,
undated. Signed: "ARTHUR TODHUNTER / NEW YORK
CITY." Black ink, watercolor, and graphite on tracing paper;
18½ × 22". Gift of Benjamin R. Emory, Lucy E. Ambach,
Katherine E. Stookey, and Leila E. Baldwin, 2001.

Coolidge and Carlson (1903–1922 and beyond)

J. Randolph Coolidge, Jr. (1862–1928)
Harry J. Carlson (1869–1957)

Minerva Davis House,
Main Street, Agawam, Massachusetts, 1923

Perspective of "HOUSE FOR MRS. MINERVA DAVIS AGAWAM
MASS." Signed: "COOLIDGE & CARLSON ARCHT'S." and
initialed and dated by the delineator: "J.E.C. 23" (probably
John E. Carlson). Graphite and colored pencil, possibly with
fixative overall, on wove paper; 12¾ × 16¹⁵⁄₁₆". Library and
Archives purchase, 1971.

Minerva Davis house about 1926.

Coolidge and Carlson (1903–1922 and beyond)
Minerva Davis House

By the 1920s, the gambrel-roof house became one of the iconic symbols of the English Colonial Revival-style suburban house, widely popularized through magazines and mail-order catalogues. At its best, the gambrel-roof form continued the lineage begun in the late nineteenth century with the Shingle Style. Although the form provides a full two stories, its low silhouette blends comfortably in a semi-rural suburban landscape.

J. Randolph Coolidge, Jr., began his adult career as an investment banker with Lee, Higginson and Company. Following his natural inclinations, Coolidge abandoned the business world to train as an architect, first at MIT, and then at the Ecole des Beaux-Arts in Paris. After practicing on his own from 1898 to 1903, he took on another MIT graduate, Harry J. Carlson, as a partner. Although the firm specialized in buildings for prestigious colleges (e.g., Harvard, Bates, Wellesley, Hamilton), domestic suburban work figured prominently in its portfolio.[1]

The house for Mrs. Minerva Davis, built in Agawam, is located in a suburban community outside Springfield, Massachusetts. The architects provided designs for the public library that Mrs. Davis funded for Agawam in 1924, and she probably had the house built at the same time.

The perspective view from the rear, probably the work of Carlson's son, John E. Carlson, illustrates the continued importance of landscaping in the ideal suburban setting. A glazed porch extends perpendicularly from the back of the house, which looks out onto a small formal garden framed by low hedges. Garden trellises with vines provide a small allée from the door at the end of the porch.

The house still stands, but in a design modified by the architects, and perhaps altered later as well. As published in *The Architectural Record* in 1926,[2] it lacks the low gambrel-roof wing on one end, and there is a garden structure on the other end. No view of the rear matching the drawing has been located. Other differences include a single, large central chimney rather than the two chimney stacks shown in the drawing. RGR

Walter F. Bogner (1899–1993) and A. W. Kenney Billings, Jr. (1901–1955)

Carl H. White Guest House,
Bennington, Vermont, c. 1928

In 1926, New Jersey businessman Carl White purchased a sixty-one-acre farm in his hometown of Bennington, Vermont, with the intention of creating a country estate. He hired Boston architects Walter Bogner and A. W. Kenney Billings, Jr., to design all the buildings, which included a farm complex and a "mansion group" with main house, guest house, and garage. For his residence, White chose a spectacular site at the crest of a hill overlooking the surrounding countryside and the Taconic Range to the north. Bogner and Billings designed the buildings in the English country style. The grounds included elaborate gardens, scenic roadways, and a one-acre swimming pond designed by landscape architect Bremer W. Pond. The original drawings for the estate are lost; only this elevation of the modest guest house survives.

The nine-room guest house was intended to be the temporary residence of Carl White and his wife, Anne, until the mansion was completed. The guest house was conceived as a traditional English cottage with architectural features popular during the first half of the twentieth century, when the Tudor Revival style was at the height of popularity. The principal façade is dominated by a massive molded chimney crowned with decorative chimney pots. The exterior walls are whitewashed brick, intended to be planted with vines. The cottage was designed to be approached from both the south (front) and west; the latter perspective features a steep gabled end, a hallmark of the Tudor Revival style. Bogner included a tiny representation of the west elevation at the lower right of the drawing. A surviving copy of an interior sketch by Bogner and a period newspaper description provide clues about the guest house interior. A dramatic wooden ceiling supported by decorative arched trusses soared to the full height of the structure. The walls were a combination of salvaged pine paneling and plaster "in the old English handplastering effect." A one-and-a-half-story bay window contained French doors that provided access to the terraces overlooking the valley and distant hills.

Why Carl White chose Bogner and Billings as architects is unknown. The two young architects had just established their practices, and this project was likely among their first large commissions. Bogner's drawing of the White guest house demonstrates the hand of a skilled artist and experienced draftsman. He had been awarded the coveted Rotch Traveling Fellowship in architecture and spent two years studying the ancient buildings of Europe. The impressive collection of drawings and watercolor paintings he produced during this period between 1925 and 1926 are testament to his skill. In 1929, he returned to Harvard, where he had studied, to teach a class on the elements of architecture. Years later, he would support the shift in philosophy at Harvard to Modern design, abandon the traditional approach of his training and early work, and become a well-known proponent of "new" architecture in the 1930s.

In the summer of 1928, Carl and Anne White learned they were expecting their first child. Tragically, only three weeks after the birth of their son in January 1929, Anne White died. At this time, several of the farm buildings, a six-car garage, and the pond were under construction, but only the guest house was near completion. Four years later, Carl White committed suicide, stating in a note concern over meeting financial obligations.

The original elevation for the guest house, copies of three associated drawings, and several photographs were retained by Walter Bogner throughout his life. At some point, Carl White's name was erased from the drawing; the project records at Historic New England are simply identified as "An Estate at Bennington, Vermont." PG

Bird's-eye view of the White estate by Walter Bogner, about 1929.

Carl White guest house about 1929.

Elevations of "Guest house," undated. Signed: "W F BOGNER & /
A W K BILLINGS ARCHITECTS" and "Bogner," as delineator.
Graphite and watercolor, possibly with fixative overall, on tracing
paper; 10¼ × 16". Gift of the Bogner Family, 2009.

Bigelow, Wadsworth, Hubbard and Smith (c. 1928–1930)

Henry Forbes Bigelow (1867–1929)
Philip Wadsworth (1881–1961)
Edward A. Hubbard (1889–1966)
Giles M. Smith (1885–1950)

Unidentified House at Northeast Harbor, Maine, c. 1929

This short-lived association of Beacon Street architects grew out of the partnership of Henry Bigelow and Philip Wadsworth. It included men trained at MIT (and, in Wadsworth's case, at Harvard and the Ecole des Beaux-Arts in Paris). The client remains unidentified, and the house was apparently never built. Northeast Harbor, on Mount Desert Island, had developed as a fashionable enclave for affluent fair-weather residents after the Civil War, when the region began to sprout Shingle Style and English Colonial Revival vacationland "cottages" along its rugged coast. The boom lasted until the stock market crash of 1929—about the time this house was designed—which was perhaps the reason the project was abandoned. In this close-up angled view of the asymmetrical driveway approach, the rambling house is broken into intimately scaled building blocks, and seems to warmly embrace the visitor. The artist's soft-pencil free strokes enhance the snug domesticity of the ensemble. The rich wood and brick composition of chimneys, gables, clapboards, overhangs with pendants, archways, and entrance topped with a swan-neck pediment is characteristic of the English Colonial Revival of the 1920s. This drawing and another for the same project in Historic New England's Library and Archives were prepared for display at an annual exhibition at the Architectural League of New York. JFO'G

Perspective of entrance court (one of two sheets), undated. Signed by the delineator: "F[ull?]." Identified on original mat as: "HOUSE AT NORTHEAST HARBOR, MAINE / BIGELOW WADSWORTH HUBBARD & SMITH ARCHTS / BOSTON, MASS." Charcoal and graphite on laid ("Lalanna") paper; 18¾ × 12⁷⁄₁₆". Library and Archives purchase, 1995.

Arland A. Dirlam (1905–1979)

Mrs. Arland A. Dirlam House (built?),
Jerry Jingle Highway, Stoneham, Massachusetts, 1935

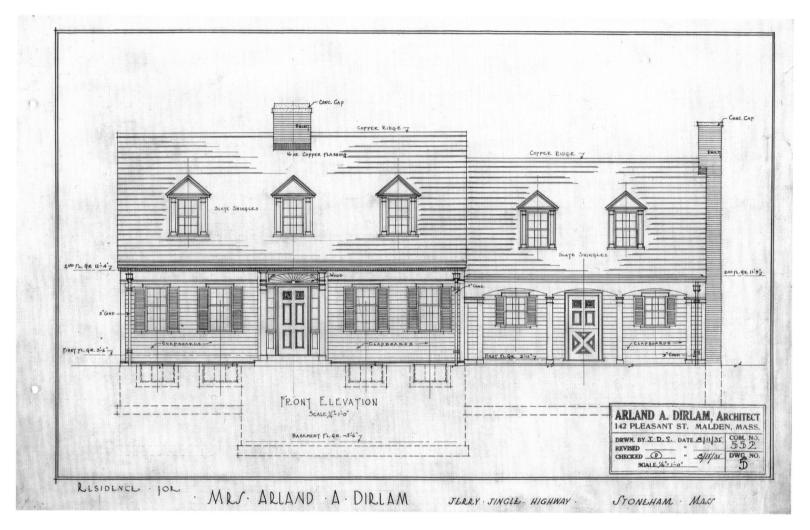

"FRONT ELEVATION" of "RESIDENCE FOR / MRS. ARLAND A. DIRLAM
JERRY JINGLE HIGHWAY STONEHAM MASS" (number five in a set
of eighteen sheets). Stamped: "ARLAND A. DIRLAM, ARCHITECT /
142 PLEASANT ST. MALDEN, MASS." Signed and dated in stamp block:
"J.D.S. 8/11/35." Black and red ink and black ink stamp on starch-coated
fabric; 13¼ × 21¼". Gift of Mrs. Arland A. (Grace) Dirlam, 1983.

"¾ DETAIL OF FRONT DOOR & DORMER" of "RESIDENCE FOR /
MRS. ARLAND A. DIRLAM JERRY JINGLE HIGHWAY STONEHAM
MASS" (number eight in a set of eighteen sheets). Stamped:
"ARLAND A. DIRLAM, ARCHITECT / 142 PLEASANT ST. MALDEN,
MASS." Signed and dated in stamp block: "J.D.S. 8/15/35." Black
and red ink and black ink stamp on starch-coated fabric; 21 × 13".
Gift of Mrs. Arland A. (Grace) Dirlam, 1983.

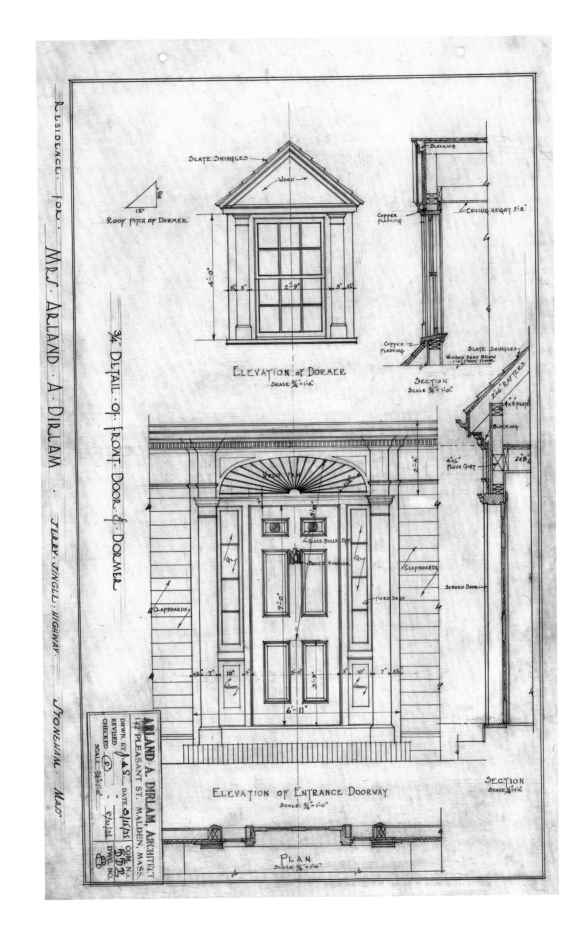

RESIDENCE · FOR · MRS · ARLAND · A · DIRLAM · JERRY · JINGLE · HIGHWAY · STONEHAM · MASS

¾" DETAIL · OF · FRONT · DOOR · & · DORMER

SLATE SHINGLES
WOOD
ROOF PITCH OF DORMER
BLOCKING
CEILING HEIGHT 7'-8"
COPPER FLASHING

ELEVATION OF DORMER
SCALE ¾" = 1'-0"

COPPER FLASHING
SLATE SHINGLES
WINDOW SEAT BELOW 1'-6" FROM FLOOR

SECTION
SCALE ¾" = 1'-0"

2"x6" RAFTERS
4"x4" PLATE
BLOCKING
4"x6" FLUSH GIRT
2"x8"

WOOD FAN
GLASS BULLS EYE
BRASS KNOCKER
GL
FIXED SASH
CLAPBOARDS
SCREEN DOOR
GL
CLAPBOARDS
WOOD
WOOD

6'-11"

ELEVATION OF ENTRANCE DOORWAY
SCALE ¾" = 1'-0"

SECTION
SCALE ¾" = 1'-0"

PLAN
SCALE ¾" = 1'-0"

ARLAND · A · DIRLAM, ARCHITECT
142 PLEASANT ST. MALDEN, MASS.
DRWN. BY J.A.S.   DATE 2/16/35
REVISED
CHECKED   P   COM. NO. 5D2
SCALE ¾" = 1'-0"   DWG. NO.

197

Arland A. Dirlam (1905–1979)
Mrs. Arland A. Dirlam House (built?)

Arland Dirlam was born in Somerville, Massachusetts, attended Tufts University in Medford, Massachusetts, for whose campus he later designed a number of buildings. After travels and special study at the Ecole des Beaux-Arts in Paris and the American Academy in Rome, he earned a Master of Architecture degree at Harvard. In 1931, he established his own practice in Malden, Massachusetts. During a long and distinguished career, in which his firm worked on more than one thousand projects, he gained a reputation primarily as an ecclesiastical architect, designing dozens of churches throughout New England, including award-winning Park Place Congregational Church in Pawtucket, Rhode Island, and University Church in Cambridge, Massachusetts. Among his many offices was the presidency of the Church Architectural Guild of America. In 1954, Dirlam contributed a chapter on ecclesiastical architecture to a collection of essays titled *Religious Symbolism.*

Dirlam's office, like any modern full-service firm, found time to turn out other building types, including residential projects like this small English Colonial–Federal Revival house—apparently designed for his own use but perhaps never erected. Executed by one of the draftsmen, identified only with the initials "J. D. S.," the accomplished line work on these sheets is representative of the best traditional drafting-table graphics of the period. They are skilled renderings of the standard American dream home. Joy Wheeler Dow, in his book *American Renaissance* (1904), championed such designs as rooted in what he considered the American tradition, as embodying "Anglo-Saxon home-feeling" in contrast to what he snubbed as "newly invented architecture." The home builder's repertory today continues to favor the English Colonial Revival style. JFO'G

David J. Abrahams (1901–1958)

Unidentified Suburban House, 1940s

David Abrahams trained at MIT (Class of 1922), worked in the office of the William J. L. Roop Corporation (1923–26), during which time he designed Mr. Roop's own small house, then set out on his own busy practice. He was active in local chapters of the American Institute of Architects and served as Director of the Boston Architectural Center. His firm was responsible for a number of commercial buildings as well as local synagogues. He died of a heart attack after attending the ground-breaking of his Temple Emanu-El in Marblehead, Massachusetts.

Abrahams's much-published residential work in the surroundings of Boston during the 1930s and 1940s, for which he often won awards, exemplifies the transitional character of that period in twentieth-century American architecture. It ranges from the English Colonial Revival of the J. Marshall Hubbard house in West Harwich (1938) to the neo-Federal design of the Harriet Wood house in Melrose (1935) to the Moderne for Robert Frazier in Winchester (1938), all in Massachusetts. And it includes at least two International Style proposals. One, a dream project for "postwar living" planned for a Newton, Massachusetts, site that was published as a perspective drawing in the *Architectural Record* for July 1944, parallels in its stark geometry the European Modernism imported to this country by Walter Gropius and others. Such houses assume boxy forms wrapped in textureless wall surfaces opened by horizontal strips of sharply incised windows. They lack ornament and achieve three dimensions by the manipulation of volumes. In Abrahams's hands, however, in both the published drawing and in the one shown here, the design was regionalized by the use of local materials, by firmly setting the house on the ground, and by the presence of stone walls connecting it to the surrounding landscape. The rounded corners used sparingly here were often seen on works in the early years of Modern design, a nod, perhaps, to contemporary streamlining.

Colored pencil over photomechanical printing appeared in the transitional period of early Modernism as a medium that combined the hand and the machine. The use of bright colors bathed in sunshine seems intended to romanticize the design, to take away the bleached starkness of the forms that many then perceived as an undesirable aspect of such Modern residences. JFO'G

Perspective of an unidentified suburban house, undated. Stamped: "DAVID J. ABRAHAMS / ARCHITECT / 260 TREMONT STREET / BOSTON MASSACHUSETTS." Signed by the delineator: "RL[?]B." Colored pencil and graphite applied to a photomechanical image printed on thin paper; 14 × 24". Gift of Jean S. and Frederic A. Sharf, 2005.

Henry B. Hoover (1903–1989)

Henry B. Hoover House,
Trapelo Road, Lincoln, Massachusetts, 1937

Aside from its remarkable quality, Henry Hoover's small, assured pencil sketch depicting his proposed house in the late afternoon sunlight is notable for several themes that it represents in the story of New England architecture. When completed two years later, the Hoover house became the first Modern residence in Lincoln, inaugurating a period when that community was one of the leading incubators of Modernism in America. In fact, Hoover's purchase of this hillside site in February 1934 and this sketch of July 1935 place him in the forefront of the experimentation that introduced such Modernism not only to Lincoln, but to New England as a region.

An additional level of significance derives from the fact that Hoover's proposed house was also the first instance of a Modern architect choosing Lincoln as the community in which to live and build his own home, a trend soon followed by Walter Gropius, Marcel Breuer, Walter Bogner, G. Holmes Perkins, and many others.

Hoover's placement of a bold International Style residence in a verdant landscape with a living court, fountain, and flanking garden wall, illustrates his unique ability to bring together nature and the Modern house, which was fostered during his lengthy experience working in the field of landscape architecture.

Finally, the drama of this design's expansively glazed, south-facing living room reveals Hoover's embrace and extension of an often overlooked Modernist plan concept (following historical precedents): the placement of a residence so that one approaches from the north and passes through a largely blank entrance façade—often concealing vestibule, corridor, closet, and powder room—to discover the sunlight, the main living spaces, an outdoor south-facing terrace, and, in an optimal location like this one, a distant view beyond.

Born in Iowa, raised in Idaho, and educated as an undergraduate architectural student at the University of Washington in Seattle, Henry Hoover enrolled in Harvard's School of Architecture in 1924. While there, he embarked on an unusual career path, working not for an architect but for a landscape architect, Fletcher Steele (in whose office he was still employed at the time of this drawing a decade later). Upon graduation, Hoover won the first Eugene Dodd Medal for excellence in freehand drawing and watercolor, and then landed successive traveling fellowships that took him to Europe for the next two years.

Hoover's extended stay in Steele's small office coincided with Steele's interest in and experimentation with Modernist landscape design, about which Steele published and lectured (and which elicited the admiration of the young Dan Kiley, Garrett Ekbo, and James Rose, all future Modernists). Although the interaction and the intertwined responsibilities and influences between Steele and Hoover remain open to speculation, Steele biographer Robin Karson wrote that "The scope, quality and sheer quantity of Hoover's work were notable (even for the period) and marked a considerable change in Steele's office procedures." Steele "looked to him for new ideas . . . letting him develop designs at his own pace and rework them according to his own judgment." Among the sites where the young architect had a hand in shaping aspects of concept and detail are Naumkeag, in Stockbridge, Massachusetts, with its iconic blue stairs and sweeping Modernist handrails, and the amphitheater at the public library in Camden, Maine, with its orientation to the water.

Although the built version of Hoover's house would be less dramatic in both its glazing and its structure than this early sketch—and subsequently would be modified by Hoover in a well-designed expansion and revision of 1955—this drawing nevertheless conveys a key characteristic of the architect's designs over a long, prolific career: the fragmentary openness of the house to the landscape. In fact, with its chimney towering above two isolated panels of brick wall, the large voids at the center and corners of the house (latticed with steel-framed windows), and its freestanding piece of garden wall, this drawing suggests a picturesque ruin as seen in the late eighteenth-century sketches of Hubert Robert. GW

Henry B. Hoover house about 1940.

Perspective of "VIEW FROM LIVING COURT / HOUSE OF HENRY
B. HOOVER / AT LINCOLN MASSACHUSETTS." Signed and dated:
"H. B. HOOVER ARCHITECT JULY 1935." Graphite with ink spot
on tracing paper; 7½ × 8". Promised gift of the Family of Henry
B. Hoover: Henry B. Hoover, Jr., Lucretia Hoover Giese, and
Elizabeth Hoover Norman, 2009.

Henry B. Hoover (1903–1989)

Terrace for the Edgar Moor House,
Tabor Knoll, Lincoln, Massachusetts, 1964 (demolished)

Relatively few architects of the Modern era were capable of rendering so effectively the lush variegated foliage that Henry Hoover creates as a background for the minimal geometry of this garden terrace. Representing the pavilion that he designed for the Moor house and garden, this modestly-sized tour de force of pencil draftsmanship could hold its own with the luxuriant, legendary drawings of two Modernists of the previous generation, Frank Lloyd Wright and Marion Mahony.

Rather than depicting the entire garden in perspective, Hoover cuts a cross section through the sloping hillside and terrace for a more conceptual representation, without the pavilion's forecourt, planting beds, and flanking walls. His masterful stippling of the forest serves to foreground the simple architectonic insertions: a thin horizontal roof floats before the deeply shaded canopy of the forest, and a long blank fragment of wall rises from the hill, breaks back to pass behind the fountain and pavilion, and terminates abruptly on the slope at a point that leaves the pavilion off center.

The pavilion's shadows reveal that its roof is open above the fountain and its basin. Slender columns are rendered with fine shading that demonstrates Hoover's precise handwork (as well as his acute eyesight!). These are 3½" diameter steel pipe columns that the architect often used (at times in combination with other posts as slender as 2¼" in diameter and with 1¼" diameter steel handrails). The wall's faint coursing suggests its concrete-block material, which, as built, was well detailed in standard Hoover fashion, being given a cast, reinforced-concrete cap.

It is instructive to compare this drawing's dramatic juxtaposition of abstract minimalism and rich natural scenery to that of an iconic representation of a Modern residence, the well-known photomontage that Mies van der Rohe's students created to depict the proposed Resor house in Jackson Hole, Wyoming. Their cutting and pasting of a photograph of the mountainous landscape onto a spare line drawing of the house's floor and ceiling makes a memorable image (while it avoids the necessity for skillful rendering). In terms of the structures being illustrated in the two drawings, the Resor house surely would have sacrificed livability for its extreme simplification. By contrast, Hoover is paring down a garden pavilion, not a residence. His houses themselves tend to avoid such minimal enclosure and simplicity, and often assume more complex forms: L-shaped plans shaping an exterior court, splaying wings responding to the topography or solar orientation, roof heights varying to accommodate the uses of the rooms within.

With respect to Hoover's design approach, even this minimal pavilion with its square plan is a hybrid, not a pure form: the floating roof is supported by full-height columns for the most part, but at the back wall, four short post extensions rise from the wall along the rear column line, whereas in a more polemical design the wall might have run amidst an unbroken column grid or else might have supported the roof directly.

Known as Tabor Knoll, Hoover's pavilion, garden, and house were all demolished in the 1990s. GW

The Moor terrace in 1992.

Within the drawing, handwritten: MR. EDGAR MOOR / TABOR KNOLL - END OF TERRACE   1/8" = 1'-0"

Rendered elevation, identified as: "MR. EDGAR MOOR /
TABOR KNOLL – END OF TERRACE," undated and unsigned.
Graphite on tracing paper; 8⅜ × 11". Gift of the Family of
Henry B. Hoover: Henry B. Hoover, Jr., Lucretia Hoover
Giese, and Elizabeth Hoover Norman, 2009.

Henry B. Hoover (1903–1989)

Mr. and Mrs. Everett A. Black House,
Mine Brook Road, Lincoln, Massachusetts, 1968

Henry Hoover's Black House appears in this rendering as a glass and wood enclosure with terraces and steel railings, set above and cantilevered beyond a nearly solid base, to which stairs lead up from grade. The deeply shaded floor-to-ceiling glazing of the upper level emphasizes its openness. A mysterious light panel that appears off center in the living room hints at one of the unique features of this sizable house: an open atrium at the heart of the building.

Hoover orchestrated a complexity of built form and open elements at this house, including a panoply of in-between spaces that mediate between the full enclosure of the house itself and the surrounding open landscape. A partially covered porte cochere spans between garage and storage sheds at the north (on the far side of the house in this drawing). Inside the house, a solid wall conceals the unexpected outdoor atrium. On the other side of the atrium are the main interior living spaces, from which the balcony extends to overlook the landscape.

To the east, on the main floor, the master bedroom suite has its own balcony (now enclosed). To the west are service spaces, a patio, and pool. The narrow windows of the base identify the children's bedrooms. (In the design as built, larger windows appear in what became a wood-framed lower level.)

This drawing's depiction of a base—presumably of masonry—below the raised volumes of the main floor suggests the similar theme found in Hoover's grand Shearer house in New Hampshire (1955), with its extensive use of locally quarried granite for walls, stairs, foundations, and terraces. The stonework there recalls the heavy base of an old mill or of an archaeological discovery, upon which an airy modern structure has been perched. While the most simplified version of this concept may have been Philip Johnson's Wiley house of 1953, where a steel and glass box sits across a stone plinth, Hoover's more complicated forms respond both to the site and to the functions that are housed within.

Design revisions made after this drawing would reverse the orientation of the roof, so that the low gable slopes to the sides instead of to the front and back. Also, four wide shallow piers were located at the edge of the balcony—seeming to be segments of a mostly missing wall—to support the thin roof above, where they emphasize the outer plane of the projecting balcony. Such fragments of wall deliberately frame the view instead of letting the panoramic landscape run by without interruption. GW

Mr. and Mrs. Everett A. Black house in 1979.

ELEVATION TOWARD SWAMP
⅛"=1'

MR. AND MRS. EVERETT A. BLACK   HOUSE IN LINCOLN, MASSACHUSETTS

Rendered elevation of "MR. AND MRS. EVERETT A. BLACK /
HOUSE IN LINCOLN, MASSACHUSETTS / ELEVATION
TOWARD SWAMP." Signed and dated: "Henry B. Hoover 9/68."
Graphite and stamp on tracing paper; 17⅛ × 22". Gift of the
Family of Henry B. Hoover: Henry B. Hoover, Jr., Lucretia
Hoover Giese, and Elizabeth Hoover Norman, 2009.

Royal Barry Wills (1895–1962)

Illustration for Better Houses for Budgeteers *(revised edition, 1946)*
by Royal Barry Wills, Architect, c. 1940

Perspective, undated. Signed: "Royal Barry Wills / Architect."
Gouache and charcoal on green laid paper; 18¾ × 25½".
Gift of Royal Barry Wills Associates, 2009.

Dr. John Dreyfus House,
Adams Street, Quincy, Massachusetts, 1954

Perspective, undated. Signed: "RBW." Graphite and
colored pencil on thin paper; 20 × 31½". Gift of Royal
Barry Wills Associates, 2009.

Royal Barry Wills (1895–1962)
Illustration for Better Houses for Budgeteers *(revised edition, 1946)*
by Royal Barry Wills, Architect, c. 1940

Dr. John Dreyfus House

Throughout a career that lasted from 1925 until his death, Royal Barry Wills swam boldly against the tide of canonical architectural history. He trained as an engineer at MIT (Class of 1918), worked as a design engineer for Turner Construction Company, then struck out on his own as an architect. Despite his technical background, he largely eschewed the Modernist design revolution raging all around him. A native New Englander, he devoted himself almost exclusively to domestic commissions, focusing on regional variations of the English Colonial Revival, and especially the suburban Cape Cod cottage. His output was large, and his publications many. Despite the fact that he worked in what some critics thought of as a reactionary mode, *Life* magazine in 1946 dubbed him "the nation's most popular architectural author," and the American Institute of Architects elected him a Fellow in 1954. His successful practice, which survives into the present under the direction of his son, Richard Wills, represents a viable chapter in a comprehensive history of twentieth-century American architecture that has yet to be written.

The large vibrant perspective of the Dreyfus house in Quincy well exemplifies Wills's approach to domestic design and architectural presentation. A quick, colored pencil rendering signed with the architect's large, scrawled initials, it depicts a traditional suburban house wrapped around a huge beech tree. The stone, shingle, and vertical board exterior is capped by low, broad gabled forms that press the spreading L-shaped plan onto its site. Such a presentation exemplifies David Gebard's characterization of the drawings of this period as "loose and free, suggesting the architect's . . . romantic effort to symbolize a nonurban world."

Wills promoted himself and his work through several popular books, one of which was *Better Houses for Budgeteers* (1941; revised and enlarged 1946), a work whose discussion of the "minimum plan" anticipated in more frugal times the "not-so-big-house" movement of recent years. Wills reproduced in that publication this drawing of a snug two-bedroom Cape Cod cottage for a family with income in the vicinity of $4,000 a year. Its principal rooms are arranged mostly on one floor joined to a one-car garage by an arcaded porch. A stairway (to a guest room or storage area) divides living and sleeping areas. Spaces are tight, but Wills, consistent with his love of the aura of the colonial, insists on a fireplace in the living room even in minimum plans such as this, for "a house without one is as soulless as a man bereft of humanity." Such a fireplace also produced the

massive chimney that crowns the exterior gable. The book includes pages of illustrated "dollar savers."

This drawing shows the white-painted shingle exterior dramatically highlighted. It was rendered for reproduction in sharp contrast of charcoal and gouache on green paper, called "easy on the eyes" by one reviewer, which may have been at least partially dictated by the production process. JFO'G

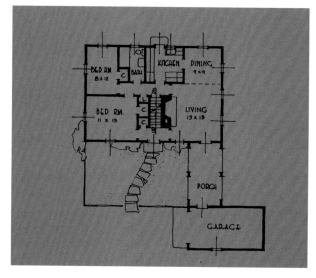

TOP: *John Dreyfus house.* BOTTOM: *Floor plan reproduced from* Better Houses for Budgeteers.

Stanley B. Parker (1881–1965)

Design for a Gazebo with Parts Salvaged from
38 Quincy Street, Cambridge, Massachusetts, 1951

Stanley Brampton Parker, an architect in Boston and Cambridge and author of two books on linear perspective, produced this drawing in 1951, during the controversy over Harvard University's intended demolition of the Lieutenant Charles Henry Davis house at 38 Quincy Street.

In 1950, Harvard University announced plans to raze two houses on Quincy Street to construct a Modernist lecture hall designed by Jean Paul Carlihan of Shepley, Coolidge, Richardson and Abbott. Many alumni, already in shock over the appearance of Walter Gropius's Graduate Center (1949), erupted in anger at this further assault on Harvard's architectural traditions. However, the architectural historian Denys P. Myers (Class of 1940) raised a different concern, calling 38 Quincy Street "the most charming example of Romanticism in nineteenth century domestic architecture still extant in Cambridge . . . a felicitous and quite sophisticated blend of Italianate, Gothic and classic elements." He pointed out that the university had recently destroyed a house of greater architectural merit to move the "rather commonplace" Dana-Palmer house. He noted that "appreciation for our nineteenth century domestic architecture is still too rare, and the attitude of the university . . . is sadly evidenced by the failure to carry out even a minimal restoration of Memorial Hall tower." Finally, he urged that if the house could not be moved, it should be recorded in measured drawings and photographs.

When the university proved deaf to Myers's pleas, Cambridge architect Stanley B. Parker offered to salvage some of the fragments of 38 Quincy Street for a gazebo that he hoped to construct at his summer house in Plymouth, Massachusetts; he apparently prepared this drawing to support his request. The university agreed, and there is photographic evidence that some architectural details were removed when the house was demolished in 1951. However, there is no evidence that the proposed gazebo was ever built, and the fragments have seemingly disappeared.

Thirty-eight Quincy Street was one of several houses designed by the leading early academic designer in Cambridge, the idiosyncratic Henry Greenough (1807–1883). Greenough was a brother of sculptors Horatio and Richard Greenough and grew up in an artistic family in Jamaica Plain, Massachusetts. After withdrawing from Harvard in 1826, Henry worked in his father's real estate business and supplied designs for his father's buildings, although nothing is known of his training in architecture or building. A talented dilettante, Greenough designed seven houses in Cambridge between 1844 and 1856, while spending long periods in Europe; he was fortunate in having eleven siblings and several former classmates to provide him with commissions. He also designed the Cambridge Athenaeum in 1851 and collaborated with George Snell on the Museum of Comparative Zoology in 1859.

Stanley Parker had a checkered academic career. Harvard admitted him with conditions in English, German, and French, but placed him on academic probation in the spring of his freshman year. He left college in 1903, having earned his only consistently good grades in his architecture courses. His talent for drawing must have stood him in good stead, however, because he found a position in the office of Cram, Goodhue and Ferguson in the fall of 1903. He then worked as a draftsman for several other prestigious Boston architects, including Guy Lowell (1904–07), Allen W. Jackson (1907–09), and James Purdon (1909–13), firms that specialized in high-end residential commissions and buildings for institutions.

In 1913, Parker entered the firm of Charles M. Baker, an MIT-trained architect who specialized in designing schools and public buildings and remodeling colonial houses. Parker left Baker's office in 1918 to join Albert Farwell Bemis's town planning and design firm, The Housing Company, which planned and built emergency housing estates during World War I.

After the war, Parker opened an office in Boston, and wrote that he designed "small office buildings, school houses, swimming pools, gymnasiums, one theatre . . . but mostly dwelling houses" in the early Georgian Revival style, from which "I have not felt at liberty to depart more than occasionally."[1] He spent eighteen years in the office of William T. Aldrich, a Boston architect whose many prestigious commissions included the Worcester Art Museum, the Rhode Island School of Design, and many country houses. Aldrich also taught at Harvard's School of Architecture, the Rhode Island School of Design, and the School of the Museum of Fine Arts, and evidently he assigned Parker to research the geometry of linear perspective. The Harvard University Press published Parker's book, *The Vertical Vanishing Point in Linear Perspective,* in 1947.

During World War II, Parker found a surprising use for his drawing skills. The Radio Research Laboratory at Harvard employed him to develop "the orthogonal perspective of various confidential experiments in radar countermeasures." Parker closed out his career designing alterations and additions for private clients and completing a few commissions for Harvard University, of which the most significant was the Eda Kuhn Loeb Music Library, Harvard's last Georgian Revival building in Cambridge (1955). CMS

Detail of Apron

Plan

Roof Framing

Elevation

Section

Scale in feet

~ GAZEBO ~ POSTS AND APRON SALVAGED FROM SIDE PORCH AT 38 QUINCY ST. C

38 Quincy Street, Cambridge, Massachusetts, about 1947.

Perspective, plans, elevation, section, and details of "GAZEBO — POSTS AND APRON SALVAGED FROM SIDE PORCH AT 38 QUINCY ST. CAMBRIDGE / HENRY GREENOUGH /ARCH'T (1807–1883)." Signed and dated: "SP del. April 1951." Graphite, watercolor, gouache, and black ink stamp on paper-faced wood pulp board; 15⅜ × 23⅝". Library and Archives purchase, 2006.

Walter P. Crabtree, Jr. (1899–1975)

Colonial Apartments (not built),
Newtown, Connecticut, c. 1960

Walter Crabtree, Jr., studied at Syracuse University and the Yale School of Architecture and probably also trained with his father (1873–1962). He practiced in the Hartford area for forty-five years, designing schools and hospitals among other public works. All three of his sons (Malcolm, Walter III, and John) became architects.

The technique here is characteristic of renderings of commercial projects of the period. Crabtree's delineator created this large, overly dramatic one-point perspective, with the attached houses seen through the dark foliage frame spotlighted by sunshine, to sell a rather ordinary communal residential complex in a vaguely neocolonial style. The project, apparently intended for a site on Main Street in Newtown, was never realized. The cars and the "Marilyn Monroe" figure in the foreground point to a date in the late 1950s or early 1960s. JFO'G

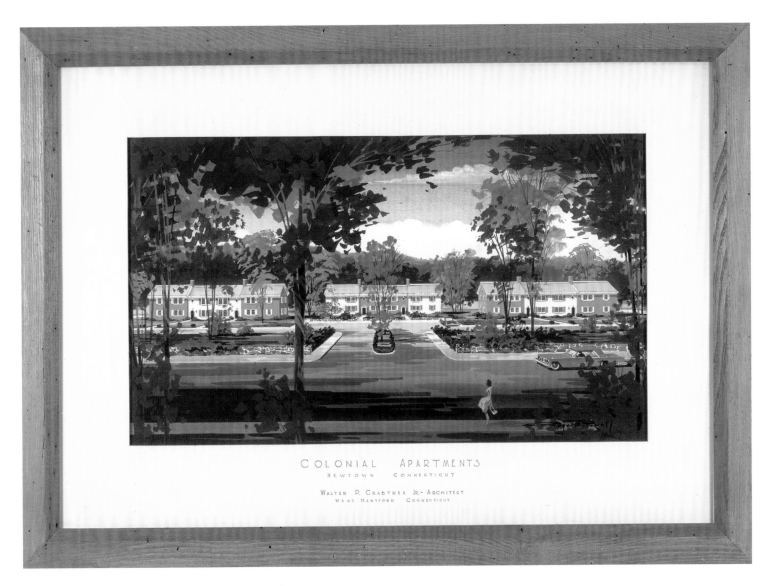

COLONIAL APARTMENTS
NEWTOWN CONNECTICUT

WALTER P. CRABTREE JR.- ARCHITECT
WEST HARTFORD CONNECTICUT

Presentation perspective in original frame, undated. Identified
on original mat as: "COLONIAL APARTMENTS / NEWTOWN
CONNECTICUT / WALTER P CRABTREE JR — ARCHITECT /
WEST HARTFORD CONNECTICUT." Signed by delineator:
"Roger S. Powell [?]." Watercolor/gouache on watercolor board
(F. J. Head Water Color Board . . . Hand Made 100% Rag Content
Facing . . . Manufactured by National Card, Mat and Board
Company Chicago Los Angeles . . . No. 88 Cold Pressed);
21⅞ × 29¹⁵⁄₁₈". Gift of Peter G. Anderhaggen, 1999.

Edwin B. Goodell (1893–1971)

Mr. and Mrs. Frederick L. Dabney House (not built),
Westport, Massachusetts, c. 1965

Edwin Goodell studied at MIT (Class of 1915), then became a junior partner with Cram and Ferguson. A trip to Europe in 1931 set him "on a quest to define a new honest style for his time," according to his grandson, Edwin Goodell, and led him "to question the validity of the historicist work he had been doing in Cram's office." He practiced with Parsons, Wait and Goodell, then Andrews, Jones, Biscoe and Goodell, and, after 1955, under his own name. His Richard and Caroline Field house in Weston, Massachusetts, of 1934, has been called the first regionalist Modern house in New England. At the same time, he was widely known for his work in historic preservation, and took pride in his restoration of the West Parish Meetinghouse in West Barnstable, Massachusetts. He also learned from his own eighteenth-century house in Wayland, Massachusetts, much about the traditional solar orientation that influenced his layout of the Dabney house. With its hip roofs and rough stone accent wall and chimney, it too stylistically expressed a regionalist point of view, but it also reflected the environmental concerns of the past and the future, anticipating as it did the green movement of today. In the oval beside the floor plan, Goodell diagrammed these concerns, explaining the orientation of the house to the movement of the sun in summer and winter, thereby justifying the large areas of glass that open the southern exposure to solar rays. These simple pencil diagrams on tracing paper reflect the scientific rather than artistic approach to design in those years, on which Goodell seems to have concentrated. The plan does not show either an approach drive or a garage or carport attached to the house. The design remained only a project: the client, according to his son, found Goodell's offering too small, and opted for a Techbuilt house by Carl Koch that still stands in Dartmouth, Massachusetts. JFO'G

Plan, elevations, and orientation diagram for "PROPOSED HOUSE for MR. & MRS. FREDERICK L. DABNEY at / WESTPORT, MASSACHUSETTS," undated. Signed: "EDWIN B. GOODELL JR. ARCHITECT." Graphite on tracing paper; 19¾ × 21⅝". Gift of Steve Oles, 1985.

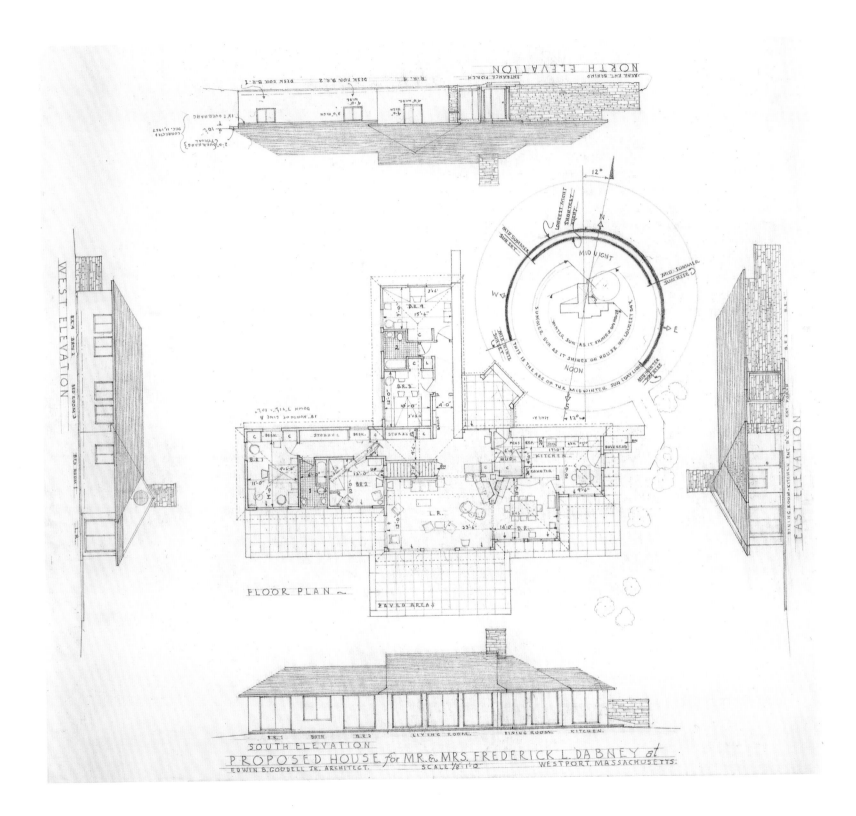

NORTH ELEVATION

WEST ELEVATION

EAST ELEVATION

FLOOR PLAN

SOUTH ELEVATION

PROPOSED HOUSE for MR. & MRS. FREDERICK L. DABNEY at

EDWIN B. GOODELL JR. ARCHITECT.   SCALE 1/8"=1'-0"   WESTPORT, MASSACHUSETTS.

217

Huygens and Tappé (1962–1980)

Remmert W. Huygens (1932–2009)
A. Anthony Tappé (b. 1928)

Dr. William Mauran House,
Congdon Street, Providence, Rhode Island, 1972

Remmert Huygens was born and educated in the Netherlands, came to the United States in 1956 to work with Marcel Breuer, then set up his own office in Boston. In 1962, he was joined by A. Anthony Tappé, a graduate of the School of Architecture at MIT, in partnership. After nearly two decades Tappé left to found his own firm. Huygens donated his archive containing records of some of the more than five hundred projects worldwide with which he was involved to Historic New England. Although his firm turned out institutional and commercial buildings, resorts, and other large commissions, residential work was a prime concern. The drawings for two very different houses shown on the following pages can perhaps suggest but in no way capture the richness of the domestic output of such a busy practice.

The house for William and Grace Mauran, or "Fort Mauran" as some neighbors disparagingly called it, was an award-winning design, an emphatically Modern building set into an area of traditional houses. As such, it was the subject of considerable discussion at a Providence Preservation Society conference focused on issues of contextual compatibility. At that meeting, Huygens justified the design by explaining the local inspiration. A nearby monument to Roger Williams and large greenhouses, he said, led him to ask the clients if they would like a "monumental greenhouse." Be that as it may, some inspiration for the Mauran house might have come from Roche–Dinkeloo's well-published 1967–70 Knights of Columbus headquarters building in New Haven, Connecticut, for the exterior seems to be a domestic reworking of that skyscraper's round corner towers, which embrace large areas of glass.

The Mauran interior is open and spatially complex. After the visitor enters through the one-story street front, according to the architect, "the distant view of the city . . . and the State Capitol comes unexpectedly. The central, sky lit [two-story] atrium has steps leading down through planting to the children and guest bedrooms." These drawings, by Huygens himself, are polished presentations in pencil on tracing paper, a common technique of the modern architectural office. JFO'G

Perspective of the front of the Mauran house. Signed
and dated: "R Huygens '71." Graphite on tracing paper;
15⅛ × 22". Gift of Remmert W. Huygens, 2006.

Perspective of the rear of the Mauran house. Signed
and dated: "R Huygens, '71." Graphite on tracing paper;
19 × 23⅝". Gift of Remmert W. Huygens, 2006.

William Mauran house in 1977.

Huygens and Tappé (1962–1980)

Remmert W. Huygens (1932–2009)
A. Anthony Tappé (b. 1928)

Dr. and Mrs. Paul Harwood House,
Crosstrees Hill Road, Essex, Connecticut, 1973

Unlike the design for the Mauran house (see pages 218–21), "where," Remmert Huygens wrote, "distinct parts are arranged as an abstraction," the Harwood house spreads out beneath the "unifying [hip] roof" found on many of his other domestic projects. The Dutch were early on great admirers of the work of Frank Lloyd Wright, and Dutch-born Huygens seems to have embraced that interest. In contrast to the Mauran design, this drawing shows an ample residence, in the manner of Wright's much-published later exurban work, placed on a gently sloping site with hip roofs floating over terraces perched above water's edge. This and other similar houses from the office were erected of materials "used according to their nature and chosen for appropriateness of the particular circumstance," as Huygens wrote, echoing Wright. The presentation also uses a partial or broken frame, a device used by Wright's draftsmen. To compare the drawing to the photograph of the finished house is to see how Huygens slightly exaggerated the Wrightian horizontals in his perspective view. JFO'G

Harwood house.

Perspective of the Harwood house. Signed and
dated: "R Huygens '73." Graphite on tracing paper.
Gift of Remmert W. Huygens, 2006.

Introduction: Drawings for New England Domestic Architecture, c. 1800–c. 1980

ENDNOTES

1. David Gebhard, "Royal Barry Wills and the American Colonial Revival," *Winterthur Portfolio* 27 (Spring 1992): 45–74.

2. For overviews of the history of architectural drawing in the United States, see David Gebhard and Deborah Nevins, *200 Years of American Architectural Drawing* (New York: Whitney Library of Design for the Architectural League of New York and the American Federation of Arts, 1977), and Deborah Nevins and Robert A. M. Stern, *The Architect's Eye: American Architectural Drawings from 1799–1978* (New York: Pantheon, 1979). For drawings from specific parts of New England, see William H. Jordy and Christopher P. Monkhouse, *Buildings on Paper: Rhode Island Architectural Drawings, 1825–1945* (Providence: Bell Gallery, List Art Center, Brown University, 1982); Lisa Koenigsberg, *Renderings from Worcester's Past: Nineteenth-Century Architectural Drawings from the American Antiquarian Society* (Worcester: American Antiquarian Society, 1987); James F. O'Gorman, *On the Boards: Drawings by Nineteenth-Century Boston Architects* (Philadelphia: University of Pennsylvania Press, 1989); and James F. O'Gorman and Earle G. Shettleworth, Jr., *The Maine Perspective: Architectural Drawings, 1800–1980* (Portland, Maine: Portland Museum of Art, 2006).

3. This formulation comes from Richard J. Betts's study of Alberti's *De Re Aedificatoria* published in Arturo Calzona et al., *Leon Battista Alberti* (Florence: Leo S. Olschki, 2007), 419–36, esp. 433.

4. For more about this process, see James F. O'Gorman, *ABC of Architecture* (Philadelphia: University of Pennsylvania Press, 1998).

5. Samuel Sloan, *The Model Architect* (Philadelphia: E. S. Jones & Co., 1851), 1:37.

6. See Lois Olcott Price's book, forthcoming from Oak Knoll Press and the Henry Francis du Pont Winterthur Museum, on the technology and preservation of architectural graphics, *Line, Shade, and Shadow: The Fabrication and Preservation of Architectural Drawings*.

7. For the latter, see Kenneth Hafertepe and James F. O'Gorman, eds., *American Architects and Their Books to 1848* (Amherst: University of Massachusetts Press, 2001), and Hafertepe and O'Gorman, eds., *American Architects and Their Books, 1840–1915* (Amherst: University of Massachusetts Press, 2007).

8. For a survey of drafting tools, see Maya Hambly, *Drawing Instruments, 1580–1980* (London: Sotheby's Publications, 1988).

9. See Sarah Allaback, *The First American Women Architects* (Urbana: University of Illinois Press, 2008). This catalogue suffers from the lack of drawings by female architects. There are no original drawings in the collection from the years covered here.

10. See Mary N. Woods, *From Craft to Profession: The Practice of Architecture in Nineteenth-Century America* (Berkeley: University of California Press, 1999).

11. See Pauline Saliga, "The Types and Styles of Architectural Drawings," in *Chicago Architects Design*, John Zukowsky and Pauline Saliga, eds. (Chicago: The Art Institute; New York: Rizzoli, 1982) or David G. DeLong, "A Note on Architectural Drawings," in H. W. Janson, *History of Art: A Survey of the Major Visual Arts from the Dawn of History to the Present Day* (New York: H. N. Abrams, 1977), 737–39. Models have been much used for presenting architectural projects, but the expense of building them precludes their appearance in domestic work other than the most lavish.

12. See James F. O'Gorman, *The Perspective of Anglo-American Architecture* (Philadelphia: The Athenaeum of Philadelphia, 1995), and the "Prolegomenon" to his *On the Boards*.

13. Edward Shaw, *Civil Architecture*, 4th ed. (Boston: Marsh, Copen and Lyon, 1836). Benjamin Linfoot, *Architectural Picture Making with Pen and Ink* (Philadelphia, 1884), 5–13.

14. *Boston Daily Globe*, 19 February 1886, 8.

15. St. Botolph Club records, 1879– , Massachusetts Historical Society, Boston. The Sturgis drawings were shown in his memory; he had died two years earlier. For more on this exhibition, see Christopher Monkhouse's essay in this catalogue.

16. Gebhard and Nevins, introduction to *200 Years of American Architectural Drawing*.

17. For a brief survey of the national context, see David P. Handlin, *American Architecture* (London: Thames and Hudson, 1985) and his *The American Home: Architecture and Society, 1815–1915* (Boston: Little, Brown, 1979). Alan Gowans's *Styles and Types of North American Architecture: Social Function and Cultural Expression* (New York: Icon Editions, 1992) covers the field in more detail.

18. Lois Price's forthcoming book (see note 6), and A. O. Halse, "A History of the Developments in Architectural Drawing Techniques" (DEd diss., New York University, 1952).

19. Robert D. Andrews, "Conditions of Architectural Practice Thirty Years and More Ago," *The Architectural Review* 5 (November 1917): 1.

20. Gerald Allen and Richard Oliver, compilers, *Architectural Drawing: The Art and the Process* (New York: Whitney Library of Design, 1981), 88.

Suitable for Framing: Architectural Drawings as Works of Art

The author wishes to thank the following individuals for their assistance in the preparation of this essay: Suzanne Folds McCullagh, Renée Melton, and Robert Lifson, The Art Institute of Chicago; Kim Wade, Bar Harbor, Maine; Joshua Torrance, Woodlawn Museum, Ellsworth, Maine; and Carole Plenty and Betsy Hewlett, Mount Desert Land and Garden Preserve, Seal Harbor, Maine.

ENDNOTES

1. Jacob Simon, *The Art of the Picture Frame: Artists, Patrons and the Framing of Portraits in Britain* (London: National Portrait Gallery, 1996), 7.

2. Perhaps the first occasion for the removal of the architectural perspective of the Bowen House, Roseland Cottage, for exhibition purposes was in 1976, when it was lent to an exhibition on the Gothic Revival in America organized by the Museum of Fine Arts, Houston. See Katherine S. Howe and David B. Warren, *The Gothic Revival Style in America, 1830–1870* (Houston: Museum of Fine Arts, 1976). Most recently it was included in the 2003–05 traveling exhibition mounted by the Society for the Preservation of New England Antiquities (now Historic New England) called *Cherished Possessions: A New England Legacy*. The accompanying catalogue illustrates the perspective and related drawings. See Nancy Carlisle, *Cherished Possessions: A New England Legacy* (Boston: Society for the Preservation of New England Antiquities, 2003), 305–7.

3. For a comprehensive discussion of architectural perspectives in America prior to the Bowen House perspective, see James F. O'Gorman, *The Perspective of Anglo-American Architecture* (Philadelphia: The Athenaeum of Philadelphia, 1995).

4. The author is grateful to Richard C. Nylander, Curator Emeritus, Historic New England, for bringing this group of related drawings to his attention.

5. For an eighteenth-century English precedent, it is worth mentioning that Sir William Chambers appears to have commissioned the French topographical artist Jean-Laurent Legeay in 1768 to provide a perspective portrait in red chalk of Chambers's Casino at Marino, near Dublin, housed in an elegant neoclassical frame from his own design, as a wedding present for his esteemed patron who commissioned the Casino in the late 1750s, James Caulfield, the first Earl of Charlemont. For an illustration of this framed perspective, see John Harris and Michael Snodin, eds., *Sir William Chambers, Architect to George III* (New Haven: Yale University Press, 1996), 27.

6. For a discussion of John Doggett's frames, see Carlisle, *Cherished Possessions*, 233–39. As Doggett's manuscript account book is preserved in the library of the Henry Francis du Pont Winterthur Museum in Delaware, a close study may eventually throw more light on this unidentified drawing.

7. The perspective for the summer cottage of Dr. J. Heald in Lovell, Maine, was included in the exhibition and accompanying catalogue authored by James F. O'Gorman and Earle G. Shettleworth, Jr., *The Maine Perspective: Architectural Drawings, 1800–1980* (Portland, Maine: Portland Museum of Art, 2006), 95 (not illustrated).

8. For a discussion and illustration of the Lightner residence, see Geoffrey Blodgett, *Cass Gilbert, The Early Years* (St. Paul: Minnesota Historical Society Press, 2001), 70–73. Also see Larry Millett, *AIA Guide to the Twin Cities* (St. Paul: Minnesota Historical Society Press, 2007), 444–45.

9. A similar scenario exists for the pastel presentation perspective of 1884 for the Commodore William G. Edgar house in Newport, Rhode Island. Possibly prepared by artist/architect Stanford White as a present

for his patron to hang in the front hall, it remained there until 1982, when the then owners took it with them to Florida. By that date the original frame and mat had been replaced and hence obliterated any trace of what White might have envisioned for it, if he was indeed the author of the perspective. More is the pity in view of Stanford White's distinguished career as a designer of picture frames, in addition to architecture.

10. The owner who retained the original drawing did provide the present owner with a photographic reproduction of the Gilbert pastel.

11. Simon, *The Art of the Picture Frame*, 46.

12. For the best overview of Emerson's summer cottages, see Roger G. Reed, *"A Delight to All Who Know It": The Maine Summer Architecture of William R. Emerson* (Portland, Maine: Maine Citizens for Historic Preservation, 1995).

13. "The Architectural Drawings at the Exhibition of the Salmagundi Club-II," *The American Architect and Building News* 19, no. 527 (13 February 1886), 77–78.

14. The pastel of the Curtis cottage was illustrated in color on the back cover of Reed, *"A Delight to All Who Know It,"* but cropped to eliminate its original mat and frame. When the drawing was lent to the Portland Museum of Art, for O'Gorman and Shettleworth, *The Maine Perspective*, the original mat and frame, in the interest of conservation, were removed.

15. "Briefly" is the operative word, because Curtis quickly transferred ownership of the house to the Boston physician Dr. Francis Peabody. His descendants still own the property, which has the picturesque name of Shellheap, alluding to the shells left over from Indian encampments on the site.

16. When Joseph Curtis died in 1928, the pastel was described on page 10 in the estate inventory as "Seashore Cottage by Amateur Artist." For a recent history and guide to the lodge and garden, see Letitia S. Baldwin, *Thuya Garden, Asticou Terrace and Thuya Lodge* (Seal Harbor, Maine: Mount Desert Land and Garden Preserve, 2008).

17. For a recent history of the Poland Spring House, see Poland Spring Preservation Society and Jason C. Libby, *Poland Spring* (Charleston, S.C.: Arcadia Publishing, 2009).

18. Earle G. Shettleworth, Jr., *The Summer Cottages of Islesboro, 1890–1930* (Islesboro, Maine: Islesboro Historical Society, 1989), 20–24.

19. A copy of the modest printed catalogue, *St. Botolph Club Architectural Exhibition 1890*, is preserved with other papers and publications pertaining to the club presently on deposit with the Massachusetts Historical Society in Boston. The author is grateful to James F. O'Gorman for bringing this publication to his attention.

20. "S. S. Howe" may have been a misreading for "L. L. Howe," Lois Lilley Howe (1864–1964), a student of C. Howard Walker, who graduated from MIT in 1890. Midwesterner Robert Closson Spencer, Jr. (1864–1953), graduated in 1886 with a B.A. in mechanical engineering from the University of Wisconsin, where he befriended Frank Lloyd Wright in his senior year. Shortly thereafter he moved to Boston, where he enrolled in 1887 at MIT (for one year) before serving as a draftsman in the office of Wheelwright and Haven (1888–89), followed by a similar stint in the office of Shepley, Rutan and Coolidge (1890–91). That his drawing skills were appreciated can be judged from his receiving, in 1891, the eighth Rotch

Traveling Fellowship, affording him two years of study and sketching in Italy, France, and England. Paul Kruty, "Robert Closson Spencer, Jr.," *American National Biography* (New York: Oxford University Press, 1999), 20: 458–59.

21. Boston Society of Architects and Boston Architectural Club, *Catalogue of the Architectural Exhibition Held in the New Public Library Building, October 28 to November 4, Inclusive, in Conjunction with the Annual Convention of the American Institute of Architects* (Boston, 1891), 38.

22. Shettleworth, *The Summer Cottages*, 20–24.

23. *Official Catalogue of Exhibits, World's Columbian Exposition, Department K, Fine Arts* (Chicago: W. B. Conkey Company, 1893), 57.

24. Wilkinson's 1903 perspective of the Samoset Hotel in Rockland, Maine, was included in O'Gorman and Shettleworth, *The Maine Perspective*, 91 (not illustrated).

The Development of the Architectural Profession in New England: An Overview

ENDNOTES

1. See Carl Bridenbaugh, *Peter Harrison, First American Architect* (Chapel Hill: University of North Carolina Press, 1949).

2. For Banner and examples of his architectural drawings, see the three-part series by Elmer D. Keith and William L. Warren in *Old-Time New England* 44, no. 4 (April-June 1955): 93–102; 47, no. 3 (October-December 1956): 49–53; and 49, no. 4 (April-June 1959): 104–10.

3. See Harold Kirker, *The Architecture of Charles Bulfinch* (Cambridge, Mass.: Harvard University Press, 1969).

4. See Fiske Kimball, *Mr. Samuel McIntire, Carver, The Architect of Salem* (Portland, Maine: Southworth-Anthoensen Press, 1940).

5. See Mary N. Woods, *From Craft to Profession: The Practice of Architecture in Nineteenth-Century America* (Berkeley: University of California Press, 1999).

6. See Martha J. McNamara, "Defining the Profession: Books, Libraries, and Architects," in *American Architects and Their Books to 1848*, Kenneth Hafertepe and James F. O'Gorman, eds. (Amherst: University of Massachusetts Press, 2001), 73–89.

7. Kenneth Hafertepe, "*The Country Builder's Assistant:* Text and Context," in Hafertepe and O'Gorman, 129–48.

8. Christopher Monkhouse, "Parris' Perusal," *Old-Time New England* 58, no. 2 (October-December 1967): 51–59, and Edward F. Zimmer, "The Architectural Career of Alexander Parris (1780–1852)" (PhD diss., Boston University, 1984).

9. Jack Quinan, "Some Aspects of the Development of the Architectural Profession in Boston Between 1800 and 1830," *Old-Time New England* 68, no. 1–2 (July-December 1977): 32–37.

10. Shaw had an exceptionally successful career as the author of several important builders' guides. See Earle G. Shettleworth, Jr., "Edward Shaw Architect and Author," introduction to a reprint of Shaw's 1854 *The Modern Architect* (New York: Dover Publications, 1995). For William F. Pratt, see Faye S. Wolfe, "Three Essays on William Fenno Pratt," in *Paradise Built: The Shaping of Northampton's Townscape, 1654–2004* (Northampton, Mass.: 350th Anniversary Committee, City of Northampton, 2004).

11. Masons and housewrights in large cities banded together to establish rules of work and publish itemized pricing guides for work in their trades. In Portland, Maine, for example, price books are known to have been developed as early as 1760, and published in 1805 and 1819. See Laura Fecych Sprague, Amy Cole Ives, and Earle G. Shettleworth, Jr., *Joiners and Their Price Books in Portland, Maine, 1760–1819* (Portland, Maine: The Association for Preservation Technology International in collaboration with the Maine Historic Preservation Commission, 2003).

12. Boston architect Gridley J. F. Bryant understood the importance of detailed specifications to ensure that a building was constructed as he intended. See Roger G. Reed, *Building Victorian Boston: The Architecture of Gridley J. F. Bryant* (Amherst: University of Massachusetts Press, 2007).

13. For Preston, see Jean Ames Follett-Thompson, "The Business of Architecture: William Gibbons Preston and Architectural Professionalism in Boston during the Second Half of the Nineteenth Century" (PhD diss., Boston University, 1986). For Richardson, see James F. O'Gorman, *Living Architecture: A Biography of H. H. Richardson* (New York: Simon & Schuster Editions, 1997).

14. See Margaret Henderson Floyd, ed., *Architectural Education and Boston* (Boston: Boston Architectural Center, 1989); Bettina A. Norton, *To Create and Foster Architecture: The Contributions of the Boston Architectural Center: A Catalogue of the Centennial Exhibitions* (Boston: Boston Architectural Center, 1989).

15. Walter Muir Whitehill, "A Centennial Sketch," in *Boston Society of Architects: The First Hundred Years, 1867–1967*, Marvin E. Goody and Robert P. Walsh, eds. (Boston: The Boston Society of Architects, 1967); Henry H. Saylor, "The A.I.A.'s First Hundred Years," *Journal of the American Institute of Architects* (May 1957).

16. See Wheaton A. Holden, "The Peabody Touch: Peabody and Stearns of Boston, 1870–1917," *Journal of the Society of Architectural Historians* 32, no. 2 (May 1973): 114–31.

17. Michael A. Tomlan, "Popular and Professional American Architectural Literature in the Late Nineteenth Century" (PhD diss., Cornell University, 1983).

18. James Lawrence, "Changing Perspectives: Beaux-Arts to Modern" in Floyd, *Architectural Education and Boston*, 86.

19. Robert S. Sturgis, "Urban Planning: Changing Concepts," in Floyd, *Architectural Education and Boston*, 109–18.

20. For a brief overview of this period, see Walter Muir Whitehill, *Boston: A Topographical History* (Cambridge, Mass.: Belknap Press of the Harvard University Press, 1968).

Preserving on Paper: Historic New England's Collection of Architectural Records

ENDNOTES

1. For discussions of William Sumner Appleton's life and career, see Lorna Condon, "William Sumner Appleton," in *American National Biography*, John A. Garraty and Mark C. Carnes, eds. (New York: Oxford University Press, 1999), 1:565–67; Charles B. Hosmer, Jr., *Presence of the Past: A History of the Preservation Movement in the United States Before Williamsburg* (New York: Putnam, 1965) and *Preservation Comes of Age: From Williams-*

burg to the National Trust, 1926–1949 (Charlottesville: Published for the Preservation Press, National Trust for Historic Preservation in the United States by the University Press of Virginia, 1981); Michael Holleran, *Boston's "Changeful Times": Origins of Preservation & Planning in America* (Baltimore: Johns Hopkins University Press, 1998); James M. Lindgren, *Preserving Historic New England: Preservation, Progressivism, and the Remaking of Memory* (New York: Oxford University Press, 1995); Katharine H. Rich, "Beacon," *Old-Time New England* 66, no. 3–4 (January–June 1976): 42–60. Also see Appleton's autobiographical entries for the successive editions of *Harvard University Class of 1896* (1899 et seq.) and his professional papers in Historic New England's Library and Archives.

2. Harvard College, Class of 1896, *Class of 1896—Report VI* (1921), 14, Harvard University Archives.

3. William Sumner Appleton, "Destruction and Preservation of Old Buildings in New England," *Art and Archaeology* 8, no. 3 (May-June 1919): 164.

4. *Bulletin of the Society for the Preservation of New England Antiquities* 2, no. 2 (August 1911): 21–22; Ernest L. Gay, "Librarian's Report," *Bulletin of the Society for the Preservation of New England Antiquities* 4, no. 1 (August 1913): 20; William Sumner Appleton, "Report of the Librarian," *Old-Time New England* 11, no. 2 (October 1920): 80.

5. Ernest L. Gay, "Librarian's Report," *Bulletin of the Society for the Preservation of New England Antiquities* 3, no. 3 (February 1913): 8; *Bulletin of the Society for the Preservation of New England Antiquities* 7, no. 1 (May 1916): 30; *Bulletin of the Society for the Preservation of New England Antiquities* 10, no. 1 (October 1919): 31.

6. Abbott Lowell Cummings, "SPNEA's Library: A Survey of Its Growth, 1910–1974," unpublished manuscript, Historic New England Library and Archives; Frederic C. Detwiller, "Thomas Dawes's Church in Brattle Square," *Old-Time New England* 69, no. 3–4 (January-June 1979): 1.

7. George Parker Winship, "Report of the Librarian," *Old-Time New England* 12, no. 1 (July 1921): 38; Letter from Lawrence Park to potential donors, 20 May 1921; Letter from William Sumner Appleton to W. R. Greeley, 4 June 1921, both letters in the institutional archives, Historic New England Library and Archives.

8. The collection of Eleanor Raymond's photographs came as a bequest of James E. (Jack) Robinson, III.

9. Thomas G. Frothingham, "Report of the Librarian," *Old-Time New England* 28, no. 4 (April 1938): 138.

10. Letter from William Sumner Appleton to Herbert W. C. Browne, 6 July 1939, institutional archives, Historic New England Library and Archives.

11. Ellie Reichlin, "Preserving Architecture on Paper," *SPNEA News* 45 (Summer 1988): 3.

12. Buchanan Charles, "Report of the Librarian," *Old-Time New England* 37, no. 1 (July 1946): 16.

13. Buchanan Charles, "Report of the Librarian," *Old-Time New England* 38, no. 1 (July 1947): 6–12; for a discussion of Browne's library, see Elizabeth C. Leuthner, " 'A Small Archs. Library': The Herbert W. C. Browne Collection," unpublished manuscript, Historic New England Library and Archives.

14. Martha J. McNamara, "Defining the Profession: Books, Libraries, and Architects," in *American Architects and Their Books to 1848*, Kenneth Hafertepe and James F. O'Gorman, eds. (Amherst: University of Massachu-

setts Press, 2001), 73–89; Wendell D. Garrett, "Report of the Librarian," *Old-Time New England* 56, no. 1 (July–September 1965): 32; Robert E. Moody, "Report of the Librarian," *Old-Time New England* 59, no. 1 (July–September 1968): 24.

15. "Library Operations," *Old-Time New England* 66, no. 3–4 (Winter-Spring 1976): 7–8.

16. Ernest L. Gay, "Librarian's Report," *Bulletin of the Society for the Preservation of New England Antiquities* 4, no. 1 (August 1913): 21–22; "The Halliday Collection of Historic Photographs," *Bulletin of the Society for the Preservation of New England Antiquities* 7, no. 2 (December 1916): 21.

17. Abbott Lowell Cummings, "SPNEA's Library: A Survey of Its Growth, 1910–1974."

Pages 40–41
Asher Benjamin: *Frontispiece of an Unidentified House*
ENDNOTES

1. Joseph Howard Account Book, Kent Memorial Library, Suffield, Connecticut.

2. For these and following references to the building documents, see Phelps and Gorham Papers, New York State Library, Albany, New York.

REFERENCE

William N. Hosley, Jr., "Architecture," in *The Great River: Art and Society of the Connecticut Valley, 1635–1820* (Hartford, Conn.: Wadsworth Atheneum, 1985), 66–67, and catalogue entries 24 and 26.

Pages 42–43
Asher Benjamin: *Jonathan Leavitt House, Greenfield, Massachusetts*
ENDNOTES

1. Franklin County, Massachusetts, Deeds, 10:332.

2. Direct Tax, 1798, 18:449, New England Historic Genealogical Society, Boston.

3. *Memoirs of Jonathan Leavitt . . . Who Died at New-Haven the 10th of May, 1821, aged Eighteen Years . . . By a Sister* (New Haven, 1822), 27.

4. Middlesex County, Massachusetts, Deeds, 112:290.

Pages 44–45
Attributed to Asher Benjamin: *Unidentified Building*
ENDNOTES

1. Asher Benjamin, *Practice of Architecture* (Boston, 1833), iii.

2. See Florence Thompson Howe, "More About Asher Benjamin," *Journal of the Society of Architectural Historians* 13, no. 2 (October 1954): 16, citing a letter from Benjamin to Gideon Granger, Postmaster General of the United States under Thomas Jefferson.

3. See Jack Quinan, "Asher Benjamin as an Architect in Windsor, Vermont," *Vermont History* 42, no. 3 (Summer 1974): 181–94.

4. Asher Benjamin Collection, Historic New England Library and Archives.

Pages 46–48
Samuel McIntire: *Unidentified House*
REFERENCES

"Brick Buildings in Salem from the Gazette of February 4th, 1806," *Essex Institute Historical Collections* 1, no. 2 (Salem, Mass.: Essex Institute, 1859): 55–56.

"Contract and Expense Account for Building the Samuel Fowler House, Danversport, 1810," *Old-Time New England* 21, no. 4 (April 1931): 185–87.

Fiske Kimball, *Mr. Samuel McIntire, the Architect of Salem* (Salem, Mass.: Essex Institute, 1940; reprint Gloucester, Mass.: Peter Smith, 1966), figure 155, discussed 91.

Dean T. Lahikainen, "Gardner-Pingree House, Salem, Massachusetts," *Antiques* 137, no. 3 (March 1990): 718–29.

————. *Samuel McIntire: Carving an American Style* (Salem, Mass.: Peabody Essex Museum, 2007), 108–12 and 120–35.

Paul F. Norton, "Samuel McIntire of Salem: The Drawings and Papers of the Architect/Carver and His Family, 1988," unpublished manuscript, nos. 93–96, Phillips Library, Peabody Essex Museum, Salem, Mass.

Matthew Adams Stickney, *The Fowler Family: A Genealogical Memoir of the Descendants of Philip and Mary Fowler, of Ipswich, Mass.: Ten Generations, 1590–1882* (Salem, Mass.: printed by the author, 1883), 190.

Bryant Tolles, *Architecture in Salem: An Illustrated Guide* (Salem, Mass.: Essex Institute, 1983), 17, 24, 42.

Henry F. Waters, "Memoir of Samuel Page Fowler," *New England Historical and Genealogical Register* 46 (October 1892): 339–45.

Pages 49–51
John Grove Hales and Unattributed: *James A. Rundlet House, Portsmouth, New Hampshire*
REFERENCES

Richard M. Candee, *Building Portsmouth: The Neighborhoods and Architecture of New Hampshire's Oldest City* (Portsmouth, N.H.: Back Channel Press, 2006).

Claire W. Dempsey, Research Binder on the Rundlet-May House (1979), Historic New England Library and Archives.

James L. Garvin, "Academic Architecture and the Building Trades in the Piscataqua Region of New Hampshire and Maine, 1715–1815" (PhD diss., Boston University, 1983).

The author wishes to thank Richard M. Candee for sharing his research on John Grove Hales.

Pages 52–53
Unattributed: *Unidentified Doorway*
ENDNOTES

1. Ellen Susan Bulfinch, *The Life and Letters of Charles Bulfinch, Architect* (Boston, 1896), 75–76.

2. Robert C. Alberts, *The Golden Voyage: The Life and Times of William Bingham, 1752–1804* (Boston: Houghton Mifflin Company, 1969), 157.

3. George B. Tatum, *Penn's Great Town* (Philadelphia: University of Pennsylvania Press, 1961), see 162 and figure 53 (aquatint of Washington Hall).

Pages 54–55
Joseph C. Howard: *Unidentified Greek Revival House*
ENDNOTES

1. See *Vital Records of Roxbury, Massachusetts, to the End of the Year 1849* (Salem, Mass.: Essex Institute, 1925) for marriage of parents and birth of Joseph C. Howard. For record of his death at Roxbury, see Massachusetts Vital Records, 1841–1910, Deaths, 27:104.

2. See Edward F. Zimmer, "Luther Briggs and the Picturesque Pattern Books," *Old-Time New England* 67, no. 3–4 (Winter–Spring 1977): 36–38. Howard's letter written from Nashua, New Hampshire, is in the collection of the Pembroke [Mass.] Historical Society.

Pages 56–57
Edward Shaw: *William Wilkins Warren House, Arlington, Massachusetts*
REFERENCES
Boston Evening Transcript, 11 April 1846.
William Wilkins Warren, *Autobiography and Genealogy of William Wilkins Warren* (Cambridge, Mass.: J. Wilson, 1884).
The author wishes to thank Richard A. Duffy and William H. Mahoney for their assistance in the preparation of this entry.

Pages 58–59
Edward Shaw: *Unidentified Gothic Revival House*
REFERENCES
Edward Shaw, *The Modern Architect; or, Every Carpenter His Own Master* (Boston: Dayton and Wentworth, 1854).
Edward Shaw, *Rural Architecture* (Boston: James B. Dow, 1843).
Earle G. Shettleworth, Jr., "Edward Shaw, Architect and Author," in *The Modern Architect* (New York: Dover Publications, 1995).

Pages 60–63
William F. Pratt: *Augustus Clarke House, Northampton, Massachusetts*
ENDNOTES
1. Northampton, Massachusetts, 350th Anniversary Committee, *Paradise Built: The Shaping of Northampton's Townscape, 1654–2004* (Northampton, Mass.: 350th Anniversary Committee, City of Northampton, 2004), 51–59.
2. The house was identified using an 1860 map of Northampton, the Northampton map in the 1873 atlas of Hampshire County, the 1875 bird's-eye view of Northampton, and deed research for Hampshire County, Massachusetts, 728: 233.

Pages 64–65
Joseph C. Wells: *Henry C. Bowen House, Roseland Cottage, Woodstock, Connecticut*
REFERENCES
Barbara J. Beeching, "Henry Chandler Bowen and Roseland Cottage: Success in Nineteenth Century America," *Connecticut History* 38, no. 2 (Fall 1999): 127–49.
Bowen Family Papers, Historic New England Library and Archives.
Nancy Carlisle, *Cherished Possessions: A New England Legacy* (Boston: Society for the Preservation of New England Antiquities, 2003), 305–7.
The Crayon 7, no. 7 (September 1860): 270.
Andrew Jackson Downing, *The Architecture of Country Houses* (New York: D. Appleton, 1850).
Susan L. Porter, "At Home with the Bowens," *Historic New England* 7, no.1 (Summer 2006): 2–7.

Pages 66–67
Charles Roath: *Unidentified Townhouses and Store*
REFERENCES
James F. O'Gorman, *On the Boards: Drawings by Nineteenth-Century Boston Architects* (Philadelphia: University of Pennsylvania Press, 1989).
Earle G. Shettleworth, Jr., *An Index to Boston Building Contracts Recorded in the Suffolk County Registry of Deeds* (Augusta, Maine: E. G. Shettleworth, Jr., 1995); *1830–1839, 1840–1844* (1996); *1845–1849* (1997).

Pages 68–70
Gervase Wheeler: *Unidentified Italianate Villa*
REFERENCES
Andrew Jackson Downing, *The Architecture of Country Houses* (New York: D. Appleton, 1850).
James F. O'Gorman, *Henry Austin: In Every Variety of Architectural Style* (Middletown, Conn.: Wesleyan University Press, 2008), 198–200.
Sandra L. Tatman and Roger Moss, *Biographical Dictionary of Philadelphia Architects, 1700–1930* (Boston: G. K. Hall, 1985), 849–50.
Renée E. Tribert and James F. O'Gorman, *Immigrant's Progress: The Architectural Career of Gervase Wheeler in America, 1847–60* (Middletown, Conn.: Wesleyan University Press, forthcoming).

Pages 71–73
Joseph Hayward: *Oakes Ames House, North Easton, Massachusetts*
REFERENCE
Information on Joseph Hayward was derived from census data.

Pages 74–75
Alexander R. Esty: *Unidentified Italianate House*
REFERENCES
Alexander R. Esty obituary, *Boston Transcript*, 5 July 1881.
General Resource and Special Collections files, Esty, Alexander Rice, Framingham History Center, Framingham, Mass.
Frank A. Kendall, "Alexander Rice Esty, Architect (1826–1881), His Early Surroundings, His Professional Associates, His Friends, and His Architectural Works," undated manuscript, Esty, Alexander Rice, Vertical File, Framingham Room, Framingham [Mass.] Public Library.
The author wishes to thank Donald C. Carleton, Jr., Dana Dauterman Ricciardi, and Kevin Swope for their assistance in the preparation of this entry.

Pages 76–91
Luther Briggs, Jr.: *Ephraim Merriam House, Jamaica Plain, Boston; Stores and Tenements for Matthew Bartlett, Boston; James F. Bigelow House, East Abington, Massachusetts; P. D. Wallis House, Boston; Ell Addition to the House of H. Emerson, Boston*
ENDNOTE
1. Edward F. Zimmer, "Luther Briggs and the Picturesque Pattern Books," *Old-Time New England* 67, no. 3–4 (Winter–Spring 1977): 36–55.
REFERENCE
Luther Briggs, Jr., obituary, *Dorchester Beacon*, 21 October 1905.

Pages 92–95
Nathaniel J. Bradlee: *Unidentified House*
REFERENCES
Nathaniel J. Bradlee obituaries, *Boston Evening Transcript*, 17 December 1888; *Scientific American, Architects and Builders Edition*, April 1889.

Pages 96–97
Henry M. Francis: *Student Drawing*
REFERENCES
Henry M. Francis Collection, Historic New England Library and Archives.
Henry M. Francis collection of architectural drawings, Fitchburg [Mass.] Historical Society.
The authors wish to thank Susan Roetzer for her assistance in the preparation of the Francis entries.

Pages 98–99
Henry M. Francis: *Charles F. Harding House, Fitchburg, Massachusetts*
ENDNOTE
1. An excellent detailed inventory of his work appeared in the *Fitchburg Daily Sentinel* on 14 October 1908.

Pages 100–102
John Hubbard Sturgis: *Measured Drawings of the Hancock House, Boston*
ENDNOTE
1. Margaret Henderson Floyd, "Measured Drawings of the Hancock House by John Hubbard Sturgis: A Legacy to the Colonial Revival," in *Architecture in Colonial Massachusetts*, Abbott Lowell Cummings, ed. (Boston: The Colonial Society of Massachusetts, 1979), 87–111.
REFERENCES
Lorna Condon and Richard Nylander, "A Classic in the Annals of Vandalism: The Battle to Save the John Hancock Mansion Ignites Boston's Preservation Movement," *Historic New England* 6, no. 1 (Summer 2005): 2–8.
Arthur Gilman, "The Hancock House and Its Founder," *Atlantic Monthly* 11 (June 1863): 692–707.
Walter Kendall Watkins, "The Hancock House and Its Builder," *Old-Time New England* 17, no. 1 (July 1926): 3–19.

Pages 103–5
Unattributed: *Unidentified Library*
REFERENCES
Charles Wyllys Elliott, *The Book of American Interiors* (Boston: James R. Osgood and Company, 1876).
Photographic Collections, Historic New England Library and Archives.

Pages 106–9
Gridley J. F. Bryant: *James M. Beebe and Gardner Brewer Townhouses, Boston,* and *Thomas Wigglesworth House, Manchester, Massachusetts*
REFERENCE
Roger G. Reed, *Building Victorian Boston: The Architecture of Gridley J. F. Bryant* (Amherst: The University of Massachusetts Press, 2007).

Pages 110–11
Edward Dow: *Walter Aiken House, Franklin, New Hampshire*
REFERENCES
Boston Daily Advertiser, 21 February 1877.
"Death of Edward Dow," *Concord* [N.H.] *Evening Monitor*, 1 August 1894.
Robert Piercy Dow, comp., *The Book of Dow* (Claremont, N.H.: Robert P. Dow, John W. Dow, Susan F. Dow, 1929).
Andrew Jackson Downing, *The Architecture of Country Houses* (New York: D. Appleton, 1850).
D. Hamilton Hurd, ed., *The History of Merrimack and Belknap Counties, New Hampshire* (Philadelphia: J. W. Lewis, 1885).
Independent Statesman [Concord, N.H.], 9 August 1877.
Merrimack Journal, 8 March 1878.
George Moses, ed., *New Hampshire Men* (Concord, N.H.: New Hampshire Publishing, 1893).
James Amasa Wood, *New Hampshire Homes: Photographic Views of City, Village, Summer, and Farm Homes of New Hampshire Men and Residents of the Granite State, With Descriptive Sketches of the Same* (Concord, N.H.: James A. Wood, 1895).

Pages 112–13
Peabody and Stearns: *William Sumner Appleton, Sr., House, Holbrook Hall, Newton, Massachusetts*
REFERENCES
Susan Abele, *Newton's Nineteenth Century Architecture: Newton Centre, Oak Hill, Chestnut Hill, Commonwealth Avenue* (Newton, Mass.: Historic Newton, Inc., 1985).
David Gebhard and Deborah Nevins, *200 Years of American Architectural Drawing* (New York: Whitney Library of Design for the Architectural League of New York and the American Federation of Arts, 1977).
Wheaton Arnold Holden, "Robert Swain Peabody of Peabody and Stearns in Boston: The Early Years, (1870–1886)" (PhD diss., Boston University, 1969).
Annie Robinson, *Peabody & Stearns: Country Houses and Seaside Cottages* (New York: W. W. Norton, 2010).
————. "The Resort Architecture of Peabody and Stearns: Northeast Harbor, Maine, and Newport, Rhode Island" (master's thesis, Tufts University, 1999).
Moses Foster Sweetser, *King's Handbook of Newton, Massachusetts* (Boston: Moses King Co., 1889).

Pages 114–15
McKim, Mead and White: *William Watts Sherman House, Newport, Rhode Island*
REFERENCE
Jeffery Karl Ochsner and Thomas C. Hubka, "H. H. Richardson: The Design of the William Watts Sherman House," *Journal of the Society of Architectural Historians* 51, no. 2 (June 1992): 121–45.

Pages 116–17
John M. Allen: *Rev. John C. Brooks Cottage, Marion, Massachusetts*
REFERENCES
John H. Ackerman, ed., *Reflections on a Town* (Marion, Mass.: Sippican Historical Society, 1991).
Christopher Monkhouse, "Suitable for Framing: Architectural Drawings as Works of Art," in this catalogue.

Henry F. Withey and Elsie Rathburn Withey, *Biographical Dictionary of American Architects (Deceased)* (Los Angeles: New Age Publishing Co., 1956), 17.
Mark Wright, "H. H. Richardson's House for Reverend Browne, Rediscovered," *Journal of the Society of Architectural Historians* 68, no. 1 (March 2009): 74–99.
The author wishes to acknowledge the assistance of Mark Wright in the preparation of this entry and Judith Westlund Rosbe for her assistance with this entry.

Pages 118–21
John Calvin Stevens: *Joseph A. King Cottage, Great Diamond Island, Casco Bay, Maine*
REFERENCES
Earle G. Shettleworth, Jr., *John Calvin Stevens on the Portland Peninsula, 1880 to 1940* (Portland, Maine: Greater Portland Landmarks, Inc., 2003).
John Calvin Stevens, Architectural drawings and records collection, 1879–1966, Maine Historical Society, Portland, Maine.
John Calvin Stevens and Albert Winslow Cobb, *Examples of American Domestic Architecture* (New York: William T. Comstock, 1889).
John Calvin Stevens II and Earle G. Shettleworth, Jr., *John Calvin Stevens, Domestic Architecture, 1890–1930* (Portland, Maine: Harp Publications, 1990).

Pages 122–23
Arthur Little: *Addition to the George R. Emmerton House, Salem, Massachusetts*
REFERENCES
Caroline O. Emmerton, *The Chronicles of Three Old Houses* (Boston: Thomas Todd Co., 1935).
Little and Browne Archives, Historic New England Library and Archives.
Little and Browne photograph album, Boston Athenaeum.
W. Knight Sturges, "Arthur Little and the Colonial Revival," *Journal of the Society of Architectural Historians* 32, no. 2 (May 1973): 147–63.

Pages 124–25
Little and Browne: *Henry Clay Frick Estate, Eagle Rock, Prides Crossing, Beverly, Massachusetts*
REFERENCES
Correspondence between H. C. Frick and Arthur Little, Frick Family Archives, Pittsburgh, Pennsylvania.
Joseph E. Garland, *Boston's Gold Coast: The North Shore, 1890–1912* (Boston: Little, Brown, 1981), 124–44.
Little and Browne Archives, Historic New England Library and Archives.
Martha F. S. Sanger, *Helen Clay Frick: Bittersweet Heiress* (Pittsburgh: University of Pittsburgh Press, 2008).
————. *The Henry Clay Frick Houses* (New York: Monacelli Press, 2001).

Pages 126–27
Little and Browne: *Addition to the William S. and John T. Spaulding House, Sunset Rock, Prides Crossing, Beverly, Massachusetts*
REFERENCES
Harold D. Eberlein, "The Formal American Country House: Residence of W. S. and J. T. Spaulding, Prides Crossing, Mass., Little and Browne Architects," *The Architectural Record* 36 (October 1914): 294–304.

Barr Ferree, "The House and Garden of W. S. Spaulding, Esq.," *American Homes and Gardens* 7 (October 1910): 375–81.
Little and Browne Archives, Historic New England Library and Archives.
Frederic A. Sharf, *Art of Collecting: The Spaulding Brothers and Their Legacy* (Boston: MFA Publications, 2007).
Frank Lloyd Wright, "Gallery for Storage and Exhibition of Japanese Color Prints and Collections of W. S. Spaulding, Boston, Massachusetts, 1914," set of eleven drawings (elevations, sections, floor plan, studies), numbers 1902.001–1902.011, Archives of the Frank Lloyd Wright Foundation, Taliesin West, Scottsdale, Ariz.
"The W. S. Spaulding Gardens, Prides Crossing, Mass.," *The Architectural Record* 28 (October 1910): 273–76.

Pages 128–29
James A. Clough: *Building for Michael H. Baker, Holyoke, Massachusetts*
ENDNOTES
1. James A. Clough obituary, *Transcript* [Holyoke, Mass.], 23 May 1917.
2. The location of the Baker building was confirmed using city directories and Sanborn Insurance Company maps. Directory searches also provided names of the earliest known occupants.

Pages 130–33
Jacob Luippold: *Philip Albret House, Dorchester, Boston,* and *Unidentified Building with Store and Apartments*
ENDNOTE
1. Information on Jacob and John Martin Luippold was derived from Boston city directories and census data. No obituary or other genealogical information has been located.
REFERENCE
Jacob Luippold Collection, Historic New England Library and Archives.

Pages 134–35
Ogden Codman, Jr.: *Paneled Room in The Grange, the Codman House, Lincoln, Massachusetts*
ENDNOTE
1. Ogden Codman, Jr., to Fiske Kimball, 17 March 1935, Ogden Codman Manuscript Collection, Boston Athenaeum.
The author wishes to acknowledge Stuart A. Drake for his on-going support of her research on Ogden Codman, Jr.

Pages 136–37
Ogden Codman, Jr.: *Unidentified Interior*
ENDNOTE
1. Letter from Edith Wharton to Ogden Codman, Jr., 27 May 1897, Codman Family Manuscripts Collection, Historic New England Library and Archives.

Pages 138–41
Ogden Codman, Jr.: *Martha Codman House, Berkeley Villa, Newport, Rhode Island*
ENDNOTE
1. Ogden Codman, Jr., to Robert Tritton, 23 December 1936, Ogden Codman Manuscript Collection, Boston Athenaeum.

Pages 142–43

William F. Goodwin: *Frederick W. Paine House, Brookline, Massachusetts*

ENDNOTES

1. Records of the Olmsted Associates, Job #1363, Frederick Law Olmsted National Historic Site, Brookline, Mass. The landscape plan and historic photos of the property are available through the Library of Congress and its American Memory web site indexed under the Town of Brookline.

2. For an account of the career of his father, William A. Goodwin, see Elizabeth Igleheart, "William A. Goodwin 1822–1896," in *A Biographical Dictionary of Architects in Maine* (Augusta, Maine: Maine Historic Preservation Commission, 1991), 6.

3. Little information has come to light on Goodwin's career beyond information gleaned from directories and census data. He formed a brief partnership with Henry E. Siter and lived in Newton with his wife, the former Ann H. York.

4. The building permits for the Town of Brookline, Mass., record it was William G. Rantoul.

Pages 144–47

Longfellow, Alden and Harlow: *James A. Noyes House, Cambridge, Massachusetts*

REFERENCE

Margaret Henderson Floyd, *Architecture After Richardson: Regionalism Before Modernism—Longfellow, Alden, and Harlow in Boston and Pittsburgh* (Chicago: The University of Chicago Press, 1994).

Pages 148–51

Samuel Rantin and Son: *John McCarthy and William Kallady House, Roxbury, Boston, Massachusetts*

ENDNOTES

1. Biographical information on Rantin was derived from Boston city directories and census data.

2. *New England Master Builder*, 13 February 1897. The only known copies of this short-lived real estate journal are in the Library of Congress.

Pages 152–53

Charles A. Platt and Thomas A. Fox: *Harriet Crowninshield Coolidge House, Dublin, New Hampshire*

REFERENCES

Keith N. Morgan, *Charles A. Platt, The Artist as Architect* (Cambridge, Mass.: MIT Press, 1985).

Keith N. Morgan, ed., *Shaping an American Landscape: The Art and Architecture of Charles A. Platt* (Hanover, N.H.: University Press of New England, 1995).

William Morgan, "Monadnock Summer: An Architectural and Cultural History of Dublin, New Hampshire," unpublished manuscript.

Susan Faxon Olney, introduction to *A Circle of Friends: Art Colonies of Cornish and Dublin* (Durham, N.H.: University Art Galleries, University of New Hampshire, 1985), 12–31.

The author wishes to acknowledge the assistance of John W. Harris, Dublin [N.H.] Historical Society, and Mary Ellen Moore, current owner of the Coolidge house, in the preparation of this entry.

Pages 154–55

Fox and Gale: *Unidentified Apartment Building*

ENDNOTES

1. Untitled editorial, *The American Architect and Building News* 76, no. 1383 (28 June 1902): 97; Rosalind Pollan, Carol Kennedy, Edward Gordon, "Fenway Project Completion Report," Part Two, Fenway Inventory Forms (Boston, 1984), 95–97.

2. For the MIT class years of Fox, Gale, and Jenney, see "Register of Former Students with Account of the Alumni Associations," *Bulletin of the Massachusetts Institute of Technology* 50, no. 3 (May 1915): 182, 189, 268. For the Rockingham County building, see Carol Walker Aten, *Postcards from Exeter* (Portsmouth, N.H.: Arcadia, 2003), 31. For the Weston Library project see "Building Intelligence," *The American Architect and Building News* 66, no. 1242 (14 October 1899): xii. For Fox and Gale's circa 1915 Copley Square subway kiosk and other "stairway coverings," see [Boston Transit Commission], *Twenty-First Annual Report of the Boston Transit Commission, for the Year Ending June 30, 1915* (Boston, 1915), 41.

3. Fox and Gale photograph album, Historic New England Library and Archives. Amy Friend, *Rediscover Weld at Larz Anderson Park: A Self-Guided Walking Tour* (Brookline, Mass., 1999), n.p. The firm's work on one of the estate's outbuildings is reported in "Building Intelligence," *The American Architect and Building News* 77, no. 1390 (16 August 1902): xii.

REFERENCES

Fox and Gale photograph album, Historic New England Library and Archives.

Massachusetts Committee for the Preservation of Architectural Records, *Directory of Boston Architects, 1846–1970* (Cambridge, Mass.: Mass COPAR, 1984).

Papers of John Singer Sargent and Thomas A. Fox, 1882–1932, Boston Athenaeum.

Douglass Shand-Tucci, *Built in Boston: City and Suburb, 1800–2000* (Amherst: University of Massachusetts Press, 1999), 101–30.

Henry F. Withey and Elsie Rathburn Withey, *Biographical Dictionary of American Architects (Deceased)* (Los Angeles: Hennessey and Ingalls, Inc., 1970), 218.

Pages 156–57

Fox and Gale: *Charles A. Stone House, The Terraces, Rocky Point, Plymouth, Massachusetts*

ENDNOTES

1. Donna D. Curtin, "References to the Stone Estate at Rocky Point in the Old Colony Memorial" (Spring 2009), unpublished manuscript, Plymouth Antiquarian Society, Plymouth, Mass.; "Guests of Mr. Stone," *Boston Daily Globe*, 10 July 1910, 16.

2. Previews Incorporated, "Rocky Point," undated (c. 1940s) realtor's brochure, facsimile copy in the collections of the Plymouth Antiquarian Society. The author would like to thank Donna Curtin for sharing her research files; Maggie Mills, "Remembrance of Estates Gone By: A Nostalgic Stroll Down Rocky Hill Road," *Old Colony Memorial*, 1 November 1979; "Get the Facts About Pilgrim Station," http://www.pilgrimpower.com/about-the-pilgrim-facility.html.

3. J. Randolph Coolidge, Jr., "The Recent Exhibition of the Boston Architectural Club," *The Architectural Review*, 11 (May 1904): 149–52. The designer of this house was Alexander S. Jenney, sometime partner of Fox and Gale.

4. "John Cotton Clapp, 1837–," *American Series of Popular Biographies*, Massachusetts Edition (Boston, 1891); Boston city directories; "Personal Mention," *The American Architect and Building News* 87, no. 1533 (13 May 1905): vii; John C. Clapp, Jr., "The Second Prize House," *Ladies' Home Journal*, August 1905, 9; "Infirmary Needed for Sick Horses," *Boston Daily Globe*, 17 July 1902, 12, makes reference to Clapp's commission for "a drinking fountain for animals."

REFERENCES

"House at Plymouth, Mass.," in Frank M. Day, ed., *American Country Houses of To-day* (New York: Architectural Book Publishing Company, 1912), 80–84.

Massachusetts Committee for the Preservation of Architectural Records, *Directory of Boston Architects, 1846–1970* (Cambridge, Mass.: Mass COPAR, 1984).

Keith N. Morgan, ed., *Shaping an American Landscape: The Art and Architecture of Charles A. Platt* (Hanover, N.H.: University Press of New England, 1995).

Stone Estate Inventory Form, May 1996, Massachusetts Historical Commission, Boston, Mass.

Sam Bass Warner, Jr., *The Province of Reason* (Cambridge, Mass.: Belknap Press of Harvard University Press, 1984), 52–66.

Pages 158–60

Edward Pearce Casey: *Hildreth K. Bloodgood House, New Marlborough, Massachusetts*

ENDNOTES

1. "Edward P. Casey Noted Architect," obituary in *New York Times*, 3 January 1940.

2. The design for the Bloodgood house appeared in *The American Architect and Building News* on 10 March 1906. The construction date derives from a building survey form prepared for the Massachusetts Historical Commission, Boston, Mass.

REFERENCE

Jon Swan and John Sisson, *A Pictorial History of New Marlborough: A Visual Reminiscence, 1735–1940* (Mill River, Mass.: New Marlborough Historical Society, 2005).

The author wishes to acknowledge Melanie Sharp Bolster and Bradford Wagstaff for their assistance with this entry.

Pages 161–63

A. H. Davenport and Company: *Unidentified Interior*

ENDNOTES

1. Alexander T. Hollingsworth, *Blue and White China* (London: The Chiswick Press, 1891), 17–19.

2. Ralph L. Power, *Boston's Special Libraries* (New York: Prentice-Hall, Inc., 1917), 44–45.

Pages 164–65

A. H. Davenport and Company: *Unidentified Room Model*

ENDNOTES

1. Anne Farnam, "A. H. Davenport and Company, Boston Furniture Makers," *Antiques* 109 (May 1976): 1048–55.

2. See plan and elevation drawing in the Lancaster City and Maritime Museum (UK), accession number LANLM.1955.20.8 at http://collections.lancsmuseums.gov.uk/narratives/object.php?irn=148.

Pages 166–69

Edwin J. Lewis, Jr.: *Unidentified Stable and Pietro Terrile Garage, Winthrop, Massachusetts*

REFERENCES

Edwin M. Bacon, ed., *Boston of To-day* (Boston: Post Publishing Company, 1892), 290.

Henry F. Withey and Elsie Rathburn Withey, *Biographical Dictionary of American Architects (Deceased)* (Los Angeles: Hennessey and Ingalls, Inc., 1970), 370.

Pages 170–71, 174–77

Frank Chouteau Brown: *Unidentified Bungalow; R. M. Tyler House, Wellesley, Massachusetts; Unidentified House on the Connecticut River; and Unidentified House, Dublin, New Hampshire*

REFERENCES

The American Institute of Architects, *Pioneers in Preservation* (Washington, D.C.: 1990), 11–13.

Frank Chouteau Brown Collection, Historic New England Library and Archives.

Henry F. Withey and Elsie Rathburn Withey, *Biographical Dictionary of American Architects (Deceased)* (Los Angeles: Hennessey and Ingalls, Inc., 1970), 81.

Pages 172–73

Frank Chouteau Brown: *Thomas Dreier House, Snug Gables, Enclosing Fence, Winchester, Massachusetts*

REFERENCES

Boston city directories, 1920–1931, Boston Public Library.

Frank Chouteau Brown, "A House for Work and Play," *Country Life* 44, no. 4 (August 1923), 40–42.

Thomas Dreier, *The Power of Print and Men* (Brooklyn, N.Y.: Mergenthaler Linotype Co., 1936).

Scott Taylor Hartzell, " 'Mr. Library' loved the idea of exploring, sharing ideas," *St. Petersburg Times,* 26 January 2005.

Albert N. Marquis, "Thomas Dreier," in *Who's Who in New England* (Chicago: A. N. Marquis, 1915).

U. S. Census, 1920, 1930.

Winchester, Massachusetts, Annual Reports, Reports of Assessors, 1919–1938.

Winchester, Massachusetts, Poll Tax lists, 1921–1934, Winchester Town Archives.

Pages 178–79

Arthur Asahel Shurcliff (né Shurtleff): *Alexander Cochrane Garden, at The Hague, Hamilton, Massachusetts*

ENDNOTES

1. Cochrane's Commonwealth Avenue home was designed by McKim, Mead and White (1887) and his Prides Crossing house by William Ralph Emerson (1884).
2. He changed his last name from Shurtleff to Shurcliff in 1930, in order, he said, to conform to the ancient spelling of the family name.
3. Shurcliff graduated from MIT in 1894, from Harvard University in 1896, and he trained and practiced in the Brookline, Mass., firm of America's premiere landscape architect, Frederick Law Olmsted, between 1896 and 1904, before going out on his own.
4. Arthur A. Shurcliff (then Shurtleff), "Planting Plan for Rose Garden for Alexander Cochrane, Hamilton, Mass.," 17 December 1914, corrected to 28 January 1915, Historic New England Library and Archives.

Pages 180–81

Parker Morse Hooper: *Earle Perry Charlton House, Pond Meadow, Westport Point, Massachusetts*

ENDNOTES

1. For biographical information on Parker Morse Hooper, see obituary, *Camden Herald,* 19 May 1966, 8; also see James Ward, *Architects in Practice, New York City, 1900–1940* (New York Committee for the Preservation of Architectural Records, 1989), 36. Additional biographical information regarding Hooper's practice is based on collections of mounted photographs removed from his Camden home, Hill Acres, which are now housed in the collection of the Maine Historic Preservation Commission in Augusta, Maine, and Historic New England's Library and Archives.
2. *The National Cyclopedia of American Biography* (New York: James T. White & Company, 1953), 38: 370–71.
3. According to a telephone conversation with the author in November 1981, Westport Point neighbor and close friend of the Charltons, Judge Hugh Morton, recollected that his mother told him about Ida Charlton's insistence on the architect introducing dormer windows into the slate roof.
4. A photograph of the second Otto Eggers perspective dated 1916 is among the mounted photographs of Hooper's work at Historic New England.
5. For biographical information on Otto Eggers, see Steven McLeod Bedford, "Eggers and Higgins," in *Macmillan Encyclopedia of Architects*, Adolf K. Placzek, editor in chief (New York: Macmillan Publishing Co., 1982), 2:12.
6. In 1922, Eggers and Higgins became partners in the firm of John Russell Pope. Bedford, *Macmillan Encyclopedia* 2:12.
7. Minor L. Bishop, ed., *Architectural Renderings by the Winners of the Birch Burdette Long Memorial Prize* (New York: The Architectural League of New York, 1965), 16.
8. Bishop, *Architectural Renderings*, 16.
9. The mounted photograph of the 1915 rendering is in the collection of Historic New England.

Pages 182–83

Halfdan Hanson: *Alterations for the John B. Drake House, Gloucester, Massachusetts*

REFERENCES

Halfdan M. Hanson Collection, Historic New England Library and Archives.

Halfdan M. Hanson obituary, *Gloucester Daily Times*, 13 September 1952.

Phyllis Ray, "Biographical Sketch," unpublished manuscript, Historic New England Library and Archives.

Pages 184–85

George F. Marlowe: *Houses for the Gardiner Building Association, Gardiner, Maine*

REFERENCES

R. C. Rybnikar, "George F. Marlowe, Jr., Babson's Early Architect," Babson College Archives and Special Collections Blog, 13 July 2009.

"The United States Housing Corporation: Project No. 59 at Bath, Maine," *The Architectural Record* 45 (January 1919): 21–25.

Pages 186–87

Arthur Todhunter Company: *Fireplace Design for the Shore Pavilion/Beach House at the Benjamin DeWitt Riegel Estate, Southport, Connecticut*

REFERENCES

Shantia Anderheggen and Lorna Condon, "Xanadu in Connecticut," *Historic New England* 2, no. 3 (Winter 2001): 8–10.

Francis Blossom, "Henry Colden Pelton, '89 Mines," *Columbia Alumni News,* 27 September 1935, 10.

Henry C. Pelton, Architect, New York City (Architectural Catalog Company, 1925).

Henry C. Pelton, Architects, New York City (Promotional brochure, c. 1931).

Louise V. Higgins, "Early Twentieth Century at Kenzie's Point: The Riegel Estate," *The Southport Packet* 17, no. 2 (April 2003): 1–7.

_____. "The Riegel Estate at Kenzie's Point West, 1920s–1940s: A Photographic Essay," *The Southport Packet* 17, no. 4 (October 2003): 1–7.

_____. "The Riegel Estate at Kenzie's Point West Continued, 1920s–1940s: A Photographic Essay," *The Southport Packet* 18, no. 1 (January 2004): 1–7.

Melanie Macchio, "Tibbitts, Armand Rhodes," in *Shaping the American Landscape: New Profiles from the Pioneers of American Landscape Design Project*, Charles A. Birnbaum and Stephanie S. Foell, eds. (Charlottesville: University of Virginia Press, 2009), 350–53.

Riegel/Emory Family Papers, Historic New England Library and Archives.

Todhunter, Inc., Collection, The Joseph Downs Collection of Manuscripts and Printed Ephemera, Henry Francis du Pont Winterthur Museum, Winterthur, Delaware.

Pages 188–90

Coolidge and Carlson: *Minerva Davis House, Agawam, Massachusetts*

ENDNOTES

1. For Coolidge, see Henry F. Withey and Elsie Rathburn Withey, *Biographical Dictionary of American Architects (Deceased)* (Los Angeles: Hennessey and Ingalls, Inc., 1970), 138. Information on Carlson is derived from *American Architects Directory,* George S. Koyl, ed. (New York: R. R. Bowker Company, 1955), 83.
2. *The Architectural Record* 80 (November 1926): 477.

Pages 191–93

Walter F. Bogner and A. W. Kenney Billings, Jr.: *Carl H. White Guest House, Bennington, Vermont*

REFERENCES

Walter F. Bogner, Professor of Architecture, unpublished biographical sketch, June 1965, Historic New England Library and Archives.

Walter F. Bogner Collection, Historic New England Library and Archives.

Carl White obituary, *New York Times,* 22 March 1933, 13.

"Will Take Two Years to Finish Building Plans," *Bennington Evening Banner*, 1 December 1928, 1.

The author wishes to acknowledge the assistance of Wendy Sharkey, Bennington Free Library, for her assistance in the preparation of this entry.

Pages 194–95

Bigelow, Wadsworth, Hubbard and Smith: *Unidentified House at Northeast Harbor, Maine*

REFERENCES

Harvard College, Class of 1902, Fifth Report (Norwood, Mass.: Plimpton Press, 1917), 296–97.

Massachusetts Institute of Technology, *Record of the Class of 1888* (Boston, 1924), 11–12.

Henry F. Withey and Elsie Rathburn Withey, *Biographical Dictionary of American Architects (Deceased)* (Los Angeles: New Age Publishing Co., 1956), 57–58.

Pages 196–98

Arland A. Dirlam: *Mrs. Arland A. Dirlam House, Stoneham, Massachusetts*

REFERENCES

Drawings and other documents of Dirlam's career are housed primarily in two places: Historic New England's Library and Archives, and Special Collections, Loeb Library, Harvard University.

Joy Wheeler Dow, *American Renaissance* (New York: William T. Comstock, 1904).

Pages 199–201

David J. Abrahams: *Unidentified Suburban House*

REFERENCES

David J. Abrahams obituaries, *Boston Herald,* 18 November 1958; *New York Times,* 19 November 1958, 37.

"House for J. Marshall Hubbard, West Harwich, Mass., David J. Abrahams, Architect," *Architectural Forum* 72, no. 2 (February 1940): 107–9.

"House for William J. L. Roop, Esq., Boston, Massachusetts," *Pencil Points* 8 (December 1927): 767.

George S. Koyl, ed., *American Architects Directory* (New York: R. R. Bowker Company, 1955), 2.

"Planning Now For Postwar Living," *Architectural Record* 96, no. 1 (July 1944): 76–77.

"A Portfolio of 30 Houses & Plans," *House & Garden,* August 1938, 42–67.

"Two-story House in Massachusetts," *Architectural Record,* 87, no. 2 (February 1940): 53–55.

Pages 202–3

Henry B. Hoover: *Henry B. Hoover House, Lincoln, Massachusetts*

REFERENCES

Lucretia Hoover Giese and Henry B. Hoover, Jr., *Henry Hoover: Modern Residences,* book in progress.

Robin Karson, *Fletcher Steele, Landscape Architect* (New York: Harry N. Abrams/Sagapress, Inc., 1989).

Fletcher Steele, "Landscape Design of the Future," *Landscape Architecture* 22 (July 1932): 299–302.

———. "New Styles in Gardening: Will Landscape Architecture Reflect the Modernistic Tendencies Seen in the Other Arts?" *House Beautiful,* March 1929, 317.

For examples of Hubert Robert, see Hélène Moulin, *Hubert Robert et Saint-Petersbourg* (Valence: Musée de Valence, 1999), and Victor Carlson, *Hubert Robert: Drawings & Watercolors* (Washington D.C.: The National Gallery of Art, 1978).

Pages 204–5

Henry B. Hoover: *Terrace for Edgar Moor House, Tabor Knoll, Lincoln, Massachusetts*

REFERENCES

For examples of Frank Lloyd Wright and Marion Mahony (Griffin), see David Gebhard and Deborah Nevins, *200 Years of American Architectural Drawing* (New York: Whitney Library of Design for the Architectural League of New York and the American Federation of Arts, 1977), and Alberto Izzo and Camillo Gubitosi, *Frank Lloyd Wright: Three-quarters of a Century of Drawings* (New York: Horizon Press, 1981).

For the Resor House, see Ludwig Glaeser, *Ludwig Mies Van Der Rohe: Drawings in the Collection of MOMA* (New York: The Museum of Modern Art, 1969), and David Gebhard and Deborah Nevins, *200 Years of American Architectural Drawing.*

Pages 206–7

Henry B. Hoover: *Mr. and Mrs. Everett A. Black House, Lincoln, Massachusetts*

REFERENCES

For the Shearer House, see "Shearer House Tour" description of the Friends of Modern Architecture, Lincoln, under events for 2008, at www.fomalincoln.org.

For the Wiley House, see Henry-Russell Hitchcock and Philip Johnson, *Architecture, 1949–1965* (New York: Holt, Rinehart and Winston, 1966), and Robert Venturi, *Complexity and Contradiction in Architecture* (New York: The Museum of Modern Art, 1966).

Pages 208–10

Royal Barry Wills: *Illustration for* Better Houses for Budgeteers, *and* Dr. John Dreyfus House, Quincy, Massachusetts

REFERENCES

David Gebhard, "The American Colonial Revival in the 1930s," *Winterthur Portfolio* 22 (Summer-Autumn 1987): 109–48.

———. "Royal Barry Wills and the American Colonial Revival," *Winterthur Portfolio* 27 (Spring 1992): 45–74.

Pages 211–13

Stanley B. Parker: *Design for a Gazebo with Parts Salvaged from 38 Quincy Street, Cambridge, Massachusetts*

ENDNOTE

1. Harvard College, Class of 1904, *Class of 1904, Sixth Class Report, 1929* (Cambridge, Mass.: Harvard University Press, 1929).

REFERENCES

Boston, Cambridge, and Plymouth, Massachusetts, city directories.

Harvard College, Class of 1904. *Second Report, Class of 1904* (Cambridge, Mass.: Harvard University Press, 1910); *Third Report* (1915); *Fourth Report* (1920); *Fifth Report* (1924); *Sixth Report* (1928); *Seventh Report* (1934); *Eighth Report* (1939); *Ninth Report* (1944); *Tenth Report* (1949); *Fiftieth Anniversary Report* (1954).

Inventory of Architecture in Cambridge, files on Stanley Parker, Henry Greenough and family, and 38 Quincy Street, Cambridge Historical Commission.

Lawrence Scientific School, student records, Harvard University Archives.

Susan E. Maycock and Charles M. Sullivan, *Building Old Cambridge: Architecture and Development* (Cambridge, Mass.: The MIT Press, forthcoming).

Denys Peter Myers, "The Fate of 38," *Harvard Alumni Bulletin,* 25 November 1950.

Stanley Brampton Parker, *The Vertical Vanishing Point in Linear Perspective* (Cambridge, Mass.: Harvard University Press, 1947).

———. "Gazebo: Posts and Apron Salvaged from Side Porch at 38 Quincy Street, Cambridge," *Harvard Alumni Bulletin,* 7 July 1951.

———. *Linear Perspective without Vanishing Points* (Cambridge, Mass.: Harvard University Press, 1961).

David H. Pottinger, "Thirty-Eight Quincy Street," *Cambridge Historical Society Proceedings* 24 (1934): 24–48.

Pages 214–15

Walter P. Crabtree, Jr.: *Colonial Apartments, Newtown, Connecticut*

REFERENCE

Walter Crabtree obituary, *Hartford Courant,* 13 March 1975.

Pages 216–17

Edwin B. Goodell: *Mr. and Mrs. Frederick L. Dabney House, Westport, Massachusetts*

REFERENCES

Frederick L. Dabney, Jr., son of the client, Frederick L. Dabney, interview with Roger Reed.

Edwin Goodell obituary, *The* [Wayland] *Town Crier,* 23 September 1971.

Edwin Goodell, grandson of Edwin B. Goodell, e-mail correspondence, 11 January 2010.

Hélène Lipstadt, "Revising Giedion," *Newsletter of the Society of Architectural Historians* 45 (June 2001): 8–10.

Pages 218–223

Huygens and Tappé: *Dr. William Mauran House, Providence, Rhode Island,* and *Dr. and Mrs. Paul Harwood House, Essex, Connecticut*

REFERENCES

Lorna Condon, "Preserving the Present," *Historic New England* 7, no. 2 (Fall 2006): 13–15.

Remmert W. Huygens Archive, Historic New England Library and Archives.

R. W. Huygens, "A Selection of Houses," maquette for an unpublished monograph, n.d., Historic New England Library and Archives.

"New House for Old Area," *Providence Journal,* 2 March 1987, C-01.

"Private House, Providence, Rhode Island," *Process: Architecture* 7 (1978): 152–55, 206, 212.

The author wishes to acknowledge Wm McKenzie Woodward, Principal Architectural Historian, Rhode Island Historical Preservation and Heritage Commission, and Donald C. Carleton, Jr., for their assistance in the preparation of this entry.

Selected Bibliography

Allen, Gerald, and Richard Oliver. *Architectural Drawing: The Art and the Process.* New York: Whitney Library of Design, 1981.

Barry, William E. *Pen Sketches of Old Houses.* Boston: James R. Osgood & Co., 1874.

Benjamin, Asher. *The Practical House Carpenter.* Boston: R. P. & C. Williams and Annin & Smith, 1830.

Blomfield, Reginald. *Architectural Drawing and Draftsmen.* London: Cassell & Company, 1912.

Brown, Frank Chouteau. *Architectural Drawing and Lettering.* Chicago: American Technical Society, 1917.

Garvin, James L. *A Building History of Northern New England.* Hanover, N.H.: University Press of New England, 2001.

Gebhard, David, and Deborah Nevins. *200 Years of American Architectural Drawing.* New York: Whitney Library of Design for the Architectural League of New York and the American Federation of Arts, 1977.

Gowans, Alan. *Styles and Types of North American Architecture: Social Function and Cultural Expression.* New York: Icon Editions, 1992.

Hambly, Maya. *Drawing Instruments, 1580–1980.* London: Sotheby's Publications, 1988.

Handlin, David P. *The American Home: Architecture and Society, 1815–1915.* Boston: Little, Brown, 1979.

Jordy, William H., and Christopher P. Monkhouse. *Buildings on Paper: Rhode Island Architectural Drawings, 1825–1945.* Providence: Bell Gallery, List Art Center, Brown University, 1982.

Linfoot, Benjamin. *Architectural Picture Making with Pen and Ink.* Philadelphia, 1884.

Little, Arthur. *Early New England Interiors.* Boston: A. Williams & Co., 1878.

Mallary, Peter T. *Houses of New England.* New York: Thames and Hudson, 1984.

Morgan, William. *The Abrams Guide to American House Styles.* New York: Harry N. Abrams, 2004.

Nevins, Deborah, and Robert A. M. Stern. *The Architect's Eye: American Architectural Drawings from 1799–1978.* New York: Pantheon, 1979.

O'Gorman, James F. *ABC of Architecture.* Philadelphia: University of Pennsylvania Press, 1998.

_____. *On the Boards: Drawings by Nineteenth-Century Boston Architects.* Philadelphia: University of Pennsylvania Press, 1989.

_____. *The Perspective of Anglo-American Architecture.* Philadelphia: The Athenaeum of Philadelphia, 1995.

O'Gorman, James F., and Earle G. Shettleworth, Jr. *The Maine Perspective: Architectural Drawings, 1800–1980.* Portland, Maine: Portland Museum of Art, 2006.

Saliga, Pauline. "The Types and Styles of Architectural Drawings." In *Chicago Architects Design,* edited by John Zukowsky and Pauline Saliga. Chicago: The Art Institute; New York: Rizzoli, 1982.

Shaw, Edward. *The Modern Architect.* Boston: Dayton and Wentworth, 1854.

Spiers, R. Phené. *Architectural Drawing.* London and New York: Cassell, 1888.

Stevens, John Calvin, and Albert Winslow Cobb. *Examples of American Domestic Architecture.* New York: William T. Comstock, 1889.

Vanden Brink, Brian. *Historic Maine Homes: 300 Years of Great Houses.* Photographs by Brian Vanden Brink with text by Christopher Glass. Camden, Maine: Down East Books, 2009.

Wharton, Edith, and Ogden Codman, Jr. *The Decoration of Houses.* New York: Charles Scribner's Sons, 1897.

Wills, Royal Barry. *Better Houses for Budgeteers.* New York: Architectural Book Publishing Co., 1941.

Woods, Mary N. *From Craft to Profession: The Practice of Architecture in Nineteenth-Century America.* Berkeley: University of California Press, 1999.

Illustration Credits

Introduction: Drawings for New England Domestic Architecture, c. 1800–c. 1980
10: Edward Pearce Casey: Long and Heppner, photographers. Historic New England Library and Archives.
13: TOP LEFT: Henry Austin advertisement: Historic New England Library and Archives. RIGHT: Luther Briggs, Jr., advertisement: Historic New England Library and Archives. Gift of Stephen Jerome. LEFT: Daguerreotype of Aaron Morse: Courtesy of the collection of William H. Skerritt.
16: TOP LEFT: Royal Barry Wills: Courtesy of Vince Lisanti, photographer, and Royal Barry Wills Associates. TOP RIGHT: Royal Barry Wills, *Better Houses for Budgeteers* (New York: Architectural Book Publishing Co., 1946): Courtesy of Architectural Book Publishing Co., and Royal Barry Wills Associates. BOTTOM: John Calvin Stevens and Albert Winslow Cobb, *Examples of American Domestic Architecture* (New York: William T. Comstock, 1889): Private collection.

Suitable for Framing: Architectural Drawings as Works of Art
20: Elevation of an unidentified residence and detail of label on reverse: Historic New England Library and Archives.
22: TOP: Joseph H. Curtis cottage: Mount Desert Land and Garden Preserve, Seal Harbor, Maine. BOTTOM: Islesboro Hotel (Inn): Historic New England Library and Archives. Gift of Andrew Spindler-Roesle.
23: Samoset Hotel: Private collection.

The Development of the Architectural Profession in New England: An Overview
26: Title pages from architecture publications: Historic New England Library and Archives.
29: TOP LEFT: Faneuil Hall Marketplace: Historic New England Library and Archives. Gift of Frederick A. Stahl. TOP RIGHT: Walter Gropius: Historic New England Library and Archives. BOTTOM: Boston City Hall: Historic New England Library and Archives. Gift of Gerhard Kallmann and Michael McKinnell.

Preserving on Paper: Historic New England's Collection of Architectural Records
30: TOP LEFT: Stations for the Boston Elevated Railway Company: Historic New England Library and Archives. Purchased with a bequest from David Cummings. TOP RIGHT: William Sumner Appleton: Historic New England Library and Archives. BOTTOM: Chapel, Mount Auburn Cemetery: Historic New England Library and Archives. Gift of Dr. William Sturgis Bigelow.
33: TOP LEFT: Jaffrey house measured drawing: Historic New England Library and Archives. Gift of Donald Macdonald-Millar. TOP RIGHT: Rachel Raymond house: Paul J. Weber, photographer. Historic New England Library and Archives. Gift of James E. (Jack) Robinson, III. BOTTOM: View along Hancock Street: Historic New England Library and Archives. Gift of James McNeely.
37: TOP: Palladio, *I quattro libri dell'architettura*: Historic New England Library and Archives. Gift of

Herbert W. C. Browne. BOTTOM LEFT: Thomas Sumner bookplate: Historic New England Library and Archives. RIGHT: Architectural ephemera: Historic New England Library and Archives.
38: Jacob Luippold house: Historic New England Library and Archives.

Catalogue Entries
40: Phelps-Hatheway house: Robert J. Kelley, photographer. Library of Congress, Prints & Photographs Division, HABS CONN, 2-SUFI, 7-3.
42: Jonathan Leavitt house: Courtesy of the Greenfield [Mass.] Public Library.
44: Hubbard-Fullerton house: Historic New England Library and Archives.
50: Rundlet-May house: William King Covell, photographer. Historic New England Library and Archives.
52: William Bingham house: Courtesy of the Library of Congress Prints and Photographs Division.
56: William Wilkins Warren house: Courtesy of the Arlington [Mass.] Historical Society.
60: Augustus Clarke house: Roger G. Reed, photographer.
64: Henry C. Bowen House, Roseland Cottage: Historic New England Library and Archives.
74: Billings house: Courtesy of the Framingham [Mass.] History Center.
77: Ephraim Merriam house: Roger G. Reed, photographer.
83: James F. Bigelow house: Illustration from Benjamin Hobart, *History of the Town of Abington, Plymouth County, Massachusetts* (Boston: T. H. Carter and Son, 1866). Historic New England Library and Archives.
88: P. D. Wallis house: Courtesy of the South End Historical Society, Boston.
102: Hancock House: Edward Lamson Henry, photographer. Historic New England Library and Archives.
104: TOP: George B. Chase library: Illustration from Charles Wyllys Elliott, *The Book of American Interiors* (Boston: James R. Osgood and Co., 1876). Historic New England Library and Archives. BOTTOM: James M. Beebe house library: Historic New England Library and Archives.
106: Beebe and Brewer townhouses: Historic New England Library and Archives.
108: Thomas Wigglesworth house: Courtesy of the Boston Athenaeum.
110: James Aiken house: Illustration from James Amasa Wood, *New Hampshire Homes: Photographic Views of City, Village, Summer, and Farm Homes of New Hampshire Men and Residents of the Granite State* (Concord, N.H.: J. A. Wood, 1895). Courtesy of James L. Garvin.
112: W. S. Appleton, Sr., house: Historic New England Library and Archives.
114: William Watts Sherman house: Historic New England Library and Archives.
116: TOP AND BOTTOM: Rev. John C. Brooks cottage: Courtesy of the Sippican Historical Society, Marion, Mass.
121: Joseph A. King cottage: Courtesy of the Maine Historic Preservation Commission.

122: G. R. Emmerton house: Historic New England Library and Archives.
124: H. C. Frick estate: Historic New England Library and Archives.
126: W. S. and J. T. Spaulding house: Historic New England Library and Archives.
128: Michael H. Baker building: Courtesy of the Holyoke Heritage State Park.
130: Philip Albret house: Roger G. Reed, photographer.
134: Paneled room in The Grange: Historic New England Library and Archives.
140: TOP: Martha Codman house, interior: Courtesy of John T. Hopf, photographer. Historic New England Library and Archives. BOTTOM: Martha Codman house, exterior: Historic New England Library and Archives.
142: F. W. Paine house: Historic New England Library and Archives.
146: J. A. Noyes house: Historic New England Library and Archives.
148: John McCarthy and William Kallady houses: Roger G. Reed, photographer.
152: Harriet Crowninshield Coolidge house: Roger G. Reed, photographer.
156: C. A. Stone house: Historic New England Library and Archives.
160: Hildreth K. Bloodgood house: Courtesy of Bradford Wagstaff.
172: Thomas Dreier house: Egan-Jacoby, photographers. Historic New England Library and Archives.
180: Earle Perry Charlton house: Courtesy of Doyle Galleries, New York.
186: TOP AND BOTTOM: Beach house at the Riegel estate: Historic New England Library and Archives.
189: Minerva Davis house: Photograph by Art Photo Co. Published in *The Architectural Record*, November 1924. Historic New England Library and Archives.
191: Carl White estate: Historic New England Library and Archives.
192: Carl White guest house: Historic New England Library and Archives.
202: Henry B. Hoover house: Russell B. Harding, photographer. Courtesy of the Hoover Family.
204: Edgar Moor terrace: Thomas Ballantyne, photographer. Courtesy of Sotheby's International Realty, Inc.
206: Mr. and Mrs. E. A. Black house: Phyllis Swift, photographer. Courtesy of the Lincoln [Mass.] Public Library.
210: TOP: J. Dreyfus house: Ken Duprey, photographer. BOTTOM: Floor plan, Royal Barry Wills, *Better Houses for Budgeteers* (New York: Architectural Book Publishing Co., 1946): Courtesy of Architectural Book Publishing Co., and Royal Barry Wills Associates.
213: 38 Quincy Street, Cambridge, Massachusetts: Courtesy of the Cambridge Historical Commission.
221: Dr. William Mauran house: Copyright Steve Rosenthal, photographer. Courtesy of the photographer.
222: Dr. and Mrs. Paul Harwood house: Photograph attributed to Remmert W. Huygens. Historic New England Library and Archives.

Index

Acknowledgments

THE EDITORIAL TEAM WISHES TO THANK THE
MANY PEOPLE WHO MADE THIS PUBLICATION
POSSIBLE. We are grateful to the individual historians
who joined the project, researched one or more drawings,
and contributed insightful entries; their names appear in
the front of the book on page 7.

The work of the following professionals ensured the quality of this publication: Julia Sedykh, book designer; Debora
Mayer, conservator; David Carmack, photographer; and
Virginia Quinn, copy editor. We are also indebted to those
institutions and individuals who provided valuable information and images for specific entries. They are acknowledged
in the endnotes for the entry.

This catalogue documents an exhibition of the same
name that was shown at the Boston University Art Gallery
at the Stone Gallery from November 18, 2009 to January 17,
2010, and at the National Building Museum, Washington,
D. C., from February 13 to August 15, 2010. The enthusias-
tic support of Professor James A. Winn, Director, Boston
University Humanities Foundation, Keith N. Morgan,
Professor of Art History and Director of Architectural
Studies, Boston University, and Marc Mitchell, Director ad
interim, Boston University Art Gallery, greatly contributed
to a highly successful collaboration. At the National Building
Museum, we are grateful to Cathy Crane Frankel, Vice
President for Exhibitions and Collections, and Chrysanthe
B. Broikos, Curator, for the care with which they arranged
the exhibition in the nation's capital.

The following Historic New England staff, interns,
volunteers, and supporters assisted with innumerable
tasks as the situation demanded: Richard Cheek, Adrienne
Sage Donohue, Joanne Flaherty, Henry Frechette, Emily
Novak Gustainis, Megan MacNeil, Stephen Pekich, Meghan
Petersen, Michael Schuetz, Julie Solz, Kenneth C. Turino,
Diane Viera, Jared Walske, and Carolyn Ziering.

We wish to especially acknowledge the work of Nancy
Carlisle, Nancy Curtis, Jeanne Gamble, Stephen Kharfen,
and Jennifer Pustz, who undertook a variety of assignments
and worked tirelessly to prepare the book for publication.

Lastly, we want to thank Carl R. Nold, Historic New
England President and CEO, for his dynamic leadership in
designating publication an institutional priority in order to
share the rich holdings of the Library and Archives with a
broader public.